W9-AOI-458

Sex and Love Addicts Anonymous

Sex and Love Addicts Anonymous

First Edition

**The Augustine Fellowship, Sex and Love Addicts Anonymous,
Fellowship-Wide Services, Inc.
BOSTON
1986**

Copyright © 1986 by The Augustine Fellowship, Sex and Love Addicts
Anonymous, Fellowship-Wide Services, Inc.
1550 NE Loop 410, Suite 118, San Antonio, TX 78209
e-mail: slaafws@slaafws.org   web: http://www.slaafws.org
All rights reserved.

First printing, 1986. Reprinting, 1987, 88, 89, 90, 91, 92, 93, 94, 95, 96, 97, 98, 99,
2000, 01, 02, 03, 04, 06, 07, 08, 09, 10, 11, 12
Last figure above indicates year of this printing.

Grateful acknowledgement is made for permission to reprint and adapt
the following:

The Twelve Steps and Twelve Traditions of Alcoholics Anonymous
are copyrighted by Alcoholics Anonymous World Service, Inc.,
reprinted for adaptation by permission of the publisher.

Material from *Knowing Woman* by Irene Claremont de Castillejo is
copyrighted by the C.G. Jung Foundation, reprinted by permission
of the C.G. Jung Foundation.

The logo is a registered Trademark of The Augustine Fellowship, Sex and Love
Addicts Anonymous, Fellowship-Wide Services, Inc.

This book is S.L.A.A. Fellowship-Wide Services Conference-approved literature.

Library of Congress Cataloging in Publication Data

Main entry under title:
Sex and Love Addicts Anonymous.
        1. Sex and Love Addicts Anonymous. I. Title.
HQ72.U53S4 1986   306.7   85-30829
ISBN 0-9615701-0-5 (cloth)
ISBN 0-9615701-1-3 (paper)
ISBN 0-9615701-8-0 (audio tape)
ISBN 0-9615701-9-9 (compact disc)

Printed in the United States of America

Contents

Personal Stories of Addiction and Recovery

Preface

Since the beginning of Alcoholics Anonymous in 1935, the Twelve Steps of that fellowship's program of recovery have been adapted to a wide variety of human problems. Among these are gambling, overeating, smoking, narcotics abuse and child abuse.

To the general hopelessness of addiction, the Twelve Steps of recovery bring an elegant simplicity. The principles in them may well be universal. They were not original with A.A., but have been found in every major religion and philosophy.

The principles are simple enough: admission of the true source of the problem (addiction to the activity itself); reliance upon God or some other source of power beyond one's own resources for guidance in recovery; willingness to inventory one's own character defects and share this inventory with another; a readiness to come to grips with basic character flaws and make restitution to others; and commitment to these principles as a continuing way of life. The summation principle, the Twelfth Step, is the affirmation of personal recovery through accepting the responsibility to take the commitment to this way of life into action by sharing it with others. And it is here that true love, which is of God, and makes it possible for one person to touch the soul of another, is found and expressed.

Given the comprehensive scope of these principles, why then is there a need for special fellowships which address themselves to specific addictive disorders? The answer seems to be that although the principles of recovery as codified in the Twelve Steps apply across the board, at a practical (and thoroughly human) level individual addicts tend to think of addiction only in terms of whatever the indulgence is that *they* can't handle. The differing addictive preferences of other addicts may seem bewildering or threatening. The alcoholic, for instance, may find the compulsive overeater's inability to control eating incomprehensible, or even laughable; the gambling addict who never wants too much to drink because alcohol makes him ill cannot understand the alcoholic who drinks to sickness, and then drinks again; the compulsive overeater who experiences an act of love and is satisfied cannot understand the feelings of the sex and love addict for whom all there is, is never enough. Each lonely addict, hungry for fellowship, and trapped in the compulsive need for some specific indulgence that only increases the yawning void within, is in a kind of pain which *he* or *she* feels only someone who has similarly experienced it in *his* or *her* form of addiction can truly understand. A fellowship of others who can truly say, "Yes, I understand—I felt that way too" is a vital part of what makes recovery possible in each avenue of addiction. Hence the need for Twelve Step fellowships specific to each addiction.

Now there is *this* fellowship, Sex and Love Addicts Anonymous, and *this* book, based on the experiences of those who found that a basic human need for close relationship with another, combined with a realization of one's sexual capacities as an expression of commitment in such a relationship, could be debased by addiction into a compulsive search for sex and romance, or obsessional entrapment in relationships characterized by personal neediness and hyperdependency—in patterns that could forever prevent really meeting the underlying need for authentic experience of self and other. The sex and love addict would come to substitute the thrill of sexual adventure or intensity of "love" for the more encompassing satisfactions, founded first and foremost on self-respect, and later realized in family, career and community. The temporary addictive escape from a painfully perceived reality would be sought more and more, until the seeking itself felt like some primitive drive for survival in pursuit of which everything, including self-worth, would be sacrificed.

Alcoholics Anonymous grew from the principle that one alcoholic could maintain recovery by reaching out to help another one. However, history also shows that the message of hope and the guidelines to recovery can be shared in book form as well as through personal contact. That "carrying the message" principle of the Twelfth Step of recovery insures that lonely sex and love addicts, desperate for recovery and armed only with a copy of this book, will have the opportunity to find that special friendship and fellowship with others which is so vital—so life giving. This book does not simply borrow from the other fellowships that have used the principles of the Twelve Steps: it is an embodiment of our own experience, from the life of one who found recovery and the adventures of those early members who struggled for self-honesty against this baffling, mind-altering dis-ease, to the shared experiences of those who stayed, learning from the mistakes of those who did not.

On January 14th, 1984, at the first Fellowship-Wide Service Conference, S.L.A.A., those sex and love addicts who had been returned to sanity and usefulness in human society and community through this program judged that this book carried their message of hope and recovery truthfully enough to be the basic text of Sex and Love Addicts Anonymous, capable of helping those still suffering from this illness.

Those of us who have lived this book from its beginning know that its real worth will not be gauged primarily by mental health professionals or literary

As a child I both hated and idolized my drunken father, and hated my mother for being so ineffective in putting a stop to the daily family holocaust. However, I also craved from her the message of "O.K.ness" which those nighttimes of nurturing gave me. I came away from early childhood with some very strange, if understandable, ideas. "The only way I know I'm loved is through experiencing physical contact." "I must never reveal my feelings, because to be 'sensitive' is to be vulnerable, and to be vulnerable is to suffer the consequences of being considered a 'weakling.' "

These early concepts linked up forcefuly with the values epitomized by the movie heroes of those times. The movie hero John Wayne, in particular, exemplified a life-strategy of straight-arming his way through life, never showing any need for emotional nurturing. Using film heroes as my models, I decided that if I never showed my feelings I'd get what I wanted, that if I was abusive towards women they would be secretly smitten. Adoring me for abusing them, they would cling to me and never leave.

As I continued my way through elementary school, this attempt to deny my own feelings had understandable consequences. My emotional "needs," of course, never really went away. They were bottled up and, festering, triggered the kind of longing that resulted in my having insatiable crushes and secret passions towards certain schoolmates, both girls and boys. One girl in particular, two years my senior, "owned" me for nearly five years. Whenever she entered a room where I was, adrenalin would rush through me, leaving me short of breath, heart pounding. She never knew it.

The objects of my passionate crushes were always cast in a madonna-on-a-pedestal kind of role. They embodied a sort of unapproachable purity. Only in fantasy, where I would cast myself in heroic roles, performing chivalrous deeds of life-saving import, could I imagine my ardor ever being revealed to these madonnas.

Another theme emerged, partly as compensation for the paralysis of being ridden with crushes, and fed by a lot of unacknowledged hatred towards my mother, and by inference all women. I cultivated a John Wayne style of blunt assertiveness, around which my self-concept of masculinity revolved. Like such film-fantasy heroes, and one of my classmates who seemed to have great success with girls, I regarded girls who were interested in me as merchandise, rather than as individuals. In my mind "madonnas" and "whores" were the only two classifications for womankind.

Ironically, being thoroughly naive about the "facts of life" until the age of eleven, in spite of lots of exciting genital play with both boys and girls during my childhood, I was quite shocked to find out about orgasm. A few school friends, grown weary of tolerating my ignorance, finally told me about "how it happens," making me an object of ridicule in the process. I confronted my

Chapter 1

Discovery of the Illness
of Sex and Love Addiction:
A Personal History

I believe that when I was small, I was a sensitive child. My response to the natural world was one of wondrous curiosity. I loved and sought for harmony above all else.

But the emotional environment around me was seldom harmonious. My father was progressing quickly downhill with the disease of alcoholism, and my mother was preoccupied with holding things together, at whatever the cost.

I was a growing, sensitive child caught between two warring adults. I tried a thousand times over to believe in a logical and emotionally consistent world. I needed a way to smooth out within myself the terrible emotional extremes and physical violence going on around me. In the midst of this turmoil, I could never really make myself believe that I was loved, nor could I ever stop wanting to believe it. I didn't even have the words to explain to myself what was happening, and so a poisonous anger was finding its way into my heart.

Frequently overcome with grief, loss and feelings of abandonment, I had few experiences which gave me a feeling that I was O.K., that I had value as the creature God had created. Very, very occasionally I *would,* spontaneously, sense my alrightness before God. Such occasional experiences of this sort, so incongruous to what was happening in the rest of my life, shone like distant, receding beacons down the dark chasm of the next twenty-five years. But these early positive experiences of myself, very private indeed, were largely forgotten, and with them their sense of cherished hope.

The only other solace in my early years resulted from physical contact with my mother. Usually she was physically undemonstrative, except for rocking me to sleep when I awakened with nightmares, and punishing me with spankings. When I was sick with fever, however, she would take me into bed with her and we would sleep like spoons, my little body tightly curled, surrounded and enveloped with the head-to-toe sensuousness of maternal warmth. This pleasure, as blissful as it was, did not register with me as sexual arousal. It was, however, in this enfolding warmth and the body caress of being held close that I felt a powerful *emotional* message: "I am nurtured, protected and wanted; I am *loved.*"

critics. The merit of this message will be most measured by those who are helped by it. It is our hope that the truth of the message will speak through the inevitable limitations of the messengers. We offer it in deep gratitude for the gift of recovery, for the experience of personal dignity, which has come to us through this Fellowship, bestowed by a Power greater than ourselves.

mother with my newly acquired street knowledge. She blanched, and finally came up with an explanation of the sex act which, according to her description, had about as much emotional content as installing plumbing fixtures. No more enlightened or human description was ever forthcoming from her.

I experienced orgasm for the first time one summer evening at boys camp. Some of the older campers had instructed me in the practice of masturbation, but I hadn't taken them seriously. Nevertheless, one night I started playing with myself and experienced strong genital sensations for the first time. When they crescendoed into orgasm the effect was so startling and unexpected that I was caught completely off guard. It was as if there were swirling lights in front of my eyes, as the power of it swept through my body. The experience was transcendental. I felt that I had tapped some secret, tabooed power which really ran the universe, but which was never acknowledged in the world.

Orgasm via masturbation became a daily staple for me right away. Unlike many people, I had not been taught religious taboos concerning masturbation since talk about such things was simply nonexistent. Therefore I was free to expand this practice without feeling that I was violating moral rules.

The stage was now set for me to embark on the active phase of what I would, much later, diagnose as my sex and "love" addiction. The old sense of emotional "O.K.ness" and security, originally derived from physical, sensuous contact with my mother, now combined with a strong genital focus. That, and a belief that I had to grab for everything I wanted, paved the way for a self-styled, would-be guilt-free promiscuity.

The pop culture of that time was already starting to pulsate with the vibratory messages of sexual entitlement conveyed in such "buzz" expressions as "new morality," "guilt-free sex," "sexual revolution," "the pill," etc., etc. Such culturally sanctioned license was ready-made camouflage, in the midst of which I entered into active addiction.

I was consciously looking for situations where I could experience sexual contact without emotional entanglements—sex without commitment. Soon I did manage a situation where I could have sex, only to find myself unable to perform due to anxiety. This heightened my apprehension about whether my body could be viable as currency in the sexual arena, not to mention fears about being gay.

The emotional insecurity from this initial failure was quickly replaced with more determination to assert myself. But all my early sexual situations were loaded with anxiety concerning my ability to live up to what I saw as my right to satisfaction. Of course I did not feel very natural or at ease in trying to arrange for sexual encounters. Inwardly I felt shy and constrained, and often depressed to the point of inertia. I did not feel myself to be attractive to others. It was only through redoubling my efforts at being assertive and bold that I could force myself through my depression and apprehension on out into the world.

Strangely, about five months after the first unconsummated sexual encounter, I found myself, without having any prior intention of doing so, telling a girl that I was deeply in love with her.

I had not anticipated this at all! Previously she had been just another person to whom I had reacted out of awkwardness with a sardonic, sarcastic, conceited attitude. I had never even thought of her in sexual terms. How amazing it was to me, then, to experience that hypnotic sense of merging with her and giving my heart away to her from the depths of my soul. Along with this feeling of discovering and sharing my deepest self with another came a transcendent feeling not unlike what I had experienced when I first discovered orgasm several years earlier. Yet no intercourse occurred on the night I discovered my heart and gave it away (or, rather, discovered my heart through giving it away).

So I had set out to achieve a sense of my own well-being through sex, without commitment, and suddenly, unexpectedly, found myself ambushed by my own emotional neediness into a committed relationship . . . *at the very first opportunity!* The power of my long denied emotional yearnings for love completely overwhelmed me. My "lover," I thought, was my "one and only," the one light in my life—made in heaven for me.

My championing of the cause of undisciplined, unemotional, guilt-free sex did not, however, disappear as a result of my great avowal of cosmic love to one woman. I still craved wanton sexual experience, and my emotional bond to another hardly made a dent on these yearnings. In fact, I cursed myself for having become involved with Lenore. In terms of what I had set out to accomplish, this should have been the last thing I wanted. Yet she spoke to my soul, at least the part of it that was rough-edged and vulnerable.

I fought against the irreconcilable turn my life had taken. All I wanted to do was have sex, and now I had a woman drawing me in at some level, and it seemed I could not resist. Of course, part of me did not want to stop it. Lenore cast me in her life in heroic, chivalrous terms. I was smitten with her enshrining me as her knight in shining armor mounted on a white steed. It seemed, for me, a realization of the heroic role in which I had cast myself. That this should actually be happening to me in the "real world" was just too much. I could not let her down. The cause was holy.

So Lenore became for me a root of emotional stability—or at least some emotional consistency, even though the thought of my being "tied down" made me feel like some caged beast. Once the blush of romance had faded I felt miserable with her—not because I didn't feel that I "loved" her, but because my own cravings pushed me toward other sexual experiences. Whenever I was not with her, I was on the make. I couldn't stop myself, and seldom wanted to. When I was locked in the embrace of still another conquest and felt my power well up and deliver itself, I would feel that *that* act, *that* embrace, was all there was in the world. Nothing else mattered.

I was hopelessly at odds with conflicting passions and pummelled myself without cease: "If you really want to just screw around, then why can't you break up with Lenore and drown yourself in what you claim you want? If you really want to be with Lenore, why can't you stop screwing and romancing around?" My sense of emotional and sexual entitlement had me feeling that I deserved both. In truth I could say "No" to neither.

I did not suspect just how deep my dependency on Lenore extended. When she left me unconditionally, some two years after we had rushed together, it was a life-threatening blow to me. I was caught in a swirl of unrelenting grief. Weight loss, lack of sleep, loss of appetite, vomiting, and thoughts of suicide were my constant companions. The horror of this "death"—a death of my "love" relationship with Lenore—was that my whole self-concept, which had come from being part of her, was also dying. My sense of "I" had come out of my sense of "We." I had no positive, personal, independent self-concept.

I denied as much of what was happening to me as possible, proclaiming loudly to myself that I could, and would, win her back, by force if necessary. However, I found a means of holding self-dissolution at bay which was much more powerful and convincing. I discovered the mind-altering potentials of alcohol.

What a great discovery! Alcohol, like masturbation before it, became a way to temporarily step off the world—to lose myself in the oblivion of instant tension release. Yet for me the discovery of alcohol as a way to pinch-hit for living life (with all its hard lessons) was probably fortunate. Lacking any other resources, at that time, from which to draw hope and meaning for the future, I might otherwise have done away with myself.

Part of the illusion alcohol gave me was the apparent ability to come closer to what I claimed I always wanted: a life of entitled, uninhibited, no-strings-attached promiscuity. That is, I could now have more exclusively sexual liaisons without having to employ the camouflage of shoddy romanticism. However, the pattern of my sexual and romantic behavior remained unaltered.

Mourning Lenore, and finding myself away at a rural college several hundred miles north from the familiar "bright lights" environment where I felt safe, I nurtured a vivid hatred at being trapped in such isolation. Keeping the hatred alive, I found I could draw a kind of strength from it, a will to survive against all odds.

Hatred as a motivating force had me packing my bags every Friday morning. After one class and an early lunch, I would hit the interstate, thumb outstretched, for the long trip south to the city. A large university was located in this city, and on one early fall weekend I attended a college dance. My whole purpose for going was to get drunk, get laid, and forget the fact that on Sunday I would have to hitch-hike back into isolation.

At this particular mixer I spotted a woman who was dancing, gyrating crazily, like some wounded moth. I sensed her arhythmical desperation, automatically reacted to it, and moved in to dance. With a load of alcohol in my system, I found it easy to match her manic, frenzied behavior with my own, and succeeded in drawing her notice. We talked and I lied to her, telling her that I was attending the local university, where she was enrolled. We did not sleep together. Little did I realize that once again, at the first opportunity, I had impulsively embarked on what was to be the next stable-yet-miserable relationship in my life. This one would make it unnecessary, at least for the moment, to go through a full grieving process over Lenore, and it would own me for the next two years.

On the surface, Lenore and Jean seemed very different. Their background, appearance, opinions, etc. were very dissimilar. I had defined the concept "love" for myself solely in terms of experiencing this strange Power which had driven me to surrender myself to Lenore so precipitously. I felt much less emotionally committed to Jean in terms of feeling that I "loved" her. She doted on me, however, and coming to expect this kind of non-stop attention, I succumbed, telling her, and trying to get myself to believe, that I really loved her. Nor did I find her sexually appealing. She struck me, physically, as quite ordinary. This lack of sexual attraction to her allowed me to use the fact that she was a virgin as an excuse to *avoid* sexual contact with her for the better part of a year. Although I outwardly championed a guilt-free, no-strings-attached sexuality, somehow I felt that by *not* having sex with Jean, I was *not* really committed to her at all.

Jean apparently worshipped me. I was the sun that rose on her life. She called me "Rich-the-miraculous," and bombarded me with attention. I had never experienced being "loved" like that, having such power over another. The more she bombarded me, the more I figured that I had her hooked, and that I could remain uncommitted without fear of losing her. She seemed incapable of leaving me.

The liberty of having Jean so deeply hooked she could not leave, and *apparently* not being hooked myself, was a situation that I did not fail to exploit. I had long been having sex with someone who lived in the same college dormitory where Jean lived, and I continued to do so. This was becoming quite obvious to Jean. Also, Jean had a friend who was just too available for me to pass up. She was one of several women over the years who physically delivered everything I thought I wanted. I got completely locked into her, although I tried to conceal it. When we were inevitably discovered, it meant the end of my relationship with Georgia, a fact I mourned. It also signalled the end of Jean's and Georgia's friendship of many years—a fact I was not capable of mourning.

I continued to resist making a statement of formal commitment to Jean. Sometimes I dropped out of sight for a while, but was unable to tell her forthrightly when I did not want to see her. I would feign illness, or a trip, or some other excuse, and just vanish. It remained for Jean to set the hook in me, and this she finally did.

We had started having sex after about a year. It was not very exciting from my perspective, but had become the path of least resistance. Overtly I felt no more committed to her than before. One evening she was not in her dormitory at the accustomed time I used to happen by (formal arrangements were unheard of with me). I had an uneasy feeling about this because she was *always* there. Casually at first, then more compulsively, I checked and rechecked to see if she was there. No Jean. The next morning I called her at 9 a.m. She had returned, and I was beside myself as to where she had been the whole night before. She could not give me a straight answer. Finally I challenged her, point blank, to tell me. She said she had slept with Bert—someone I knew slightly.

I was shattered. Jean was, I thought, *hooked* on me. This wasn't supposed to happen. Since my whole identity was constructed around being desirable and irresistible, this sent my head spinning. I kept envisioning them in bed together. It made me sick. I wanted to vomit. Yet I could not let myself erase that picture from my mind. I felt raped.

Jean observed all this carefully, and seemed conditionally contrite. I sensed after a while that I could still have her if I wanted her. The choice was no choice. We walked down to Bert's house to pick up some clothing she had left there the previous evening. Now she was disclaiming any further interest in him. She seemed as hooked on me as before—with a big difference: *I* was finally "committed."

As our relationship rambled on, Jean started to suspect the shoddy premise on which it was founded: a mutual investment in excessive emotional dependency. Also, she was becoming less able to overlook the glaring inconsistency between my stated commitment and my actual unavailability to her. Although supposedly committed to Jean, I spent most of my weekends elsewhere, in search of sexual adventure.

One typical evening I announced that I was going out alone, ostensibly to a jazz club. I spent the time instead immersed in romantic fantasies and sexual indulgence with a woman who had intermittently provided me with sex for several years. I got back to Jean's place very late. I was sure to take a shower and rinse my mouth out with mouthwash to get rid of my sex partner's body scent before climbing into bed next to Jean. The next day I was full of enthusiasm for the jazz group I had never heard.

With this scene more or less typical of many others, it's very apparent to me now that I was never able to be sure of what my feelings about Jean were, independent of addictive trappings. As much as she had invested in her fantasy of me and the super-human role I was supposed to fill in her life, she was nevertheless starting to be aware of my emotional inconsistency. A poignant scene revealed this growing awareness.

On a weekend spent at her mother's house in the country, we were driving through the countryside. She had once again mentioned a topic that had been in the air for months—marriage. I was beginning to feel the pressure towards this coming from her and her mother. As we were driving, I was feeling extremely lonely. I recall no greater loneliness than that of being with someone I supposedly loved without any deep, positive communication going on, or even being possible, between us! It's far lonelier than being by oneself.

Suddenly Jean dissolved into tears and sobbed that I didn't really love her. I felt like a cold wall of stone, awkward in the presence of her very real emotion. I found myself trying to reassure her . . . reassurances on reassurances. At that moment I felt thoroughly at odds with the protestations of my love and care, but I could not be honest because, love her or not, I really *needed* her. She was the security on which I depended for my ability to function. The commitment marriage would require was impossible, but so was doing without her. Being honest about the true scope of my feelings was not, and could not be, an option.

Sensing my ambivalence, she finally broke up with me. Six weeks later I begged her on my knees to marry me, tears streaming down my face. It was a plea for her to relieve me of the problem of *me*. Even though today I know that I was not capable of real love at that time, nevertheless, the withdrawal I suffered over Jean was even more acute and intense than what I had suffered over Lenore.

By now the pattern of my sex and "love" addiction had been set for a number of years. Only the cast of characters had changed. Naturally I did not recognize this. To me, every fresh pursuit held the promise of new and novel intrigue. I thought I was living the life that others secretly envied. "They are the gutless ones," I thought, "too scared to take a chance on living." The possibility that no durable happiness or fulfillment could ever come from living out this pointless pattern did not occur to me at all. In fact, the promise of the "next one" being *the* situation that would make me whole, or complete me in some way, was a carrot that seemed to be forever dangling in front of my nose, coaxing me onward.

With Kate the pattern was, in retrospect, achingly familiar at the outset. As the steady, security-providing situation in my life she could only be shown a small part of me. My life was now rigorously segregated into closed compartments. All of my efforts went to keeping them closed, so that my security with Kate would not be threatened by the constant romancing and seduction of others.

Kate and I endured a relatively turbulent, on again, off again relationship for several years. It was not until I got sober in Alcoholics Anonymous in late January, 1971, that the seeds of major change were initially sown. I was twenty-four years old. In the closing months of my drinking, Kate had become something of the voice of my "observing self" — a part of me that I was not too happy to discover existed. As the evidence mounted concerning my inability to stop drinking, I was finally able to become open, however narrowly, to A.A.'s help.

Yet there was something I needed to establish right away when I got sober from alcohol: that my sex and "love" life would not have to change! When I had been sober only about a month, a business trip yielded a brief but intense sexual/romantic intrigue, and convinced me that it wouldn't. It didn't.

I'm sure the fact that I could carry on my sex and "love" life as before helped make becoming sober in A.A. less frightening for me. This is not to say that I consciously resisted A.A. recovery. I became very active in this fellowship and got involved with the Twelve Steps of Recovery relatively early on. However, I could not be honest with myself in certain areas beyond my capacity and readiness to be so. The attitudes I held concerning how I pursued my sex and "love" life were so close to my view of myself as a person that I could not be expected to voluntarily question them very much—until life and circumstance might force me to do so.

During my first year of A.A. sobriety, Kate worked for a man who was also attracted to her, and who had much to offer. It was against the threat of this competition that I asked her to marry me. This was the only move that would keep her with me, I thought. So it was that Kate and I got married when I was about eight months sober. I made an inner resolve to be "faithful"—although the notion that I could or would never romance or screw around again was incredible. Despite these misgivings, my engagement, wedding, and honeymoon went off well, and this was a period when I was able to enjoy some closeness with Kate. There was even some feeling of relief that on some level I was at least taking a chance on life and living, rather than resisting it at all cost.

Addictions, however, are like internal hurricanes. Periodic lulls may occur, but a tidal onslaught may recur at any time. Six weeks after our honeymoon I had contracted VD and, not knowing whether Kate could be infected, I forced myself to tell her about it. We went through the local VD clinic together—real togetherness!

Now I was running the risk of deeper emotional involvements with my sexual partners because the old emotional vulnerability was no longer being masked by alcohol. Real emotional intrigue began to come into play. I was no longer looking merely for adventurous sexual experiences, I was searching for a whore/madonna combination, a woman who could give me sexual oblivion, yet speak to my soul.

After only five months of marriage I fell completely "in love" with Felicia, who combined desperate sexual craving with spiritual yearnings. I went with frightening speed from being coolly in control to a state in which my appetite for her was insatiable. The extent of my enslavement was revealed when I went on a trip with my wife to Nova Scotia. Inexplicably, I suffered an acute anxiety attack the second day of the trip. I felt I was facing imminent dissolution and death. I was hysterical, hunched up in a fetal position on the front seat of the car, sobbing and shaking uncontrollably. I called this a "travelling phobia." Today I know it was the result of being cut off from Felicia—not knowing what she was doing in my absence or whether she would be readily available to give me my "fix" when I returned. This was so unnerving that I compressed the two week trip into five days of manic, crazy driving. "Give Kate enough to appease her, to let her know that I'm doing my best, but get me home to my source of supply"—so ran my thoughts.

Finally, fearing that my carefully compartmentalized life was in danger of collapse, I terminated the relationship with Felicia. By a thin margin I kept it stopped, partly with the help of a new intrigue, another repetition of a now familiar pattern. After the torrid, almost out of control affair with Felicia, I became increasingly concerned with managing my tendency to become emotionally involved. Therefore I cultivated a number of "safe harbors" out of town where sexual favors, emotional intrigue, and romantic illusion could be indulged in with, I thought, relative safety. I also managed to cultivate a few situations locally where the risk of emotional involvement, which always seemed to lead to loss of control, seemed minimal.

In one of these relationships, with an older, married woman, sexual binges were coupled with a business relationship. Despite some intense, sporadic self-disgust on my part over the undisguised "meat-on-the-counter" quality of our sexual relationship, the arrangement persisted for several years. I would try to abstain sometimes, brimming over with self-loathing. But physical craving for relief of tension would warp my resolve, and I would find myself with her again, often conjuring up some fantasy or other in order to reach orgasm. I was using her as an embellished form of masturbation.

I justified this situation, as I did all others, by seeing it as my "sexual nature," my dominant drive, my primary characteristic. It was a devil to be appeased—and lived with. "Other people might not experience it this way," I thought, "but for me my sexual nature is the baseline—the foundation of who and what I most truly am." It was something I did not want to change. I was determined to take it to the grave with me, hopefully not hurting too many others along the way. No other alternative seemed at all possible, let alone desirable. Despite the accelerating nightmare, I had not yet experienced that amount of emotional pain which is needed before change is possible.

Kate got pregnant in November of 1975 by prior agreement, although my attitude had been that I never wanted to have children at all, just as I had never "wanted" to be married. Such situations represented bondage to me. Increasing responsibility could only impinge on my ability (my right!) to pursue sexual and romantic adventure. It was society that was sick, I thought, trying to force bondage upon me. I was a true pioneer of alternative modes of living—and loving. But my highly prized philosophy crumbled before the threat, once again, of losing Kate if I could not yield to her desire to have children. So, grudgingly, I complied with her wishes, without really changing my convictions one iota.

The pregnancy loomed, but the usual pattern of my behavior continued. In A.A., as in other parts of my life, I collected "rainchecks" with vulnerable, attractive women. One of these, Sarah, was especially intriguing. Sensing the danger of involvement, I tried to keep control by not sleeping with her. In spite of this, I became increasingly obsessed until the prospect of not seeing her was torment.

In February, 1976, Sarah suddenly withdrew and paid no attention to me at all for several days. I went into a state bordering on paralysis. The hook was already set very deeply. Then, just before I left town on business for a few days, I made an impulsive, last minute dash to her apartment and told her that I loved her. The relief of finally spilling the fact that I was hooked was matched only by the relief that I was going to be out of town for several days, and therefore could avoid dealing with the consequences of my newly avowed passion.

By the time I went on another trip a few weeks later, a missed connection and the resulting threat of missing the flight back home where I was scheduled to see Sarah put me extremely close to another acute anxiety attack and total loss of emotional control.

By the time Sarah and I had sex for the first time, the pent-up need, now sexualized and freely expressed, carried me into another world. I had never been able to come when a woman was giving me oral sex. With Sarah this barrier melted away. I felt introduced to a new level of the sexual mystery. Sublime sex with her once a week increased to daily maintenance doses within about three weeks time. Kate, her pregnancy really starting to show, would be up and out to work early in the morning. I would quickly climb out of bed, get over to Sarah's place and climb into bed next to her. There we would remain in a sort of timeless trance for hours, savouring each other. Looking into her eyes, I would engage her in recitations of: "I love you"; "I need you"; "You're the one I want"; "I can't live without you." An atmosphere of mutual hypnosis prevailed. Each of us seemed a candle into which the other's moth would fly.

Sarah as planned, feeling very tense. It was about half-past midnight when I arrived, Thursday—the day I finally cracked up. I remember needing endless reassurances from her that she was not leaving me now that I had inwardly committed myself to this thing which Sarah and I had created, which had long since taken on a life of its own.

Later, after only about four hours sleep, I prepared to attend Sarah's graduation. My father-in-law, as it happened, was a rather devoted alumnus of Sarah's college and was a class marshall that year. I knew that he would have been startled to see me there, and that I would not have been able to explain my presence. Inside the grounds, I spotted him early and had to watch carefully to avoid being detected. All of this while I was trying to appear nonchalant and otherwise attentive to my friends!

After the ceremonies I was to rendezvous with Sarah and her family. Sarah hung on my arm, getting me to pose with her for family pictures. I alternated between wanting to push everyone away from me and run away to safety, and trying to hide amongst them and be inconspicuous. My anxiety surged as I considered the very real possibility that my father-in-law might stroll by while his son-in-law was in a romantic pose with another woman, surrounded by a family he did not know.

After this horrendous episode I was to have lunch with friends. When we got to the restaurant, I was very near tears. I could not manage much longer. I was unable to open my mouth, let alone force any food into it. After ten minutes I excused myself from my concerned friends and went home. It was quiet there when I arrived; I was alone.

That afternoon a nap restored me somewhat, and a local merchant delivered a couch Kate and I had bought for the living room. But when Kate came home, I found myself unable to say or do anything. Kate started to pry, wanting to know if I was angry with her for something. The words just came out suddenly: "I want a separation." I couldn't believe I'd said this. She then asked, "Is there another woman?" I said, "Yes." "Is it Sarah?" I answered, "Yes."

She was furious and shocked, and I reacted from the depths of the turmoil I had been living with for many months, the power of my emotion heightened by the recent combination of circumstances which had so unhinged me. I wept, in a state of complete emotional collapse.

I was to have met Sarah that evening. Instead, Kate—her big belly wobbling—and I took a long, long walk around our town and talked, and talked, and talked. I somehow knew that nothing in my life could ever be the same again, and a part of me accepted that this was as it should be.

Kate called a sister who lived a few hundred miles away and arranged to stay with her when we separated. I felt that my guts were now open to inspection, and that in whatever time remained I wanted as much of my life

visible to the light of day as possible. We decided to remain living together only until such time as our child was born. I told her that I would continue to see Sarah because I had to; this was a non-negotiable condition. If Kate was electing to stay, she would have to accept this.

Most of the summer of 1976 was spent awaiting the arrival of our child, holding back nothing. I shared all my feelings with Kate about all that had transpired, going back as far as memory could take me—all this while continuing a progressively impassioned relationship with Sarah.

One aspect of my relationship with Sarah had been that I felt able to share my real feelings, my true self with her. Knowing her for less than two months, I had felt that Sarah knew me far better than Kate, whom I had known for eight years. And no wonder. I had been so highly mortgaged in my emotional life that I could never afford to be emotionally available to Kate. To know me was to leave me, since she would have found my promiscuity and emotional intriguing intolerable. I had, of course, an inner desire to be "known" by Kate. Yet it had only been through making vague allusions to my behavior (usually from the distant past) that I had been able to let Kate "know" me at all, while I hid from her anything that was *really* going on. I had both desires: a powerful desire to be known and loved for who and what I really was, and the desire not to rock the boat and upset a relationship which provided me security, even if I had never been happy or fulfilled in that relationship.

With my decision to withhold nothing of what I had done, the tide started to turn. The humiliation which each successive revelation brought me, and every ounce of pain these revelations inflicted on Kate, were the overdue accounts from years of a divided life. The illusion that I could forever avoid the consequences of my actions was permanently shattered.

All the consequences were now rushing together, compounded by the years they had been so rigorously managed and separated. To Kate's undying credit, she realized the importance of this dredging up of the sewer of my past—and she never flinched from her part of this process. She was seeing the reality of who and what she had been trying to make a marriage with. Her denial of our difficulties was also forever swept away.

Side by side with this brutal process were the times spent with Sarah. If my life was to be truly open, I also had to share with *her* as well as with Kate as much as possible of what was going on with me. I dared not make an exception for fear that I would descend quickly back into covert obsessive/compulsive activities, and to do this seemed to me like suicide.

I started vomiting up my festering past in mid-June, 1976, and essentially threw in the towel on a life built of closed, divided compartments. I experienced then for the first time in years some positive emotional feelings towards Kate that I was prepared to trust. My part of wanting to put our separation off until

after our child was born was grounded in what seemed genuine caring for Kate's side of this unfortunate debacle.

Therefore, I told Sarah that I really wanted to put in enough time at home to take full advantage of Kate's and my remaining time together. I told her that Kate's and my separation was not in doubt, but that the equation had changed: Kate had a lot of catching up on my life to do. The story of the two and a half months which followed is largely the story of how *unable* I was to carry out my resolve. Still, by maintaining open sharing of feelings and activities at all cost, I was able to gain perspective on just how powerless I was over managing my addictive relationship with Sarah.

Kate and I set up some ground rules. I proclaimed loudly, defiantly and self-righteously that I would continue to see Sarah and pursue full sexual and emotional involvement with her. Along with my "caring" for Kate there was much pent up frustration and need to blame her for my not being able to submerge myself in non-stop passion with Sarah! From that standpoint, I could not wait until Kate was gone, and even had fantasies of her being killed in an accident. Only part of me loathed this idea. Another part of me knew that it would be the easiest way out for me. Yet short of an "act of God," Kate was going to be around, and I knew that I would not, and could not, stop seeing Sarah while Kate and I were waiting for the baby.

Kate had only two conditions: that I would not sleep over at Sarah's place during our remaining time together, and that I would be home by 1:00 a.m. every night.

I'll never understand how Kate dealt with the pain it must have caused. She witnessed in a way that I could not (for I was too close to it) how completely manipulated I was by my own neediness for Sarah, and how completely I could rationalize my way out of facing my weakness, justifying it as "entitlement." For my part, I didn't want to stop long enough to look at the evidence of the way my moods would change radically without my being aware of it, but some evidence was starting to get through to me, regardless.

I would have a few good hours with Kate, enjoying warm feelings towards her, and a desire for sharing to continue. Then I would have a set time to see Sarah. I might feel somewhat resentful about having to see Sarah at first, because I wanted to preserve these good feelings at home. But I would leave, and once at Sarah's, I would watch this inner resolve disappear.

My perspective would alter *completely.* Now Sarah was the one with whom I was imagining myself in my golden middle years. Kate ceased to exist absolutely. As I succumbed to Sarah's sensuous force-field, I could see what was happening, but I *could not stop it.* Then I would be drawn into it entirely and feel the clock stop. An entrancing moment with her, ephemeral in real time, took on the qualities of eternity, and in such a moment all awareness of how my

mind had been altered was lost; I was overwhelmed.

At the 1:00 a.m. curfew I would return home, full of resentment about my horrendous state of affairs. Then Kate would react to my altered state: I could not be emotionally present to her—and I would see it and have to admit it. I would feel the terror of not knowing when I had stepped over the line into oblivion, of not knowing how it had happened, and of knowing that it would happen again. When I was in oblivion, it was all "I" wanted, but now I was starting to get the sense that I was oblivion's victim. I felt suddenly that I was being pursued by some diabolical force that was using me for its own purposes.

The times of seeing my powerlessness were few at first. The truth left me feeling like I was being eaten alive by my addictive relationship. It put me in touch with what the end could look like were I unable to stop: insanity, institutionalization, or suicide. I already knew that I could rule out the "more-of-the-same" possibility, because the consequences of my pattern were progressing. I could never hope to get away with it again over any duration. And yet the truth of my powerlessness told me that, even in the face of these dire consequences, I was unable to stop myself. Although seeing where I was headed with one half-opened eye, I was on the skids and they were greased.

I began to know authentic terror—observing my own insanity and, in observing it, knowing that the part of me doing the observing could be routinely overwhelmed by it. I was locked in, and condemned.

In the early stage of awareness concerning these matters, I reacted, knee-jerk style, with an attempt to terminate my relationship with Sarah. This was in early July. In some ways trying to break up with her was pre-emptive. I sensed in her an ambiguity concerning other sexual options in her life, despite her vehement protestations of undying "love." My emotional insecurity would skyrocket at the thought of her having sex or intrigue with others. I tried to deal with this fear by rationalizing it as being the projection onto her of *my own* wayward behavior and attitudes, and this bought me some short-term relief. However, the instability persisted. A power struggle was unfolding.

When I made my attempt to leave the relationship in early July, I fortified myself with positive thinking as best I could. The actual decision to leave was made on impulse while we were out for a drive, when I found myself delivering this message and feeling quite vindictive about it. When I got home, I announced the fact proudly, and promptly headed out to visit friends forty miles away to get my batteries charged. I was really going to do it, by God!

Less than twenty-four hours had elapsed when a trembling, thoroughly distressed Rich, in acute withdrawal, followed the path of least resistance and frantically called Sarah. Welcomed back into her arms and her body once again, I could only vaguely recall the impulse which had driven me to try to get out. I thought, "How could I have ever wanted to leave this?" as I again succumbed,

and was numbed.

As the summer wore on, with variations on this basic dependency and power struggle, I felt in private moments ever more despairing. I continued to maintain my "open-ness," sharing everything that I was feeling/thinking/experiencing at all costs. Once I was on a trip and nearly succumbed to having sex with a woman who had, several years earlier, given me a "raincheck" for sexual adventure. Alone with her now in her home, set way back in a hilly woodland, I ached for it. Yet the consciousness of my condition and the consequences associated with it did not leave me, although I wished it had. After an impassioned kiss and body caress, on the verge of plunging, I forced myself to get up from the couch and make two long distance phone calls—one to Kate, the other to Sarah. I explained to each what had almost happened. I knew that in making these calls I was guaranteeing that there would be emotional consequences, but these external constraints were the only things that could hold me in check. To proceed with sex would have given Sarah the ammunition with which she could destroy me. Bitterly retreating from the agitation of this unconsummated sexual titillation, I was forcing myself to learn something about the futility of setting myself up for these things if the bottom line of sexual and romantic immersion was removed as an option. I had much to learn.

Early on the morning of August 16th, I came home at the customary 1:00 a.m. After some two months of difficult waiting since learning of my relationship with Sarah, Kate was about to give birth.

Her labor was long and intense. As I watched her, I felt anguish. I felt that much of what I was witnessing was not the pain of labor, but rather an expression of the agony of the situation she was in, and for which I felt quite responsible. Yet even during transition, I skulked out of the labor room, found a pay phone, and established that all-important connection with Sarah. We would have dinner, and with Kate in the hospital, I would spend the night at her place.

It was bizarre, at dinner later, to be receiving warm congratulations from Sarah and her roommates over my new paternal status—the father of a baby girl. Kate was not mentioned.

When Kate left the hospital after four days, I knew that about two weeks remained before we would split. I was still strongly in favor of our separation. At the same time, I realized that our time left together would be the end of what had been a lengthy and tortuous process. My life was in the open now, however jagged and disparate the separate pieces might be.

The "open-ness" which I had held the line on since mid-June had largely erased the advantage Sarah had enjoyed earlier in the spring—that of knowing me, and knowing more about me, than Kate did. This open-ness concerning my

active thoughts and feelings continued to pay dividends. Although I felt more strongly than ever that the time remaining between Kate and me was precious, it was all the more glaring that, despite my stated intentions, I continued to be with Sarah a disproportionate amount of time. I could not kid myself about it, or rationalize to myself the appropriateness of it. I was being forced to note more and more the disparity between my stated intentions and my actual behavior.

Of course, I still had a vested interest in *not* seeing this discrepancy. To *really* acknowledge it was to admit my powerlessness over my sexual and emotional conduct, and this carried with it the possibility that I might have to *change.* It was far easier to continue to cast blame on external circumstances.

In September, I drove Kate and my little baby daughter several hundred miles away to Kate's sister's house. The night prior to this I had been in a musical performance at a college, and Sarah had gone with me. I had felt so exhausted and dissipated that prior to the concert I had wondered how I was going to be able to go on stage and face an audience at all. I rallied, and lost myself in the performance itself. I dropped Sarah off very late after the concert and the trip back, and said goodbye to her. She was going away to an island resort the weekend I was taking Kate and the baby north.

Somehow, on a few hours sleep, I mobilized myself for the day's journey. As we drove, I looked at Kate and then glanced back at the sleeping baby in the wicker bassinet on the back seat. I felt a flood of emotions. I began to reflect, inwardly, on how tormented my "twenties" had been. I was nearing my thirtieth birthday. What did I want for my "thirties"? I looked at Kate and my child, and felt that I wanted the security of belonging in my family. I wanted "maturity." I wanted to cast my lot *here.* This private glow lasted most of the trip. I couldn't share it with Kate, because I knew it might commit me to something I might not be able to live up to.

I flew home the following day, having helped set up the baby's new crib and said my goodbyes. Now I was full of resolve. "I must," I thought, "break up with Sarah now. She's away for the long weekend, and it's Saturday night. I've got two days to try to consolidate myself in my resolve. I'll go to any lengths, *any* lengths to be rid of her."

The first challenge to my resolve occurred on the way home. I had arranged to be met at the airport by Sarah's friends. Now this panicked me. I *knew* that I wanted my family, but I knew that my emotional convictions were soluble in Sarah's force-field and that seeing her friends could set off an inner landslide. I was frightened. Feigning enthusiasm, I ditched them as quickly as I could. I got home and walked into an empty apartment for the first time, now on my own. My cat was there, and I hadn't lost my resolve to leave Sarah.

Originally the plan had been for me to join Sarah on her long weekend after

I had returned from enacting my separation from Kate. This was to be a celebration. I knew I couldn't do this. My consciousness of wanting out was so fragile that I knew I had to nurture and protect it. Sarah called late Saturday evening and I was caught off guard. I managed to say that I was not coming to spend the rest of the weekend with her; I would see her when she got back. On Sunday I once again fortified my resolve with an all day trip to visit another family. I tried to soak up as much of their communal energy as I could, and I arrived back, still with a strong intention to split with Sarah.

It was quite late Sunday when I got home. On my answering machine was a message from Sarah. She had taken an early boat and had apparently dashed home as quickly as she could. She clearly was distraught, none too secure about what my current emotional state might be, and knew, undoubtedly, what she would have to do if it had turned against her. I was again put off balance by her message and the fact that she was at that moment less than a mile away from me. I felt invaded.

I made an impetuous decision to see her then, that very night. I called her and told her that I would be over. I knocked at the door and was greeted by her delicious, naked form under her unfastened bathrobe. She moved to hug me and kiss me and I felt myself stiffen—not my penis, but my whole body. I felt like wood; I *could not respond.* She led me into her bedroom and down on her bed. I heard myself say, "I want to see how it will work out between Kate and me; that's what I really want." I was still rigid, unable to relax. A long silence followed. Finally she said, "Why don't you just go home." As a bridge-burning gesture I took the key to her apartment off my key ring and tossed it on her desk. I may have said something like, "We're through," but I don't remember. More likely I tried to convey this feeling safely—and ambiguously—through silence. Then I turned and walked out. I arrived home still feeling strongly resolved, if somewhat traumatized, and inwardly congratulated myself that I had had the guts to face her: to look into those eyes of hers, and say what I had to say.

I had declared my intentions. Inwardly I felt that if I could create six weeks of distance between us, then I might have sufficient perspective on things to make a more far-reaching decision.

On Labor Day, 1976, I left town to visit yet another friend's family to try to further fortify myself. Back in my apartment late Monday, I planned to go way out of my way to attend an A.A. meeting where I felt that I would not be likely to encounter Sarah. I awakened Tuesday feeling needy and in withdrawal, but still my resolve held. I pulled myself together and left to attend a mid-day meeting.

I arrived at the meeting place. One quick glance around the room and adrenalin surged through me like a shock wave. It was as if I somehow "saw" her—felt the force-field of her presence—before I could actually see her. Sarah *was* there, and by the time I actually saw her I was already inside the door and highly visible. What could I do? I pretended not to notice her and went about getting coffee, planning a quick exit before the meeting ended. As I tried to make my way to the door, inconspicuously, without looking back, I was aware of her starting to get up from her seat. I was several steps along the sidewalk headed away from the building before she reached me. "Rich, STOP," she said. I tried to look aside, but could not avoid meeting the desperate gaze of those imploring, vivid dark eyes. "I'll talk to you in six weeks," I said. She got in front of me so as to force me to look right at her. "I can't go on like this; I'm just going to go crazy," she said. I did not reply but walked around her and kept walking, stomach churning, feeling ragged and war-torn.

Later that night a very rough-edged Rich called Sarah on the phone... with nothing particular to say...just needing the connection. One long, ambiguous pause and the scales tipped decisively. Twenty minutes later I was back in her body, back in her bed, soothed with sweet love noises. I forgot that I had ever been away, or ever wanted to be.

With Kate living far away, I might have been forever without the benefit of any further perception of my own desperation. However, psychotherapy, which I had begun a short time before, began to take hold at this time. I found myself, in those sessions during the first three weeks of September, railing on about how much I hated being in bondage to Sarah, and how much I wanted to be rid of this dependency on her. The word addiction was never used, but it was clear that I somehow expected my therapist to provide me with some magical key or secret knowledge which would enable me to make a break. In truth, I really wanted my therapist to make the break for me (and take up the slack herself). My awareness of powerlessness and desperation, however, only persisted during the therapeutic hour and a short time thereafter. It would vanish with the onset of that gelatinous solubility I would experience once again around Sarah.

I visited Kate three weeks later. She had cultivated the hope that I had broken up with Sarah, since I had seemed so highly resolved to do this. I had not, however, informed Kate about my subsequent failure to do so. (Once re-immersed, of course, the "failure" of my strongest resolve had not seemed like a failure.) Only on the last day of my visit did Kate and I have any communication. There was no sex.

Arriving back in town very late Saturday evening, I saw Sarah Sunday afternoon. She had established an "insurance" position with another lover during my absence. Usually I would have been consumed by jealousy, but now I responded with anger and disappointment, the full extent of which I was afraid to show. She seemed eager to keep our arrangement going with a sexual fix. Usually I was an eager taker under such circumstances, but now I felt at odds with myself, with an aggressiveness which was anything but loving. Also, amidst our intercourse I saw her with eyes tightly closed and with her hands clawing her pillow and bedsheets. I normally would have seen these as signposts of heightened ecstasy, and this would have further stimulated me. My reaction now was altogether different. I realized that I could have been anyone else, that my seeming uniqueness as a "lover" was an illusion. I was trying to trump up a sense of my singular, irreplaceable qualities as a person through engaging in one of the great common denominators of mankind. Hardly unique, I was merely another player.

Early Sunday evening, I called Kate long distance. She was still angry over my recent visit to see her, feeling that I had acted under false pretenses. Kate told me that we had spent the whole summer examining my life, and our lives together. We had discussed at depth, she said, all that had been in the past, and what might be salvagable to build on in the future. She said she could no longer tolerate seeing me while I was still with Sarah. As far as she was concerned, the summer's process was finished the day we separated. She wanted no further continuation of *that* process—no more of that kind of pain. "What about my relationship with my daughter?" I asked, grasping at straws. "Not at the expense of my sanity," Kate replied. I realized that she was right. I knew I could not argue anything else; I did not want to. I could not criticize her in *her* resolve. I respected her for it.

It was early Sunday evening, September 26, 1976, after the phone call to Kate. I was due to pick up Sarah, but feeling extremely ambivalent about this. A desire was crystallizing within me to take myself out of circulation from her and from anyone. Suddenly, I knew what I had to do. I was faced with a turning point that could not be avoided any longer. I called Sarah and told her that I was going into seclusion to make an inventory of our relationship, and that when I had completed my inventory, I would be in touch. I then said goodbye and hung up.

I went out to an A.A. meeting *alone* that evening, and felt relief at even this little assertion of freedom, meeting my own needs, rather than servicing hers. I was also somewhat in awe of the task which I knew now lay before me, for I knew full well that I had been scuttled twice previously in my attempts to break free. How could I be at all sure that I could now assert my freedom and make it stick? I knew I could not be sure. No pep talk in the world could prepare me.

Yet I had reached a point where I knew that, if I went back in one more time, I might never get back out of it again. Suicide seemed a real possibility. Even short of bodily suicide, I was aware of feeling conscious terror over the prospect of irretrievably losing my sanity. My feelings were a strange mix: humility concerning my profound frailty combined with terror of succumbing to it, combined with some resolution (the value of which I could not assess at that time) to try yet again to change. By not committing myself brashly and prematurely to an "outcome" in regard to Sarah, I bought myself some precious time; so precious, in fact, that the time seemed sacred to me.

Arriving home from the meeting late Sunday evening, I sat down at the kitchen table and started to write. Out poured the details about the nature of my crisis. Then I set down chronologically as much about my relationship with Sarah as I could. Initially, I wrote blindly, but as I went on, some form emerged. My inventory included sections dealing with both positive and negative aspects of my relationships with Kate and Sarah. As my writing continued, I began to realize that I had, in a sense, been equally ill in both relationships. I looked at the long held dichotomy with which I had beaten myself for years: "Do I want a stable commitment in my life or do I want to screw around? Why can't I settle for one or the other?" A concept emerged of how those questions had been unanswerable for me because I had never been capable of enough emotional consistency to even begin to know the potential qualities of a committed relationship. I had traded my feelings for the fool's gold of addictive intensity.

As I wrote and reflected I came to understand that my choice was not, at depth, the choice between a "Sarah" or a "Kate." I was faced, rather, with the choice to withdraw from my obsessive/compulsive pattern of sexual pursuit and emotional dependency. Encountering and facing any and all pain along the way through this process of withdrawal, I could become capable of making some decisions about how to live my life. This would now be based on the discovery of who and what I really was, which might emerge during my time alone, in full awareness of my addictive past. My ability to live my way into an answer to my dilemma could only come through voluntarily becoming available to withdrawal.

I knew full well that if I were to follow this path the pain of withdrawal would be immense. I realized that, for me, the process involved not simply ending my addictive relationship with Sarah, but the unconditional withdrawal from a whole pattern of addiction which extended back at least fifteen years. Nothing less than going through the death of all that I had been in the world up to that time—of experiencing the dissolution of my former self—seemed required. I could only glimpse what such a "withdrawal" would entail and the extent to which it would unravel me. I felt I was on the brink of a conscious commitment to it, but I also knew that I could have no guarantees for the specific results. I would have to let it take me where it would.

In this frame of mind I was not so much chasing after change. It was, rather, as though the need for change had caught up with me. I could either accept its mandate or die. In my situation this mandate was presenting itself in a form that seemed stark and clearly defined, however reluctant I might be to recognize it. Nevertheless, my current straits seemed to carry the possibility of being an opportunity for a kind of death/rebirth experience that might bear golden fruit. I embraced this possibility with fervent hope, praying all the while that I would be given Grace to further aid me in discerning my own personal truth. I had hope, and a sense of being in touch with the truth, even if I could not know in advance the ways in which a transmuted Rich—renewed, and possibly made whole—might change. My "dilemma," so terrifying on one level, began to appear as an inevitable consequence of my sex and "love" addiction: the result of an inexorable progression which could only have ended in this sort of predicament. My choice was not between two kinds of lovers. It was between the old patterns and a completely new identity for myself which I could not even envision.

I completed the bulk of my inventory in about two days, on my thirtieth birthday, in 1976. It was the most precious document I had ever, and probably would ever, write. I hugged it. I knew I had the truth on paper now. My feelings and thoughts, so easily dissolved in the neediness of an addictive onslaught, were now frozen on paper. I could retrieve them at will; they would "stand still" for me at last.

Internally I sensed that I had turned a corner. Externally I was still very frightened as to whether I would be able to act in accordance with the truths about myself and my addiction which had surfaced through the inventory process. My message to Sarah had been a unilateral one of "taking myself out of circulation." I did not want to be interrupted. However, I knew that I could not count on her "cooperation." To do so could create an illusion of "partnership" around the very issue of just how impossible the "partnership" was!

Having completed most of my inventory, I went out for a while. On returning late in the afternoon of my birthday, I found four white roses in my mailbox, with a card signed simply "S." My reaction was immediate and intense; an emotional connection had been reopened. I think I took the roses upstairs, and had them in my apartment only a few moments before I started to feel transfixed by them. I looked at them closely. The flowers were not well formed and seemed to droop a little. The white of the roses was not pure, but rather struck me as an anemic off-white, as if they might once have been red but had had the color sucked out of them. This aroused in me the strong sense of how sucked dry and bled I had felt for months in this relationship. The promise of separating from Kate had been that the tension born of managing two irreconcilable relationships would ease. Ever since Kate's departure, however, my tension had run at even higher levels. Sarah had continued to say that we would have the opportunity, after Kate left, to discover what was between us without encumbrances. As I looked at the roses, I could imagine Sarah saying things like, "What a shame you broke it off before we even had a chance to discover what we *really* had together," or, "You never really gave us a chance."

As I focused on the roses, I knew that the tension and anxiety was an immutable feature of the relationship with Sarah. It was not ancillary. The idea that the relationship was more than this tension, or could exist outside of it, was a lie, a dangerous deception. Such a concept could only serve to set the hooks deeper, as salvation and deliverance would always appear to be just around the next bend . . . ever, so elusively, just out of reach . . . if only I might try a little bit harder . . . .

I took the four roses out onto the front porch and looked at them for what seemed like a long time. I felt them crying out to me—for me. I felt rage boiling in my belly, and suddenly I took them into the street and ripped them apart, mangling with my hands all four flowers and stalks and crushing them underfoot. It was an exultant moment. Afterwards I scraped up the remains and found a trash barrel around the corner on a dead-end street. Now dispassionate, I dumped the shredded blossoms and stalks into it. I walked away. The die was cast.

I knew that I could not count on leading any kind of charmed life in effecting my resolution to break with Sarah. I screened all calls on my answering machine and was away from my apartment much of the time. I felt I had to do something to inform her of my decision. I also knew that if I put a premium on my "style" of letting her know, and wound up explaining myself into those eyes, I would probably fail. There could be no Hollywood heroics for me. If I were really intent on getting the task done, then I could afford to be cowardly about it. Therefore, I decided to write a letter.

The letter said, simply:

Sarah,

I am terminating our relationship. I have come to realize that for all the love there has been between us, and there's been much, at least an equal part of sickness, obsession and neurosis has been present also.

My long term needs have been consistently sold out to my getting my short term feel-good buttons pressed, and you are a master button presser. My own personal center has been thrown askew through my trying to constantly service your needs, which are also excessive.

My inventory has been exhaustive and has led me to the lamentable truth that you are bad news for me. Therefore, I'm getting out now.

We are all through.

If you are tempted to contact me, I ask you to re-read this letter.

Rich

I finished the rough draft of this letter on Wednesday evening, and on Thursday, September 30, 1976, I mailed it.

When I dropped this letter in the mailbox, it was *the act,* the continental divide between watersheds, a gesture of great symbolic and practical importance for me. All that happened before belonged to one phase of my life—a phase centered on active addictive behavior. All that has happened since has constituted the adventure of becoming available to, discovering, and living a new kind of life.

Chapter 2

The Beginning of Recovery and of Sex and Love Addicts Anonymous

I entered withdrawal on September 30, 1976. I was living alone for the first time in my life. Because my addictive lover, Sarah, was active in A.A. in my locale, I had to make a complete change in the pattern of meetings I attended. I had become a fairly big fish in the local A.A. pond, and this was a painful thing to do, but do it I did. I became just another anonymous stranger at outlying meetings. It was one of the healthiest shrinkages of an inflated ego that I have ever had to suffer. The sense that I was doing what was good for a deeper part of me which I had previously ignored was very soul-satisfying indeed. The pleasure this brought me was simple, but real.

Before my withdrawal I had often thought of myself as possessing a certain quantum of sexual energy that had to either find an outlet or explode. Imagine my surprise when, free of all addictive sexual activity (including, for me, masturbation), I found that my ambient state was NOT HORNINESS. My body started to "cycle down." The stridency of its sexual urges diminished, and this happened early on in my withdrawal.

This shift away from sexual satisfaction and constant arousal extended into my dream life. Normally, wet dreams were one channel through which my charged libido sought release. Yet in my seven months alone I only experienced two of them.

What a discovery, after years of anywhere from ten to twenty orgasms per week! It was not that my body was never tense; it was just that the tension was not *sexual* in nature. Some underlying current was starting to reveal itself. The existence of this deeper stratum, decidedly non-sexual in character, was something I had not suspected.

An even greater awakening came as a whole new emotional landscape appeared. Because I was no longer screwing or romancing my feelings away, they began to come through into awareness where I was able to recognize and label them. These early discoveries carried great significance for me.

Now that bottom-line addictive behavior, acting out sexually or engaging in romantic intrigue, was no longer going on, I was left without the payoffs toward which my entire life had been geared. This did not mean, however, that I was not confronted with temptations now that I was in withdrawal. In fact, the opposite was true. I was literally besieged with such situations. I saw, for the first time, how automatically and unconsciously I was continuously creating a whole gallery of possibilities for loaded sexual and emotional events.

For example, I had always been an impulsive hand-shaker and a "kisser and hugger." This low-level physical contact had been a staple for me, day in, day out. This ongoing conduct had served the immediate function of finding out where my "rain check" situations were. On one level I had been constantly sifting people through this kind of "screening," looking for prospective partners for intrigue. Although I now knew that the payoffs from such intrigues were poisonous to me, I still found myself initiating them as second nature. This had the result of swiftly pushing me right up against the possibility of acting out addictively, and faced with this, I would recoil bitterly and back off. As this type of experience was repeated over and over, I finally became aware of the specific things I did to foster such intrigues, and became conscious of the futility of continuing to do them.

I came to understand, keenly, how enmeshed in this addiction I had unwittingly been. When I was still actively addicted, this network of potential intrigues had constituted a kind of safety net, or security, for me. Now, however, a long process of grieving began. Each little victory of awareness was accompanied by feelings of acute loss and mourning, for my little addiction-fostering habits were also important parts of my whole self image. These gestures of kissing and hugging and touching were the currency of my external personality, of the way in which I related to others.

As I accepted the mandate of withdrawal, it seemed like my whole identity was being pared back further and further. I cursed God for having given me an attractive body which seemed useless to me now because I could no longer abuse it. A friend's suggestion that perhaps the reason God had given me a beautiful body was so that I would be "nice for other people to look at" was no consolation whatsoever.

Sometimes I fantasized that I would become ugly, or that my penis would fall off and I would sprout breasts, or just age and shrivel up. I experienced long periods of anguish over my crisis of identity and meaning. My life was agonizing—an agony without horniness!

Some days I would arrive home late at night, filled with exasperation over my plight. I would lie down on the living room couch and pick up a book to read. My cat would jump up on my chest and start purring, looking at me serenely. At such moments I would feel that even if I was not sure there was anything worth living for, my cat apparently found *me* worthwhile . . . loved *me*. Since there was another creature who felt I was O.K., I could not negate myself completely. The meaning in this carried some weight, because Sarah was allergic to cats, and after Kate had left I was going to have my cat put to sleep. Now her purring and her serene stare seemed a statement of gratitude to me for not having killed her. In the most difficult, despairing moments of my withdrawal, this experience was the one affirmation of my worth that I could feel.

Part of changing my pattern of A.A. meetings was not only to avoid running into Sarah, but also to avoid mutual acquaintances. I was very vulnerable to the emotional fallout from "coincidental" encounters, and I knew it. It was important not to deny my feelings of loss and neediness relative to Sarah. I had enough background in psychology to understand the danger of trying to force myself to believe I had no wanting or desire. I knew that if I did this the desire would not go away, but would gather force and probably ambush me at some particularly inopportune moment. No, kidding myself about "how much I don't want Sarah" was dangerous. It seemed far wiser to admit to having those feelings of yearning for her. At least in that situation I could keep an eye on them.

A strategy began to emerge. The question became, "Am I on good spiritual ground or bad spiritual ground?" I was on good spiritual ground if I was not looking for mischief, for a way back into addiction, however subtle. I could be feeling extreme yearning, but if I was acknowledging it and not acting on that yearning by setting up some "psychic" connection with Sarah, then my spiritual condition was good. I was on bad spiritual ground if I did anything that intentionally opened the door to further contact with her. I knew that if my spiritual condition was good, then much as I might dread running into her, *if* it happened I could probably come through it without being drawn back into the addiction. If I ran into her and was on bad spiritual ground, then the encounter itself would seem to have happened as a result of my state of mind and I would be off to the races.

In the interests of maintaining good spiritual ground, I started to keep a running list of thoughts and feelings I was encountering in withdrawal. This list consisted mainly of short one-liners, such as, "I'm still feeling acute pain and loss today, but I am not feeling self-disgust." The list became quite lengthy, and I carried it everywhere. It was like having a portable, stabilizing anchor with me at all times. Seven months after I began this list, by that time scrawled across both sides of three sheets of tightly folded paper, it went through the washing machine and that was the end of it . . . but it had served its purpose.

I also knew that to keep on good spiritual ground I had to refrain from making any inquiries about "how she was doing." *No* answer to that question could help me. If she were doing "well" it would be a blow to my ego, and if she were doing "not so well" I could construe it as an irresistible invitation to become involved again, with all attendant consequences. This way of looking at things brought me some relief. I realized that if I were not to ask about her, a day at a time, then I would be sparing myself the hatred and jealousy that I would be sure to feel if I tried to keep in touch with her situation.

This "spiritual ground" concept was tested several times in the early weeks. Once I was walking in a crowded part of town about a mile from my house. Suddenly I had a kind of "red alert" reaction before I even saw her. There she was, crossing my path about twenty feet ahead of me! The adrenalin surge was so strong that I visibly recoiled, jerked back as if my head had run into a wooden beam. Whether she saw me or not I didn't know. I was in wretched shape for a day after this, but I knew that difficult as the situation and my reaction to it had been, I was on good spiritual ground because I had *not* set out to initiate contact, not even subtly.

A few weeks later an envelope containing autumn leaves was left in my mailbox with Sarah's working address on the outside. Again conscious of not having solicited this invasion of my space, I took the leaves to a park a block away, scattered them, and threw away the envelope. This did not mean that I did not feel needy or off-balance as a result. It did mean that I continued to act in a manner consistent with not going back into the addiction. I was affirming my commitment to continuing withdrawal.

I was traveling north to visit my wife and baby every two and a half to three weeks. Kate and I would have sex on these visits, although I was extremely perplexed as to what my sexual expectations were. It seemed, on the one hand, that now that I was a "good boy" I should have the right to demand a kind of high-intensity sexuality from her which I had prized so highly in my addictive trysts, although this had generally been lacking in my sex with Kate. On the other hand, how could I be sure that my illness consisted only of a numbers and romance game with "other women?" Might it not extend, as well, to my concept of what constituted "good" sex with anyone, not least of all my wife? Side by side with this feeling of being entitled to some payoffs within my relationship with Kate existed the gnawing question as to whether the *values* I drew from in looking for such payoffs might be *themselves* a part of my illness!

One bright spot was an event that happened about three weeks after I had broken up with Sarah. In the midst of making love to Kate, I started sobbing and was able to express my deep anguish over the pain I had so uncontrollably caused her. Nothing like this had ever happened during sex before, with anyone.

When I thought of Kate, I was still faced with enigmatic, unresolved feelings about whether I wanted to get back together with her. I just told myself it was O.K. not to know the answer, and to focus attention on my own process of withdrawal and recovery.

Fiendishly, a severe temptation would often occur the day before I was to visit Kate. I was still on the road giving concerts and was often in Pennsylvania. On two occasions when I was to drive directly from a concert tour to visit Kate,

I was handed the alluring possibility of drawing the covers up around my head with an adoring, needy fan. At one concert in the fall of 1976, a woman who was home from school for the weekend came to see me play. As it turned out, she was also "on leave" from a tortured love affair. This was early in my withdrawal, and I was not good at handling this temptation because so much of me still wanted to indulge in it! I was painfully aware of the inner conflict. Even while I was playing in the concert, I spotted her in the audience. After the concert was over, there she was waiting for me, no words having yet passed between us. She came back to my room and I changed in front of her, acting quite nonchalant as I got down to my underwear. I was doing this even as I was screaming to myself inwardly, "Rich, what in God's name do you think you're doing!" Then, feeling extremely uncomfortable, I got us out of there, and we went for a late night walk around the town.

I remember mentioning something to her about this addiction I had to "love" and sex. I know I was trying to create an external barrier to my sleeping with her. After walking around for a while and getting something to eat, we returned. There was a long silence as we were standing before the guest house where I was being lodged. We were all alone; nobody was around. I grabbed her, kissed her quickly on the lips, hugged her, pushed her away and said, "I just can't," all in the same moment. I felt my body both wanting her and starting to freeze up all at the same time. I watched her puzzled face. Then she turned around and walked to her car. I just stood there watching her drive off . . . for as long as I could see the car. I just sighed and sighed and ached and felt numb and then ached some more, and went up to my room and went to sleep.

The next morning I arose for my all day drive to visit Kate. Funny, I had no regrets now. I knew I would mention to Kate what had happened, but I also knew that I had not compromised my recovery, and that I was still living an open, undivided life. Many hours later, I turned into the driveway of the house where Kate was staying. I can't describe the relief I felt, not just at seeing her, but at *knowing* how grateful I was that I had not followed through on the sexual/romantic encounter the previous evening. What had seemed to be alluringly "made in heaven" twenty-four hours earlier, now seemed to have been diabolically contrived to do me in, to get me reinvolved with the addiction.

On another concert trip a similar situation occurred. This time I had naively dropped a postcard in the mail to a woman in Philadelphia who always went out of her way to hear me play when I was in the region. I thought of her only as a loyal, devoted fan. We had never had any sexual arrangements. When I showed up at the all-women's college where I was to play, who should appear, broke and waif-like, but my wispy-haired "fan." I had already felt some sexual pressure from a few of the students at the school and felt more on guard because of it.

I had been furnished with very nice accommodations, which I had to myself, so when my vagabond friend, Sharon, told me she had no place to stay, I knew that I had a problem on my hands. The situation was thoroughly awkward, but I was determined to sleep alone, and I didn't even want her in my bedroom under the ambiguous edict of "sleeping in the other bed." I decided to come clean about this situation. I went to the student who was my liaison with the school, explained to her that this "friend" had arrived, and asked if she could be found a place to bed down for the night. This alert coed batted it right back in my court. "Oh," she said, "your friend can sleep with *you. We* don't care!" I replied briskly and emphatically, "Well, *I* care." The matter was not negotiable for me. I could see perplexity cross her face, and I imagined her to be sizing me up as the largest "square" she had happened on in years, or at least as a jerk junior grade. Nevertheless, my "fan" was found a place to stay, and I slept alone.

I was to drive into New York City the next day, en route to Vermont. Sharon needed a ride to New York, and I obliged her. In the demystifying morning light I broached the subject about what her expectations had been in traveling all that distance to hear me play. My tone was not threatening, but simply inquisitive. She readily admitted that she had planned an intrigue. I shared with her my life situation, stressing my awareness of sex and "love" addiction, and she revealed her own circumstances regarding her relationships with lovers and parents. All the intrigue and mystery, so thick the night before, was dispersed in the reality of the morning candor. I dropped her off in mid-town Manhattan and waved goodbye. She seemed moved by our sharing, and I felt grateful to be still unscathed, and wiser.

I realized that these kinds of situations were happening regularly, almost always just before I was to visit Kate. An important principle emerged from these events, that "Whenever and wherever I am vulnerable, I will be tested." The integrity of my withdrawal, and the sense of personal dignity which had started to emerge from it, was like an immune system. It is the nature of immune systems that they work only when the body is invaded, so it is the invasion itself which forces the immune system to become strong. So it was with withdrawal from sex and "love" addiction. Withdrawal guaranteed me anything *but* a charmed life. The onslaught of other temptations and "force-fields," especially at times when I felt least able to handle them, was forcing me to face at depth the stark nature of my sex and "love" addiction, and to affirm my resolve to continue to recover from it. A torturous process? Yes, but no other could have been so thorough. I was learning, and starting to get better.

"Success" in handling temptation was measured only by the outcome. The fact that I did not succumb, rather than the gracefulness (or lack of same) with which I resisted temptation, was the payoff. Furthermore, the energy available to respond to a temptation, when it was *not* shunted into addictive behavior, could be used inwardly to increase my awareness.

Most of my reading throughout the fall had been drawn from the writings of Carl Jung, because I had found in his work a seemingly compassionate and lucid understanding of much that I was experiencing. The concept that the human unconscious might not be merely a dumping ground for repressed conflicts, but could hold, as well, the creative seeds of individual wholeness and well-being, buoyed me. My dream life became for me a "transcendent function" which I felt was placing me in dialogue with my "higher Power."

So it was that in early December, 1976, I received the gift of an important dream. On that very evening, I had been subjected to yet another of the now routine bouts of intense craving and desire, stimulated by still another temptation which was compounded by the agony of seeing someone else help himself to what would formerly have been "my" territory!

In this dream I fought a gorilla, my addiction, for possession of a very nice and precious pocketknife. The gorilla was tremendously strong, and clenched this knife in his fist. I had never been without this knife and was incensed that this brute could have taken it from me. I grabbed its hand with my own and began, with all my might, to pry its fingers apart. The dream ended before I repossessed my knife (life?), but I was filled with the strong sense that my effort would be successful, because I was willing to gouge my way right through its hand if necessary.

I came away from this dream with a strong sense of the incredible tenacity and power of my struggle with this addiction. Indeed, I now felt I had reached a point in withdrawal where I had been granted the Grace of choice in my sexual and romantic life. This new state of affairs was born of the long struggle between addictive temptation and personal autonomy. The balance was tipping in my favor at last, even if just barely!

At this time I realized that a mandate was being presented to me. Now that I had been given some choice over my active sex and "love" addiction, I was going to have to find other people to work with if I was to increase my own margin of recovery. I had been alone a little over three months. I had to find others suffering from this affliction, someone to talk to. I sensed that my state of release was not irreversible. I had to forge ahead.

With this new sense of being in a state of Grace, I felt I would be shown how to find others who might be of help to me. I didn't have long to wait. Throughout the fall I had been attending A.A. meetings in many different areas, a pattern of meetings which was necessary to minimize the chance of meeting Sarah. Since some of these meetings were a good distance from my home, I was candid about revealing the basic nature of what I was going through on a number of occasions. This was not particularly difficult because the psychological pain I was experiencing was so great that I really had no choice but to express it, and I welcomed the relief which sharing afforded.

The reactions I received were varied. Some people responded to the fact that I was in pain, although they could not understand the "why" of it. Others could not understand my suffering at all because they were so filled with envy over the conditions which I reported had led to it. Even as I described the pain brought by these addictive patterns of compulsive sexual activity and emotional intrigue, these people complained that their lives did not contain "enough" of this. They could not seem to understand that an addictive appetite never gets "enough," and that insanity is *insanity* regardless of whether it is encountered in drinking or romance! Still another group of people seemed threatened and downright hostile when I shared my experiences, and I was brick-batted quite a bit. Yet this was my truth. It was all that I had, and I could not, now, turn my back on it. I had been through too much for that.

Sharing these things, regardless of whether I was met with sympathy, envy, or vilification, helped me immensely. It was by taking these risks that I continued to develop perspective on much that had happened to me. The fact that I got little or no empathy from others did not deter me because I also was becoming aware of others who seemed to have similar patterns happening in their lives. Usually they were as unaware of the signs of addiction in these matters as I had been, in my own life, just months earlier.

So it was that about five days after my symbolic dream I had the opportunity to speak at a rather large A.A. meeting. I told my story of getting sober in A.A., and mentioned that my addictive nature did not simply cease to exist after I stopped drinking. Sadly, obsession and compulsion had continued to run me, albeit in other areas. Sobriety from alcohol abuse had brought me many blessings indeed, but in itself was incomplete. I told in some detail my experiences with obsession, compulsion, loss of control, and progression (as I now identified them) in the area of sex and "love." I referred to this condition openly as "sex and 'love' addiction," because the connection between these experiences and the alcoholic ones was clear to me now. I spoke of the agony of withdrawal, but mentioned the hope of finding new meaning and identity which had carried me through this period.

The public response at this meeting was primarily hostility and defensiveness. Remarks ranged from assertions that there was no place for mention of these topics at an A.A. meeting, to off-color jokes, and to bewildered inquiries from people who were not hostile, but did not know what on God's earth I was talking about.

The value of my openness, however, became apparent after the meeting. Two people, a woman and a man, sought me out to tell me that they had *identified* with what I had said. Given well over one hundred people at the meeting, consisting of a highly vocal and hostile minority and a majority of silent, bewildered or indifferent people, I felt greatly rewarded in having met two other kindred souls.

There was also a woman with whom I had done some sharing throughout the fall. She had seen me break down and cry at a meeting the previous summer, and although I had pretty much worn her out as a resource, we still discussed our sexual and emotional lives occasionally. So there was, by mid-December, a very informal network of four of us. I started seeing Jim, the other man, quite frequently about then, and I awakened one morning with the idea of starting a group, based on the principles of Alcoholics Anonymous, but devoted entirely to this problem of "sex and 'love' addiction." I saw Jim for lunch that day, and was just about to ask him what he thought of it when he turned to me suddenly and said, "Hey, Rich, how about starting a group of *us*?"

I contacted the two women, and they agreed. We four met in my apartment in Cambridge, Mass., for our first S.L.A.A. meeting on December 30, 1976.

We drew lots to decide who would tell his/her story first. Each of us was going to try it entirely in terms of the personal identities we had formed around sex and "love" addiction. A wonderful precedent was set with those very first stories: we held nothing back. We each revealed as much of our sex and "love" addiction story as we could then recognize and recall, regardless of whatever apprehensions we had about how the others would receive what we had to say.

Jim told of getting the "quick fix" of blow jobs from the high school athletic coach, and trying to have a relationship with a woman for whom he cared a great deal, but finding himself driven by imperious physical craving to submerge himself in pornography and the local red light district.

Jill told of a string of unwanted pregnancies and backroom, or self-induced, abortions. She spoke of a series of relationships in which men were always cast as saviors. She wound up at age thirty married to a teenager who provided her with a meal ticket, a son, and, after the honeymoon wore off, emotional indifference. She was still trying to convince herself that they were compatible.

Sandy, a middle-aged woman, spoke of extorting cars from lovers by threatening to reveal their activities to their wives, and, additionally, of an appetite for young boys. She had nearly been driven to suicide some five years earlier and had finally been able to unhook herself from the active phase of the addiction.

As we proceeded around the circle (of the four of us), it was my turn last. I tried to tell my story with the same level of detail as Jim, and brought it up to date by talking about the increasingly progressive consequences I had experienced as I had continued on in this addiction. I mentioned how amazing in terms of pain and hope my withdrawal had been to that point.

That first S.L.A.A. meeting lasted about three hours, and when it was over, we were all pretty well spent. We resolved to meet again in a month's time.

After the others had left, I became aware both of how exhausted I was, and of a wonderful, expansive feeling in my chest. I shook my head in disbelief. This was the last kind of sharing I could ever have imagined during most of my life. Yet here I was, not acting out addictively and actively reaching out for others with whom to share the awareness I had found about my addiction. There was a great sense of warmth in discovering, experiencing and sharing a common bond with these three other people.

Moved by an immense gratitude and a sense of deepening commitment to what had happened that evening, which history would show was the beginning of the Fellowship of Sex and Love Addicts Anonymous, I got down on my knees. "Dear God," I said, "I never would have thought . . . chosen . . . " (followed by a deep, deep sigh). "Well, dear God, if this is *really* what you want me to be doing, then I'm willing . . . ." My head was still shaking with incredulity that I, of all people, should find myself in this position. It seemed so ridiculous in terms of my former standard, and so strange in terms of my present one.

The meetings of Sex and Love Addicts Anonymous continued on a monthly basis. However, I soon discovered that I seemed to want them more than the others. It fell to me to round up people and to find new people to attend. Between meetings, I kept busy on the telephone with Jill, Sandy and Jim, trying to foster a level of commitment to this group which I felt was necessary to maintain sexual sobriety.

Meanwhile, other areas of my life continued to unfold. For one thing, I continued to experience enticing situations which could have lured me back into the addictive quicksand. Among these was one more very serious trial concerning Sarah. The timing of this was so uncanny as to be particularly meaningful.

Kate was due to arrive for a few days visit with me, a prospect I looked forward to a lot. I had been very careful to avoid any ambiguous situations which could have re-opened a connection with Sarah. Yet the fact that I was to see Kate after a long absence left me particularly vulnerable to a sudden encounter, a "coincidence" I had repeatedly experienced.

The very morning of the day on which Kate was to arrive, the telephone rang and I found myself on the other end of the line with Sarah's roommate, Nancy. Instantly I was in a state of shock. She said she was putting a theatrical presentation together and wanted some assistance with the music. The Devil himself could not have created a more tantalizing situation! Not only did it offer a chance for musical recognition, thus appealing to my professional ego, but Nancy was beguilingly attractive. I could rationalize that it was for my career, while "proving" to Sarah how "well" I was doing without her by romancing her roommate. These were powerful motives, and this particular temptation loomed as unnervingly attractive.

All this went through my mind in a split second. I found myself replying, "I'm going to decline; it sounds like the road back to mischief to me. I hope you're well. Goodbye." I hung up the phone. I had handled it, if not very tactfully, but did I ache!

Nor was this the end of it. That afternoon, before going to pick up Kate, I went to an A.A. meeting which I had not attended in years. This was out of deference to my altered schedule. As I entered the large meeting room, I was aware of a feeling of tension, as if entering a "force-field." A shock wave passed through me. Sarah was there. I hoped she had not noticed me. I knew that if it got too difficult for me, I would leave. I was able, however, to endure the discomfort.

As the meeting ended, I turned to Jack, a man who happened to be nearby. Although I didn't like him much (he had been around making insensitive remarks during the painful end with Sarah), I riveted myself into conversation with him. I don't remember one word that passed between us, but I was glad he was there to concentrate on. While we talked, I could hear people behind me leaving the hall. I hoped that Sarah was leaving, too. When I finally ended the conversation five minutes (or was it five years?) later and turned around, I was greatly relieved to find that Sarah had left.

With the "one-two punch" to contend with (the phone call from Nancy and actually encountering Sarah) I was in a very shell-shocked, morose frame of mind as I drove out to meet Kate. I told her what had happened earlier that day. The feelings of yearning, loss and hunger were as intense as any I had experienced the prior four and a half months. Yet they passed more quickly. I was still open and current with Kate and with myself, and my new life was alive and intact.

In early February, I felt ready to ask Kate if she would rejoin me. There were several reasons why I felt I might be ready for this. First, I had been able to refrain from sex and "love" addiction for over four months. This was not a long time in absolute terms. It was, however, the longest time I had been inactive in fifteen years, and the first time I had ever been voluntarily inactive in my life!

Second, these four months had been no picnic. The testing of my integrity and resolve while in withdrawal had been incessant. I had come through it this far with increased appreciation of the tenacity and depth of the illness. I also had an increased sense of the positive, redemptive qualities of withdrawal, and some real insight concerning the whole nature and manifestation of addiction in my life.

Third, I was beyond the point of feeling that solitude was only deprivation, and was faring well. I had learned how to cook a good meal for myself, to do my laundry, to maintain my apartment. I had done many things which I had always depended on others to do for me. I had learned to take real pleasure in my ability to take care of myself.

Fourth, my solitude had become precious to me. With the help of psychotherapy I had gotten a great deal of insight into myself as an individual, not just as part of a relationship. Most importantly, I had developed a vision of personal wholeness towards which I felt able to grow.

Fifth, I was not seeking a new relationship with Kate out of desperation. This was amazing for me to realize. But it had become evident in my reaction when Kate got involved in a relationship with someone else while we were separated. When she first told me about it, I had experienced jealous pangs and anxiety. Surprisingly, however, these feelings had subsided quickly. I was so engrossed in my own recovery process that I felt complete acceptance of the possibility that she might become involved with this other person. I knew that I felt worthy, and worthwhile. If Kate were to spend her life elsewhere, it wasn't the end of me. I could have my own life and it would be good. These convictions apparently went so deep that I did not even ask about her status with this man. It simply didn't occur to me to ask.

Sixth, in trying a reconciliation with Kate, I felt that I would be giving up the remarkable experience of living alone, with its inner richness which I now regarded as a daily companion. My experience alone had been a contemplative oasis in my life. I knew that I would miss it when it ended.

Finally, I felt that I was not "through" with Kate. I realized that since I had never been emotionally available to our relationship on a consistent basis, I did not really know whether it was workable or not. This meant also that the "success" of getting back together was not measured by whether or not we stayed together. The only standard for "success," considering my past history, would be that I was now really *present* in the relationship, minus addictive distractions. If we were to get back together, I could now discover what was, and was not, there. If we were incompatible, I knew that I would be able to leave the relationshiop without regret, and without the agony of irresolution and guilt over "how things might have been different if only I had tried harder." If there *was* something there between Kate and me, I felt that I could now be available to work on it. The " success" of this, for me, would hinge on my ability to be emotionally "available" to her and to myself on a consistent basis.

These seven points could be summed up simply: In the process of being alone and going through withdrawal, I had discovered, for the first time in my life, a sense of my own dignity. It was mine, divinely given to me as I was. I no longer needed to hold another person responsible for giving it, or failing to give it, to me.

Kate agreed to my request to come back. She, too, had been through a process of reassessment, and wanted to find out for herself if we could work it out. We arrived at early May as the probable time to make the move.

With about two and a half months remaining in our separation, I had much work to do, looking for a new apartment and dealing with problems of money and other practical matters. However, my greatest concerns were: Could I continue to remain "sober," not acting out addictively by getting involved in sexual or emotional intrigues? And could I maintain my wholeness of self? I wondered and worried. Had my recovery gone far enough?

I continued to try to reinforce my sobriety with persistent efforts to find new people for the sex and "love" addiction group, S.L.A.A. I was becoming more anxious about this because two of the original people who attended the first meeting were drifting away. The third person attended inconsistently, finally drifting away later. I managed to encourage a few other people to attend, whose addictive patterns seemed obvious to me. But either I was mistaken, or consciousness of their true condition eluded them, because one or two meetings would be all they would attend.

As far as I could tell, "recovery" had not been replicated in anyone else I had seen thus far at S.L.A.A. meetings. The fact that I had hit bottom, surrendered, gone through withdrawal, and turned the corner on this addiction, while important enough personally, really meant little if the experience could not be replicated by others. Although sharing at our S.L.A.A. meetings had been cathartic for a number of people, the whole approach of viewing compulsive sexual and emotional behavior as an addiction was still largely abstract theory unless others could use this roadmap to find recovery themselves. Still, I felt myself getting stronger in both insight and steadiness of behavior as I continued to share my experiences, both before and after recovery, with others, even if they were not receptive.

Typically, a new person would come to a meeting in the midst of an intense crisis, such as a "love" affair breaking up. Such a person would seem remarkably receptive to hearing about the dynamics of addiction as long as he or she was feeling the immediate pain surrounding the situation at hand. A newcomer in this phase would often recognize other situations in his or her life which fit in with the obsessive/compulsive pattern of the present one. Inevitably, the person would experience some relief from suffering through this initial sharing.

However, once the pain started to subside, newcomers would forget anything about having a prior pattern consisting of circumstances like the most recent one. Once again they began to blame their current straits on bad luck or an unfortunate "pick," or blamed the "other" as being a bad-apple-in-the-bunch. It was as if they had never looked at these events in any other way. Often a life pattern that seemed, to me, to have been as grim as anything I had experienced myself would simply be lost to the person's conscious awareness as soon as the current crisis was over. This happened even though the awareness and focus of the S.L.A.A. meeting was strong and consistent. The outlook of the group would then appear to be unappealing and downright obnoxious to the new person. He or she would leave us, ready to go out and repeat the pattern of self-destruction once again.

As the time neared for Kate to come home, I was feeling under more and more stress. I developed hypertension, but was grateful to learn that it could be controlled with meditation.

Kate and my daughter returned on May 3rd. I was terribly apprehensive. I had been looking for another apartment for over two months and had not found anything. I knew Kate's coming back was "for real." I felt insecure and unsure—exactly the kind of feelings I had always subdued with sexual indulgence and emotional intrigue.

For two months around the time Kate came back, I had been working with a man named Dave. He was still married and appeared to care deeply about his wife, but had a pattern of promiscuity that led him to porno establishments and sexual intrigue with other men, which he said helped him avoid the emotional entrapments encountered with women. His idea was to get sexual oblivion without emotional complications.

Dave's gender preference was of no concern to me, but his compulsive pattern was. I remember when we were walking across a city park together and I told Dave my story. Dave went from seeming quite composed to weeping. He really identified with what I was trying to share with him. I was greatly heartened. Perhaps here was someone who would be able to make the surrender. We started having meetings every two weeks, and for about a month Dave seemed to be making progress.

Then the slide came which I had, by now, witnessed a number of times in others. Dave would come to the S.L.A.A. meetings en route from one rendezvous to another. Rather than building awareness, he seemed to be using the meetings solely as a place for bragging and boasting. Listening to his ongoing sexploits, I wished at times I had not become conscious in these areas so that I could also be "enjoying" the short-term hits which were his main staple of life. Finally I questioned him as to why he continued to attend S.L.A.A. meetings. I explained that the purpose of these meetings was to further the consciousness of addiction as it might apply to the sexual and emotional components of his life. I reminded him of his own tears of identification, and the obvious emotional pain he had been in, when first we met. I observed that the Dave I was seeing now was very different from the desperate one I had met some eight weeks earlier.

Listening to my observations and statement of "group" purpose, he got very incensed and left in a huff, not to return. I felt guilty. Apparently I had driven him out, and now I had no one else to work with. I was back to square one with the sex and "love" addiction group. I felt very sad, and lonely. I knew that I had had to take my stand with Dave, but I missed the companionship of our early association.

In early July, I was at an inner city noontime A.A. meeting. At its conclusion I started walking to a subway entrance about a half a mile away. Unexpectedly I found myself joined by Jack, the person I hadn't liked very much during my days with Sarah, and the person I had latched onto that Sunday afternoon months before when I had run into Sarah at an A.A. meeting. I kept walking, and Jack was clearly going out of his way to keep up with me.

I asked him, as we walked, what he wanted. I told him that I neither trusted nor liked him—that he had always seemed to go out of his way to slam me one way or another. He said that he had always respected me as someone who wasn't just blown away by adversity, and that his "slams," possibly real, had not been maliciously motivated. He observed that, except for that Sunday meeting, he hadn't seen anything of me for a long time. He wanted to know what was happening with me; his tone was friendly.

I decided to let him know as completely as I could. Although I was still scheduling and holding S.L.A.A. meetings, there were weeks when no one else came. Dave was gone, and I was feeling pretty alone and discouraged. Who was I to be particular about sharing my story with anyone?

We stood outside the subway entrance, leaning up against a concrete wall on a narrow walkway about two feet wide, and I told Jack my story. He had seen much of my slide with Sarah, although he hadn't known how to make sense of it. I spoke of it in the context of my life-pattern, drawing on other relationships to show how the addiction worked. I closed with a careful explanation of the withdrawal process: why it had been necessary for me to drop out of sight, what the process had felt like to go through, and what I felt it was now yielding. I spoke of having been given choice over my sexual and emotional life, free of gnawing dependency and lurching desperation. I mentioned that I was now living with Kate again, and that we were trying to work out a relationship now that I was free of having to act out on this addiction. I also mentioned Sex and Love Addicts Anonymous, telling him where and when the meetings were.

When I finished, I had no idea how he had received all of this. He was quite pokerfaced. He had mentioned something about having just gone through a difficult time with his girlfriend of long standing, but I couldn't tell if what I had said was relevant, and he wasn't letting on. I had told my story primarily because it seemed to bolster me, and keep my awareness alive. We parted cordially.

The next meeting night, several days later, the doorbell sounded. It was Jack. There were two of us at the meeting that night.

It turned out that Jack had ended, or had been trying to end, an addictive relationship. His lover had started screwing around on him. Realizing how desperately dependent he had been on her for four years, he was seeking refuge from this predicament by going on a sexual rampage. He was incapable of sleeping alone, and he had not been able to stay away from his lover. He felt powerless.

Jack was shocked at the implications of withdrawal, which I said meant a period of complete sexual abstinence in order to let his body cycle down (something he didn't think could ever happen). Jack wanted nothing to do with any of this. He was adamant about not being able to "give up sex." He *knew* why he needed it; it was a sedative to cushion the emotional fallout stemming from the horrendous situation he was in. He just could not conceive of stopping. We left things pretty much on that basis. I certainly was not trying to force the issue in any way. I just tried to get him to continue to look at his own experiences and to size up the options.

My initial efforts with Jack were not really different in character from those I had embarked on with others. There was, however, one difference: Jack continued to fear being drawn back into his nightmare. Also, although he continued to screw around, often sandwiching a visit to his long-term lover between other sexual intrigues in order to insulate himself emotionally from her, he was getting progressively less mileage out of sexualizing his feelings about her onto others. In late August he called a "moratorium" on having sex with women in Massachusetts. This was still an external constraint, but a step in the right direction. Of course, Jack was a traveling salesman, and was out of the state far more often than he was in it. The humor in his brave attempt to abstain did not escape us.

By mid-September some important developments were happening in my life. First, Kate and I had encountered severe emotional obstacles in our relationship of reconciliation. We were fighting a great deal. Things between us were torturous. I didn't feel that I wanted to be in the relationship, considering the rage I was experiencing, and yet I didn't trust the part of me that wanted to be done with it. How could I be sure that my feelings of wanting to run were not the addiction itself speaking? If my feelings of wanting to leave the relationship were suspect, my feeling about the alternative of staying were no less so. How could I be sure that my feelings of wanting to stay were not merely another sickening chapter in perpetuating a stable but miserable dependency, that they were not simply more of the desperate desire for emotional security at any price? In a foul frame of mind I often wracked myself with questions like these.

Full of untested expectations about what "partnership" with Kate would hold, I yearned to be cast in a heroic role at home, with sexual oblivion instantly available on demand. Unfortunately for the addict in me, true partnership is not built on fantasy or heroic expectations, nor on the availability of sex, on tap and on demand. Clearly, approaching partnership with Kate for the first time, I knew nothing about it. I was learning that the stress of reconciliation was equal to the stress of splitting up.

Thus, in September, we decided to seek marriage counseling. Once again I was looking for a way to answer that troublesome question: "Do I or do I not want to be here?" When the fights were vicious, I felt that Kate's and my whole relationship, extending as it did from my active alcoholism through my active sex and "love" addiction, must have been too rooted in sickness, and was now irretrievably crippled. I wondered if anything could be healthy about it. The past seemed so condemning. At that time I did not suspect that major issues about trust, intimacy, commitment, expectations, childcare, another pregnancy, and attitudes towards sexuality would all be covered in fine detail in our relationship of reconciliation as we travelled the road towards greater communication, understanding and cooperation; that is, towards partnership.

Also at that time I began a college program which required a two week residency on campus every six months, in addition to rigorous independent study. Having left college in an alcoholic haze some years before, vowing that I would never return, this felt like a real gamble. So these changes, Kate's and my severe emotional difficulties and the start of college, both hit about the same time.

My experience at school turned out to be extraordinary. This school was devoted to helping students plan independent study projects and carry them out. The temptations for sexual and romantic intrigue at this school were so severe that I found it necessary to plan my studies around the concept of sex and "love" addiction, to research the concept, read extensively in related fields, and write what I could on the subject. To what extent could the models from substance abuse be applied to non-substance areas? For sex and "love" (emotional dependency) I already knew the answer to this question, but the opportunity to study this whole area formally seemed like a gift to me. The most practical result of beginning this study was that my commitment to this unusual topic became public knowledge at the college. This publicity (or notoriety) had the effect of providing me with a strong external constraint to acting out on the addiction while at school. If I was describing sex and love addiction in terms of the dire consequences that resulted from it, using my own experiences as examples, it wouldn't make much sense for me to jump into bed or ride off into the sunset with anybody. I might just as well hang myself. Therefore, designing studies in the area of sex and "love" addiction helped to keep me sober while at school, and deepened my commitment to this opportunity in my life. I arrived home dedicated and revitalized.

During my two week absence, no S.L.A.A. meetings had taken place.

Clearly the meetings were not even close to being self-sufficient at this time. When I returned, I contacted Jack and a few others, and the meetings resumed, still being held every two weeks. About this time Jack finally appeared to turn the corner. Some recent encounters out of state had highlighted how unmanageable his sexual life was. He realized that he did not know how to tell what a healthy relationship with anyone might be like. He had taken a room in a nearby city, had gotten an unlisted telephone number, and was not near a bus line. He had hit bottom and was available to withdrawal, from which he was not flinching.

This turn of events was heartening to observe. It heightened my appreciation of what I had been through. I just couldn't believe, in watching Jack, that someone else was going through this. And, of course, in a way I could not believe that I myself had gone through it, and come through it.

Jack's withdrawal and recovery, which started in October of 1977, signified another major milestone in the development of S.L.A.A., which had been proceeding from meeting to meeting since its beginning in late December, 1976. It was now clear that the concept of addiction could be used by others to deal with obsessive and compulsive sexual and emotional behavior. My own recovery was no longer an isolated, idiosyncratic happenstance. Others would come to have their own transformative experiences, of equal significance to my own.

In summing up this story of my own addictive history and the very early formative history of Sex and Love Addicts Anonymous, including the founding of the first regular S.L.A.A. Group (December 30, 1976), I can report that the subsequent growth and development of S.L.A.A. has been a wonderful and moving adventure.

The lesson of this early history is that consciousness in these areas is fiendishly difficult to achieve and maintain for us as sex and love addicts. Questioning one's attitudes and behavior concerning sexuality and emotional dependency is tantamount to questioning the very ground on which we have been standing—our whole identity as human beings. Our package of assumptions about the world and our own roles in it have had to be upended in this process. Yet nothing short of this has been necessary to make us available to new life.

Largely due to the difficulty of achieving and sustaining this awareness of sex and love addiction, the Fellowship of Sex and Love Addicts Anonymous has grown slowly. Our membership has doubled each year. At the end of the first year of S.L.A.A. meetings we were essentially two members, although a total of approximately fifteen persons had attended at one time or another during the year. At the end of two years we had about four die-hards, out of thirty-five to forty people who had attended. At the end of three years this figure had doubled to seven or eight people, out of about eighty persons who had attended. At the four year point we could count approximately fifteen people who were in various phases of recovery, out of around one hundred and thirty people who attended. *

Another way to see our growth is that, whereas in the beginning only one meeting per month was in existence, by the eight year point that had grown to nine meetings per week in the Boston area, as well as numerous ongoing groups in the San Diego and San Francisco Bay areas and in a number of other U.S. cities. S.L.A.A. meetings have also commenced in Europe.

Our growth has been primarily by word of mouth to those individuals with whom we have had personal contact and who have seemed to be in trouble with this addiction. Even so, as the word has gotten around about the existence of S.L.A.A., we have been sought out for media and professional events on several occasions, which would have brought considerable publicity for the Fellowship. We have consistently weighed with great caution such opportunities to place our message before a wider public and have generally avoided doing so out of concern that such publicity would be subject to the editorial biases of others, and could lead to our being besieged with inquiries from those whose intentions might be other than that of seeking recovery from the addiction.

Our membership is a diverse group of individuals, widely varying in their social, economic and ethnic backgrounds. We also cover the spectrum in terms of individually held preferences concerning gender of our partners and sexual practices. Wonderfully, however, we have discovered that the affliction of sex and "love" addiction, in our individually shared life experiences, is a common bond which erases the significance of those differences of gender preference and sexual aims that so often serve to divide people outside of S.L.A.A.

In terms of what recovery is like, at least as much as has been written thus far could be written on any one recovery in S.L.A.A. Here are a few aspects of recovery, mine and others'. First, I have not had to act out addictively since I began recovery, a number of years ago. This means that I have been completely free of bottom-line obsessive/compulsive sex and/or emotional intrigue during this time. This sobriety has been achieved through many trials and growing pains, as well as through seasons of relatively smooth sailing. Considering my addictive history, I can only use the world "miracle" to express the significance of this singular fact.

Describing the attributes of partnership to one still locked into addiction is

---

*The January, 1986 estimate of S.L.A.A.'s reach is approximately 1,500 committed members, ninety percent of whom live on either the U.S. East or West Coasts, with the remainder spread across some two dozen interior states of the U.S. and five European countries (West Germany, Great Britain, France, Norway, and Switzerland). There are currently about 100 S.L.A.A. groups worldwide, with new groups springing up weekly.

like trying to describe color to a blind person. Yet although at one time I could not imagine what it would be like, today it is a vital part of my experience. I am still married. Indeed, my relationship with Kate is now over eight years further along since each of us decided to get back together to see what was there. It now has a degree of commitment, trust, sharing, and cooperation and (dare I say) *love* in it which exceeds what I could ever have hoped for. We have the capacity now to live, work, play, and grow together. I never would have thought, through all those years of addictive agony, that I could ever be contentedly married; yet today I am. That old question: "Do I *really* want to be here?" has been resolved.

Working out sexual and emotional issues has been long, difficult and often discouraging on both sides. Yet efforts along these lines have yielded, over time, a tremendous understanding, increasing trust, and the capacity to experience genuine intimacy together. We have sought extended counseling on two occasions to get issues on the table before us in a way that could be constructive, rather than destructive. Even through difficult times, I feel that the process of our relationship has been positive.

We have had another child since getting back together, and this has been very challenging for us. Ironically, despite every intention in the world *never* to be married or have children, I find, in my sobriety, that I am quite an adequate husband and father (partner and parent). I am no longer tyrannized by old models of husbanding and parenting. I have come to discover and appreciate my own capacities. My children love me, and do not live in fear of me.

The trials and tribulations of establishing and maintaining partnership is something being experienced more and more often in our S.L.A.A. society. For all us S.L.A.A. pioneers it is, with sanity, the first time around. Those of us who have married have been able to remain free of addiction. We have not had to escape the very real pressures of growing relationships by "falling in love" elsewhere, or by seeking sexual oblivion. Still others of us have chosen to be alone for extended periods, beyond what withdrawal in and of itself would seem to call for, because of an inner richness which we have found in the experience of our own solitude.

In all cases the withdrawal process has brought with it a deep and abiding knowledge of our own dignity as human beings. Discovering this from within has released us from the pressure to extract it from others, which, of course, can never work anyway.

In my own life the basis for relationships with others has changed absolutely. My interactions with other men were formerly marked by competitiveness and distrust. The assumption in active addiction was that sex and "love" objects were a common quest. Therefore, those of the same gender were potential adversaries. Also, the objects of my passion were seen entirely in terms of their ability to fulfill my NEEDS. They were defined by how well they functioned in this way. They were *functions,* not human beings.

Now that I am sober in S.L.A.A., I enjoy a deep human sharing with other persons of either gender or sexual preference. The experiences of addiction which bind us, in sharing, to one another in S.L.A.A. are far more compelling than the differences of gender and sexual choice which serve to divide more "normal" people. The experiences in addiction itself, faced and understood, become the common ground for a new and moving adventure, a quest for meaning of the human spirit. New meaning in life has come to us. Some of us have started new careers which are radically different from anything we could have conceived of doing previously. The discovery of personal dignity and integrity has become a new standard which we apply to our ventures. We prize a more holistic understanding of ourselves, and seek to affirm this in all areas of our lives. We find that nothing short of this is fulfilling to us.

This rendering of aspects of recovery is necessarily quite limited and somewhat arbitrary. May it suffice to say that we hope others who have been locked into addictive patterns similar to those which imprisoned us may find in these words hope for change, and may be inspired to contact us and start their own journey. If you are like us, you may be poised on the brink of immense personal discovery and healing. If so, may you join us in our experience of God's grace and redemption as we encounter these in S.L.A.A. We want you, and we need you.

Chapter 3

Living With a Sex and Love Addict

The experiences shared to this point have been those of the addict. But there have been others trapped in the addictive cycle, those who have relationships with the sex and love addict. While it was often true that "likes attracted," that both people in a relationship were truly sex and love addicts, this was not always so. We who were also victims of this disease, without "catching" it, have our own stories and struggles, before and during the addict's recovery. We would like to share our experience with you. Perhaps you may not have to suffer so long through what we, too, suffered, and can find hope for a redeemed life, with or without your addict-partner.

Probably the first question in your mind is, "How can you be so sure that you weren't sex and love addicts yourselves?" This question presented a real problem to some of us. It is not just the addict who is excited by the fantasy of illicit sex, and our discovery of or suspicions about the activities of our addict-partners seemed to justify our own adventuring, either for revenge or from the questionable reasoning, "If you can't fight them, join them."

The difference for us was that the price we paid was internal; the addict's price was extracted from those around him or her. The addict seemed to be content as long as lovers were available and unaware that they were sharing the addict's favors. For us, the same events left us dissatisfied and ashamed. We may have lost sight of them for a time, but we DID have values and conscious goals in life, as the selected comments which follow indicate.

"Before meeting R. I had a few intense, short-lived romantic 'flings.' Perhaps 'fling' is too light a word, because I took these relationships very seriously at the time, and with each one I had entertained hopes of being married. I had always wanted the security of marriage and family as far back as I could remember, so it was not really in my nature to play around lightly. Having a relationship with more than one man at a time was intolerable and impossible for me."

"My religion had led me to assume that I would marry and be faithful. I knew there was a lot of fooling around in most marriages, but I simply assumed that if we loved each other and didn't fight too much, it wouldn't happen to us."

"After the unhappy experience with J., I just didn't feel like taking the risks of dating and 'being in love' again for a while. For two years I didn't date at all. My life was pretty full with my job, doing things with the kids in my brother's family, and helping my parents, whose health wasn't too good."

"G. could not keep his promise to stay faithful, so I moved out. I still hoped we could get back together, but I just couldn't live without being able to trust my partner."

We did have some sense of values, and these were not what the addict cared about. Nevertheless, we found many ways to rationalize the behavior of our addict-partners and experienced a similar progression into sickness that threatened to destroy us. The story that follows is Kate's story. We hope you will find understanding and hope in her experience: a golden coin, first shattered, and then mended again.

*   *   *

I came from a good-sized family with parents who loved and cared for us as best they could. We lived in a nice house and went to good schools. Yet despite all this, I remember feeling inadequate, insecure, and a little weird. Some part of me felt quite unlovable just for being myself, and so I tried to earn it by being generous, forgiving, understanding, undemanding, and seemingly selfless. Although it won me a lot of friends in school, this strategy was my undoing later on. I thought that I was a good judge of character, and if I just put enough effort into figuring out and filling people's unspoken needs, I would be indispensable. Paradoxically, along with this ability to read people, I developed the ability to shut out unpleasant feelings. As long as the person I was with was happy, I was happy by definition, and the same was true for sadness. The stage was nicely set for me to fall in love with someone who needed me a great deal, but because of his own problems would not give much back to me on any kind of a consistent basis.

At the time I met Rich I was still rebounding from two previous relationships and had dropped out of college. I was sharing an apartment with a roommate and supporting myself with temporary employment at a local restaurant and bar. Rich was frequenting that restaurant-bar on a regular basis with some drinking buddies. In spite of an outward appearance of confidence, I was shy and would never have allowed myself to be picked-up by a customer. But Rich had a way about him. His gentle approach won my confidence one afternoon when he came in for a few beers by himself.

We began to see each other on a very casual basis at first, and it wasn't long until I found out that Rich was seeing a girl he had been involved with for a long time. I also had an "old college friend" out of town whom I would visit from time to time, but my relationship with Rich did not seem to conflict with that. As I look back on it now, there were early signs of Rich's addictive nature, but

I chose to ignore the intuitive caution signals inside myself.

Within a few months we started to sleep together and our "other" relationships ended. I remember thinking how attractive and experienced with women Rich was. I wanted to be the perfect sensual counterpart to his lusty nature. My awareness of my own sexual nature was limited to pleasing my man and convincing him that he was pleasing me even if that meant "faking it."

Those early years of our relationship weren't easy for either of us, although we did have our romantic moments with lots of wine and music. I had decided to continue school at the same college Rich was attending, so we skied, sailed, and cut classes together. And we had our fights. The issues invariably boiled down to one thing: I wanted more time and commitment from Rich. Little did I know that I was asking for the one thing he was incapable of giving. We would have the most intimate and closest of times together, and then he would suddenly seem totally distant, as if he didn't know me at all. He often failed to show up when he said he would, and would not even call to explain. Broken promises were patched together with all sorts of excuses, some more honest than others. I always took him back because I loved him and wanted desperately to believe in his intentions, even when they were not consistent with his actions. I knew that something was not right with us, but I rationalized that all couples went through this sort of thing, which is true to *some* degree. I told myself that Rich was an independent spirit, and that I needed to be less possessive and "hold love with an open hand."

At this time Rich was trying to make a living as a musician, and I supported us for the most part. I lived with various roommates and Rich spent more and more nights with me and fewer at his own apartment. I was aware that as a musician he had access to an ample supply of booze and women, but I chose to focus on the romance of supporting the "starving artist" both financially and emotionally. "Besides," I thought, "what other woman in a similar situation would be as understanding and as giving as I was?" I loved being needed, and I thought that by filling that need we would be bonded for life.

The more I put into the relationship, sometimes at my own emotional expense, the more I wanted out of it, and the less I was willing to even consider breaking it off despite the glaring inconsistencies. One time when our relationship was particularly rough I got him to confess that he had recently slept with two other women. Confronted with the actual fact instead of my endless suspicions, I rallied into action and took off to a neighboring state to seek solace with an old boyfriend. I purposely left no word of my whereabouts in the hope that Rich would be contrite and fearful of losing me. I spent three days with the old boyfriend, sleeping with him out of spite and need. I returned home to find notes from Rich, full of apologies and saying that he desperately wanted me back. I was elated—it had worked!

I kept one of the notes for a long time to remind myself that I did have some power in the relationship, but we soon relapsed into our old patterns. The only difference was that Rich would not take the risk of being that open with me again. Over the years there were other scenes that played out the same feelings repeatedly. I never again resorted to the tactic of sleeping with someone else, but I would flirt from time to time and wished with all my heart that I had the strength to break off my relationship with Rich. Sometimes we would decide it was over and not see each other for a few days, only to be drawn back together by our mutual neediness. At some frightening level, we were both terribly weak.

One day in the middle of winter, Rich picked up the book *Alcoholics Anonymous* and decided to do something about his drinking. Although anyone with a trained eye could see that his drinking was clearly alcoholic, I was very threatened by that admission. Somehow it seemed like such a public admission of a private devil: what would my family and other people think? Eventually the sense of relief triumphed over fear, but it was soon replaced by my jealousy over all the time he spent at meetings of A.A. Then I started to attend meetings with him and was overwhelmed by the honesty, power of example, and amazing courage of these people. I realized that the influence on Rich was a good one, and that our mutual lives would be saved. If his alcoholism was at the root of so much of his/our troubles, then staying sober through A.A. could only bode well for the future.

Certainly Rich's sobriety had a profound and positive influence on him, but it also took away the excuse I had been using for much of our discord. The fights and emotional distancing did not stop with his sobriety, and I began to realize that not drinking by itself was not going to provide all the answers.

That summer we travelled together to Colorado and had some wonderful adventures together. These times were broken only by Rich's spells of "travel anxiety," which I later found out were really resulting from being denied access to some of his women friends who were left behind. When we returned, we took up residence in a small apartment, and things went from bad to worse. I started working for an attractive man fifteen years older than I was. I rapidly developed a school-girl crush on him, and was amazed to find that the feelings were mutual. When I was with him, I felt respected, attractive, witty, intelligent, and totally appreciated. It was like being offered water after walking across the desert. I was in tremendous conflict and told Rich of my feelings toward this man. Rich was very upset and offered to try harder to give me love and care instead of the criticism and hostility that had become a daily diet. I was so moved by his offer that I decided to try to cool my strong feelings and give Rich and myself another chance.

However, my decision was short-lived as Jim was not about to give me up easily, and I found I couldn't push him aside. He told me he needed me, that I was the "only light in his life" (he was recently divorced), and that he would wait to sleep with me until I was free of Rich. My job with him was such that we could structure our time between job-related meetings, so our days were increasingly spent doing more play and less work. Two weeks of that culminated in one evening together that convinced me I must make a decision. I was beginning to feel schizophrenic with my two lives/loves and I knew that I was not capable of keeping it up any longer. I arrived home in tears that evening and told Rich I was falling in love with Jim and could no longer hang on to the shreds of our relationship, which was going nowhere.

I thought Rich would be relieved finally to have the freedom he craved. Instead, he seemed stunned and went numbly out to an A.A. meeting. When he returned, we talked some more and he asked me to marry him. This is what I had wanted for so long. And yet I had doubts about the sincerity of his offer because of the circumstances. But, after four years of a stormy relationship and eight months of sobriety and much emotional bloodshed, I finally had "my man" and so I said, "Yes."

Having made the decision, we saw no reason to have a long engagement and made plans to be married the next month. Strangely enough, during that month before our marriage Rich seemed at peace with himself and committed in a way I had never known. On the other hand, having told Jim of our plans, I had days of mixed feelings and apprehension which forced me to wonder if this marriage was what *I* really wanted. But the overwhelming desire to be married and my eternal optimism won out over the nagging doubts.

We had a small, simple wedding followed by a warm reception and a long weekend in a little cabin at a nearby resort. Rich introduced me to everyone as his wife and I was happy at last. For a brief time I was able to shut down the voice in my head which kept asking, "How long can this last?" I got my answer to that question three months later when the issue of VD raised its ugly head. Rich found himself in the uncomfortable position of confessing that he had had a one-night stand a month earlier and that VD was a possibility. The tests turned out negative, but I can never forget the feeling of humiliation I had, waiting in the clinic, having to answer questions about my marital sex life.

I don't remember all the rationalizations I used to keep my new marriage intact, but I managed to convince myself that it was a fluke occurrence and at least Rich wasn't romantically involved with anyone else. But my unhappiness was deep inside me, and when Rich asked me a few months later if I was really happy, he saw through my protestations that "of course we were happy because we loved each other." He suggested I see a therapist and go to Al-Anon to help me with my long-suffering martyr complex. I did go to an outpatient clinic which did not prove to be particularly helpful, but I did benefit from one part of the experience. I had to go through three initial intake sessions on a one to one basis where I had a chance to tell my life story. During one of those sessions, I broke down and wept when I realized that the person I was talking about was *me*. Up to that time, it had been too threatening to face my unhappiness. If I did, I might have to change a basic coping strategy in my life, and I wasn't ready for that yet.

My experience at Al-Anon was a lot less confrontive and easier to assimilate than group therapy at the clinic. It was tremendously helpful in relieving the burden of guilt I had about Rich's drinking, and it was wonderful to be with people who understood alcoholism without attaching social stigma to it. Finally, it was to be the beginning of a gradual process of self-awareness that did not revolve around the alcoholic in my life. Although I put too much effort into trying to rescue other people in the program whose suffering seemed worse than mine, I did manage to channel some of my energy into understanding myself. I attended meetings once a week and made a few friends, one of whom is still very close. I tried hard to lump Rich's problems and his promiscuity under the label of alcoholism, a disease over which I had no control. For quite a while I lived one day at a time and tried to believe in a higher Power who had my best interest at heart. My only definition of "unacceptable behavior" was physical abuse. Since I hadn't experienced that, I felt blessed. Although now I no longer attend meetings, the principles of Al-Anon permeated my life for almost ten years and had a most healing effect. It certainly started me on the path of becoming honest with myself and gave me the strength to weather the storm that was yet to come.

The first four years of our marriage were not unlike our courtship except that Rich was sober and working his A.A. program. We still had our intimate times of soul-sharing followed by painful, power-driven arguments which would leave me shaken and wondering if this pattern would ever change. I worked very hard at accepting the state of our marriage and, with Rich's help, denied my intuition that I was sharing him with other women. "After all," I rationalized, "we're married, and *that* surely would have an effect on Rich's outside activities." Once, during that time, Rich told me of a relationship he had had with a woman in A.A. that had lasted a few months after we were married. But he told me two years after the fact, and I took his confession to be a sign of closeness and an indication that he would not do it again. I wanted very much to put aside any suspicions I had about Rich's late nights, and Rich was only too eager to help me do this.

Sometime before my thirtieth birthday I decided that I wanted to have a child badly enough to make it an ultimatum. The question of children was a decision that Rich seemed to want to postpone indefinitely. In the deepest part of myself, I knew that I was not willing to give up the idea of having a family in order to maintain my marriage. I knew that even if I could talk myself out of wanting a child for that year, eventually my bitterness towards Rich for depriving me of something so essential would corrode and destroy our marriage. Rich must have known that my resolve was not an empty threat. Rather than lose me, he gave in. Rich thoroughly enjoyed trying to make a baby because we had sex so frequently. We succeeded after the second month and I was in seventh heaven. Rich seemed pleased too, and I thought that this pregnancy, this baby, would bond us closer together.

Whatever fights we had after that point, I was quick to rationalize as the effect of increased pressure on Rich in view of his impending fatherhood. But as time went by and I grew larger with child, I began to want assurance that Rich really loved me and wanted to participate in this experience. Instead, he grew more distant and protective of himself. He stayed out late at night and told me how much he needed A.A. Again, I knew something was wrong and this time my unconscious wasn't about to let me off the hook. I had a very frightening dream one night about Rich being totally involved with another woman and leaving me. It was so real and upsetting that I cried and cried and told him about it the next day. It seemed incomprehensible to me that he could ever love another woman enough to actually leave me, especially after all we had been through. He, of course, true to form, denied that there was any truth in my dream. On my part, I tried to write it off to my insecurities and a "suspicious" nature. Actually, I am not at all suspicious by nature, and I soon convinced myself that my suspicions were ungrounded.

We started to attend birthing classes. The first evening, they showed a movie of a couple who went through labor together. The contrast of this loving couple and their mutual support with our strained and increasingly painful relationship was too much for Rich. He told me he wasn't sure if he could go through the rest of the classes with me. The following evening, the dam broke. Rich told me he wanted a separation, and I was hurting enough to agree with it, but not before I knew if there was someone else in his life. He told me there was a woman with whom he had been totally involved for the past five months. He told me he couldn't stand dividing his life any more, that his sanity was at stake, and that he was incapable of breaking off with this person. I was stunned, enormously relieved, and extremely angry all at the same time. The relief of knowing that there was an explanation for his past behavior and that I wasn't crazy was overwhelming. At least, if he separated from me, it wasn't because he couldn't tolerate me and our future child. It was because there was a secret seductress in the wings who had him under her spell. Then the anger and outrage filled me, and I yelled and screamed at him, hoping that it would lessen the intense pain of betrayal that I felt. Somehow I felt that if I could concentrate on the rage and believe that he was truly an uncaring and wicked person, I could save myself the immense suffering of losing someone I really loved.

A writer expressed well what I was feeling:

> Jealousy is not necessarily a mere egotistical desire to possess for one's very own, not just a selfish unwillingness to share. It is the anguish of despair; the whole-ness one thought one had found with the loved one is shattered. The golden coin of love lies smashed to pieces at one's feet. One is overwhelmed with fear; it is burning with the intensity of one's desire for wholeness and one's desolation at its betrayal. *

As Rich's system of deception crumbled, there came a strong desire on both our parts to know all. The enormous wall between us finally had a crack in it, and it was time for it to come tumbling down. We walked and talked late into the night and on into the next day. Rich told me of all his affairs and filled me in on details of his current love. I felt numb. It was as if, after the initial blow, I couldn't be hurt anymore. Instead, a morbid curiosity took over and I listened as if I was hearing the confessions of a man on the street.

A part of me was fascinated by the intrigue, as I struggled to fit the new pieces of our relationship into some sort of cohesive whole. I found that I kept separating who "he" was and who "we" were because the two seemed to mix about as well as oil and water. I wondered if I had ever really known him. I ques-tioned every intimate moment we had ever had together, wondering if he had really been making love to me, or if he was thinking of some other woman. Rich helped by telling me which were the times when he really did feel close, and when he was really distracted. It put a whole new light on our most bitter fights: they were almost always during times when Rich was upset about a new rela-tionship. Two of our worst and almost violent fights had happened during trips away. With my new-found information, it was obvious that I had been an inno-cent victim of Rich's tremendous tension over another involvement.

My sexual life had always been pretty uncomplicated and above board. So when Rich started talking about "sexual currency" and sending out "available" messages, I was amazed and almost uncomprehending. I had thought naively that only prostitutes and gigolos engaged in such practices. Who were all these people out there dressed in regular clothes and leading "regular" lives that were sending and receiving all these sexual messages? I was appalled at how many available and needy women there were, and how few scruples they had about one-night-stands or relationships with married men. In fact, two of the people on Rich's list had been close friends of mine who were no longer living in the area. That meant I had the unpleasant task of reassessing my friendships with them. At times Rich's need to confess was tempered with concern for my

---

*Irene Claremont de Castillejo, *Knowing Woman*. (New York: Harper Colophon Books, 1973), p. 128. Reprinted by permission of the C.G. Jung Foundation.

emotional welfare. I had lost all perspective on what my pain tolerance was and therefore could not always know if what I was hearing from Rich was exceeding what I could stand. Sometimes when this would happen I would sort of automatically tune out and disassociate from it. I didn't know what our relationship might be, if any, after such a lengthy catharsis. But I knew that whatever happened, we were on an unalterable course of honesty with each other regardless of the cost.

I decided to stay with Rich until after the baby was born and then go to live with my sister and her family. Rich was agreeable to this. At last he seemed to feel free to share in the birthing process of our child: a paradoxical fact in light of his emotional mortgage to his current passion. He told me that he couldn't possibly stop seeing Sarah, and that he would continue to see her during the time we continued to live together. I knew from his description of how hooked he was that that was true, and that if he were ever to resolve his relationship with Sarah, it would have to run its course. I set down some guidelines that I dredged up from the shreds of my self-respect, and he agreed to them.

And so we began a horrendous two months of waiting for the baby to be born. At the time we had agreed to this arrangement, I was so big with child I was sure I would have the baby at least a month sooner and felt certain that I could put up with anything for four weeks. My parents were shocked, and angry, and hopeful that I would start divorce proceedings. My sisters and brother and a few close friends were also very angry, but suspended judgement to let me work out for myself what I needed. I put a great deal of energy into explaining Rich's behavior as compulsive and neurotic so as to remove him from the arena of moral judgement.

Those two months were like a daily roller-coaster. I desperately wanted to take a consistent stance of "injured party" or "understanding wife" or "vengeful bitch." Yet my emotions whipsawed me around, leaving me confused and almost crazy at times. Sometimes I felt terribly depressed and thought of suicide. It seemed as if my whole world had been turned upside down and I couldn't find firm footing anywhere. The responsibility of the baby growing inside me helped somewhat to ground me, but then I also felt terribly guilty about what the upheaval and stress might be doing to the baby in utero. Sometimes I felt like a self-righteous, liberated woman who had every excuse to leave her marriage for good and take up with any new man that turned my fancy. But mostly I felt jealous, insecure, and full of hate towards Sarah. I knew I couldn't compete with her in bed since she seemed to be offering Rich nothing less than absolute sexual ambrosia. I didn't even want to compete in this area as I was in no mood to sleep with him most of that summer anyway. I resented tremendously the sexual availability that is such an integral part of being a mistress. After all, when you don't have to live with someone day in and day out, it's relatively easy (and powerful) to be in the position of granting sexual favors. I knew that in many ways Sarah and Rich were a total mismatch because of their conflicting lifestyles and attitudes, but they had the bond of complete mutual addiction which seemed to override all other considerations. In the height of my need to be close to Rich at any cost, I even had brief times of counseling him about his relationship with Sarah.

Of course, at that time the problem had not been labeled as an addiction, and there was no S.L.A.A. perspective through which to view all of this. I felt that most of the time I walked around with a great sign on my forehead which said, "I hurt." My concept of a loving God also suffered during this time. I felt betrayed and angry that my higher Power would let this happen to me. Why me of all people? I didn't deserve this. What kind of punishment was this anyway, and for what sin? I had been a loving and faithful wife and I certainly didn't deserve this kind of pain for all my efforts. How come my love for Rich hadn't succeeded in making him whole? How come it wasn't strong enough to counterbalance his own unhappy childhood? I knew that there was much in his background that could be a cause for his addiction, but still I thought that somehow *my* love could fill up all those holes and that he would then blossom into the man I was waiting for. Like the popular song I sang to myself, "I love the light, I love the changing season, I love without much thought to reason. I'd give it all if I could make you see, I love the man who waits beside you, I love the man who hides behind you." Then I would weep for all the lost promise. And if I were feeling at all optimistic, I would cling to the hope that something fine and enduring would come out of all this pain, that my prince would finally cast off his cloak of darkness and come into the light.

Finally the time came for my baby to be born. As it happened, Rich was out with Sarah that evening, and had come home late telling me of some nightmare that Sarah had had. But I was going into labor and, for once, I just didn't care about anyone else but myself and my unborn child. I knew that I was soon to be delivered, literally and figuratively, of all this pain. The birth of our baby was my ticket to freedom. My labor was long and quite painful and the concept of "natural" childbirth began to seem like a cruel joke. I had always envisioned myself as having a high threshold of pain, but the long hours wore me down and the emotional distress I had been under took its toll. Finally I gave in to anaesthesia and an hour later a beautiful baby girl was handed to me to breast feed. I was ecstatic. She was perfect! And I loved her with every ounce of energy I had left. Rich took off to announce the news and check on Sarah, and I stayed in a bubble of maternal bliss for the next three days. Rich was too emotionally mortgaged out at this time to really participate in the joy, but I didn't care. Soon I would be on my way to Vermont, and I had an infant who needed me totally.

The day of my departure dawned bright and clear. Rich and I packed the crib and some other essentials, and drove to Vermont. We shared relief that this painful period was over, and uncertainty about what this move would mean for our future. Rich seemed to be hinting at trying to break off his relationship with Sarah and having some time alone, but I was skeptical, with just a glimmer of hope. My sister and her children received us with open arms and I felt I was home at last. Rich flew back to Boston the next day, and we officially began our separation.

I lived with my sister and her family for eight months. It was just what the doctor ordered. I was in a lovely house in the country surrounded by a caring family with a baby to occupy my time and energy. The tide had truly begun to turn for me and I felt blessed. However, I knew I wanted to rebuild my life and could use the help of a therapist. Fortunately my sister knew of an excellent one. In the first few sessions I put all my energy into explaining to my therapist the nature of *Rich's* problem. The therapist turned to me and said, "But you haven't told me anything about yourself—where are *you* in all of this?" Where was I indeed? Was I still defining myself primarily through the success or failure of my marriage? Having established that I was lost to myself, we wasted no more time on Rich and began to delve into *my* childhood to see if we could find out about *Kate* long before she ever met Rich.

Rich and I arranged that he would come up for a short visit three weeks after our separation had begun, and I found myself looking forward to this with mixed emotions. Somehow I believed that Rich was not seeing much of Sarah. His letters hadn't mentioned her and I hoped that the impact of our separation had really taken hold. The visit turned out to be very difficult. We made love and talked and walked, but something was not right. It wasn't until the end of his stay that I realized how much time he was still spending with Sarah, and I realized I couldn't tolerate this any longer. I called him the day after he returned and told him I didn't want to see him if he was going to continue his relationship with Sarah. It was a painful decision for me to make, since I had no assurance that he was capable of ending his relationship even if he wanted to. But I had had enough of sharing Rich during the summer to last a lifetime.

True to form, Rich took my ultimatum with apparent calm and said he would get back to me about his decision. A few long days passed. Finally, I called him. He told me there was a letter in the mail to me which I would be receiving the next day. The letter was a written confirmation of his decision to end his relationship with Sarah. In fact, he had already told her that the relationship was over. His voice sounded disant and flat over the phone. He told me that "stopping" with Sarah didn't necessarily mean "going" with me. More than anything, he wanted to have some time alone. I was relieved at his decision and also knew that there was nothing I could do about his feelings of loss. I remember wondering if I even wanted a relationship with this half-person. Was I now supposed to fill in the hole that Sarah had carved out so he would feel less empty? And I wondered if the spark between us could ever be reignited after such emotional bankruptcy—maybe we would be better off as friends instead of husband and wife.

A few weeks later he came to visit and we began, very slowly and tentatively, to explore rebuilding our relationship. About six weeks after that visit he called one evening to tell me of his idea about promiscuity being an addiction. I was skeptical at first as it seemed to be an over-simplification of a very complicated problem. He told me he was trying to start a group and I thought it was doubtful that he would be able to find others who had shared his experience. However, my lack of enthusiasm did not deter him, fortunately, and S.L.A.A. went through its birthing pains without me.

During my stay with my sister, I had one very brief, mild flirtation, but as much as I wanted to retaliate and show Rich I was not going to be forever available to him, my heart wasn't in it. Rich and I were already starting to commit ourselves to each other again and I didn't want to muddy that process with another man. I also wasn't all that attracted to him. But I did want Rich to be jealous and I wanted to be courted again. Unfortunately, I felt just as insecure and shy as I always had. I had fantasies of how much fun it would be to really sleep around and enjoy myself without the constraints of marriage. I kept saying to myself, "Now's your chance to find somebody else and nobody would blame you for doing it." But the reality was that on another level I was absolutely terrified about being unmarried and meeting available men. So while my fantasies remained active, I remained faithful, more by default than by choice.

After the months of separation and occasional visits, we decided that we should try to live together again. I returned to Cambridge with a nine month old baby and equal amounts of hope and apprehension. I had left my loving sister and her family, my therapist, my existence in the quiet and beauty of the country, to return to an uncertain future with a man who had identified himself as a sex and love addict. Those first few months back together turned out to be a big adjustment for us both, bigger than either of us had anticipated. It wasn't just the apartment that neither of us liked, or Rich's return to school while trying to figure out a way to support us. It was that our new relationship, built on sporadic weekend visits, now had to work in the everyday realities of getting along with each other.

The self-discovery and growth that Rich and I had achieved during our separate lives had to survive the testing grounds of a committed relationship. I wanted very much for things to work out between us to prove that my original choice of mate had been right all along. But the ghosts of our past lives together would re-emerge unexpectedly, and I would doubt all the changes we had been through and wonder why we were still together. In our sex life, I was determined not to engage in any sexual practice that Rich had experienced with another woman—especially Sarah. That didn't leave a lot of options, and it seemed no matter what I did, I thought that Rich was comparing me with his past lovers. Even if he wasn't, *I* was always comparing myself to my fantasies of what his sex life had been with other women. Also, since Rich was now depending on me solely for his sexual gratification, the dice were really loaded against us.

After an uneasy summer during which our dreams of the great reunion had been pretty well trampled, we decided to try marriage counseling. We had come to the point where we both wondered if the only glue holding us together was our neurotic and needy past. Both of us were very wary of continuing on in some unconscious, addictive way. As for me, I knew that something had changed deep inside me. I knew that I could never again love Rich with the same abandon of those early years. Something had died inside me. Perhaps it was the innocence of not knowing the darker side of his nature, or the dream I had clung to for so long that "love would conquer all." Even as I mourned the passing of that innocence, I realized that this might be my ticket to a freer and happier relationship—one that was no longer rooted in "being there no matter what."

Marriage counseling was a mutual statement that our marriage was again in trouble. This time the enemy was not another woman or a bottle of booze. The enemy was inside, with a potential for destruction greater than all of the external enemies. Fortunately, we had two very competent counselors, one male and one female. Together Rich and I laid out our history as a couple and identified some issues we wanted to work on. But before we even got a chance to work on them, another issue raised its head: I was pregnant again, quite by accident. And neither of us felt emotionally ready to handle another child, with our relationship shaky, and while still getting used to one baby. But ready or not, I wanted to have the baby and I wasn't really open to any alternatives. Rich felt trapped and upset and we spent a number of helpful sessions exploring our feelings surrounding having a second child. We both agreed that we wanted a second child if we were to remain together. It was the whole question of having an additional strain on our relationship at a time when neither of us had any guarantees of our future together that made it so difficult.

It became apparent in those sessions that whatever decisions were to be made would have to be the result of really being able to hear the other's points of view—not just listen, tolerate, and dismiss the other. That realization was the beginning of a long process of breaking the habit of dismissing each other's feelings by labeling them as neurotic or immature. As one counselor said, "You seem to communicate with each other well—you are both very articulate—but there's no real contact between you." It took me a while to fully understand the distinction, but it proved to be very valuable. So it became apparent that we both really needed to be heard and understood by the other, and whenever that happened the process itself became the victory, and the decision (of whatever issue) seemed like a by-product.

We also spent a lot of time trying to work through the conflicts surrounding our sex life. We found that our frustrations and bitterness surfaced more easily in the safe environment of counseling. I had hoped that one of the counselors would somehow step in and tell Rich that his demands were excessive. I wanted a referee to keep score and announce the winner. Of course, no such thing happened, and we were left face to face with each other, trying to respect the other's needs and thereby come up with a compromise that would make us both feel like winners instead of losers. For us, the sexual arena was loaded with treachery and a lot of defensive maneuvering. This caused us a lot of pain and a sense of futility.

There were times when we left the sessions feeling further apart and closer to divorce than when we came in. But ultimately our strong commitment to counseling, coupled with a strong determination on both our parts to see if there was any real glue that was holding us together, won out. We came to a stopping point after seven months. The baby was due soon and we felt like we wanted to try it on our own again. Our problems were by no means resolved in any final sense, but at least we had gained a new perspective on our conflicts, a perspective that included the sure knowledge that we really did care for one another.

Our second child was born and it was a joyous experience for us both. When I remembered the stress we were both under when our first child was born, I realized what a long way we had come in just two years. I knew, if we could manage to have enough trust and faith to keep on, that time and shared experiences would be the great healer.

Rich's continued involvement in S.L.A.A. was a great source of comfort to me as it continued to allay my fears of his straying. At the same time, it was very difficult at first to have him share his litany of temptations with me. He told me his reason for doing so was not to hurt me, but to provide an external constraint for his fantasies. I understood this in part, but there were still times when I felt too vulnerable to hear about them. It was particularly difficult when he happened to run into Sarah. Our relationship would feel the reverberations from that for days. I knew that he loved me, but it took a long time to believe that I was more than just a mother or a friend to him. I had wanted to excite the same kind of passion in him that Sarah had. I didn't want to be relegated to the position of being his nice, understanding, tolerant wife.

In retrospect, I think I expected too much too soon. In addition to S.L.A.A., Rich was still seeing his therapist, and I was often on the defensive as he worked out his internal problems. There is always a grain of truth in any criticism, and

I would fight tooth and nail to defend myself, especially when that "grain" took on huge proportions. I returned to individual therapy for a time to help me understand that my imperfections were not abominations, and I did not have to be so defensive.

Another year went by, and we began to reap the rewards of working so hard on our relationship. We grew increasingly committed to each other as the effects of our mutual past had less and less impact on our daily lives. We had worked out a fairly comfortable agreement as far as our sex life was concerned and had managed to find one weekend away from our children and responsibilities to simply enjoy each other again. We were coping with external worries over money and employment but that seemed possible, too.

Paradoxically enough, the newfound security in our relationship helped to give me the courage to face another major discontent in our lives together. Everything in me railed at disturbing the peace once more, but I couldn't help it. I had felt for a long time that I was doing 90% of the parenting of our two little ones and I began to resent that fact tremendously. Rich told me he loved the children very much and enjoyed being with them when he felt loving, but unfortunately those occasions never seemed to coincide with the times when I really needed help. I became increasingly frustrated by his endless list of things that always had to come before taking care of small children. This was no partnership in parenting, I realized. This was Kate pretending she was a single parent and feeling envy over the shared parenting that other friends were having. And so, once again I gave Rich an ultimatum. Although it appeared to center around childcare, the issue really centered around *us* once more. And once again it was going to take both of us to work out what we wanted and expected from one another. For me, this meant giving up the myth of being a self-sufficient person who doesn't need anyone and therefore can never be disappointed. Rich began to see that he could respond to my need for him without feeling manipulated or overwhelmed. We went into counseling again, but this time were not satisfied with the help we got. Our joint decision to terminate therapy prematurely (by the therapist's definition) turned out to be unifying and strengthening for us. Rich was really beginning to help me out, and the change was causing me to trust our ability to work out our own problems in a way I never had before. The transition wasn't perfectly smooth, but then, transitions never are. The point was that we had rallied to overcome our differences and had shown ourselves willing and capable for the task.

Almost two years later, I am overwhelmed at the process of transformation. There is no question in my mind that we would not be together today if Rich hadn't been so capable of changing. This is a blessing, one which I could not have anticipated early on in our relationship. I also know that my *own* growth as a person was the result of suffering tremendously in a love relationship which has served as a crucible for my development.

> But if jealousy can be made to see; if a capacity and willingness to understand dwell in the heart at the same time as one is torn to shreds by jealousy, then the agony of despair can be lifted to another plane where its white heat can fuse again the scattered pieces of the golden coin; can make possible the return of love through the acceptance of one's desolation and the humility of forgiveness. Wholeness is restored, but this time the wholeness is within the sufferer himself. *

Sometimes Rich and I look at each other and wonder how we can be the same people who met each other fourteen years ago and who separated six years ago. Interestingly enough, when we got back together after our separation, we got new wedding rings as we had never really liked our old ones. That gesture seemed to us an outward symbol of an inner change that was only beginning to actualize. The image of our relationship that comes to mind is that of a plant which got pruned at a certain point and then sprouted off in a newer, stronger direction. The roots of the plant are still there, only the growth they are nourishing is a healthy, vibrant one. The time, from the point of pruning, which seems so drastic and potentially life threatening, to realizing the viability of the whole new shoot or sprout, can not be condensed by time-lapse photography. There were no short-cuts for us and now I'm grateful for that fact because time has a healing quality which is an experience unto itself. If someone had asked me five years ago about the chances of having a true loving parnership with a recovering S.L.A.A., I would have said I just didn't know. Today, as a result of my own experience, I can honestly affirm that possibility.

And so, dear reader, just for today my story ends with a "happily ever after" by my own definition. I would not presume to define your definition or your process, be it mutual or individual. My story has been shared not purely for its ending but for its process. The writing of it is to let you know you are not alone and that there is hope.

*   *   *

The experience of others of us has been similar to the pattern Kate found in her life. Many of us had the feeling of "needing to be needed" that left us clinging to the addict, certain that if we made ourselves necessary, or "indispensable" to the addict, we would be "safe." We, too, have sacrificed our personal dignity and hidden behind self-deception in order to make the relationship work, no matter what the cost. We became skilled at rationalizing away each new infidelity, wanting to believe in the denials or the apparent remorse of

---

* de Castillejo, *Knowing Woman*, p. 128.

our addict-partners. We *wanted* to blame the seducer or seductress, or even preferred to blame ourselves ("I shouldn't have made him/her angry." "I should be a better lover; if only I was sexier."), rather than hold the addict responsible for his or her own behavior and trusting our own misgivings. We were too afraid of losing the one we loved, to whom we had sacrificed so much!

Recovery and reconciliation, too, can seem as difficult as living with the addiction. The addict's demands for sexual satisfaction can appear unreasonable, yet we are fearful that rejection will be used as an excuse to look elsewhere for a more cooperative lover. We envy those in relationships who do not have to bear the painful intimacy of knowing about all the former lovers, or each day's temptations. ("If he/she is so often tempted, how real can my partner's commitment to OUR relationship be?") The need to be honest about how we really feel—and to be willing to accept that same honesty from our partners—demands trust and self-confidence that are often hard to summon at all, much less to deliver on a consistent basis.

Even the addict's necessary involvement with S.L.A.A. has been a source of real discomfort for us at times. So much of our security had been based on being needed. Now it seemed that the addict could and would go it alone, and if he/she needed anyone, it was the Fellowship, not us. It was painfully apparent that if we demanded that our partners choose between us and S.L.A.A., then WE would be the losers. And yet the needs of every other S.L.A.A. member at times seemed to take precedence over ours. Newcomers to S.L.A.A. are often attractive and needy, and we wondered if *our* partners might not be vulnerable to this temptation within the Fellowship.

Then, too, our privacy was always on the line, it seemed. We cringed inwardly as we imagined these strangers hearing about the most intimate details of our lives, of our sex life being discussed at meetings. Then there was the fear of what friends and family would think if they knew about any of this. What might they imagine, hearing even the simple fact that the one to whom we were married or committed was "a member of Sex and Love Addicts Anonymous"? Even the thought was humiliating.

We have learned by painful experience that life with a sex and love addict cannot and will not be without growing pains and often severe conflict. This is true even, and perhaps *especially,* in recovery. If we try to keep the surface of the relationship smooth, we begin to compromise our own feelings. These silent sacrifices, first voluntary and then increasingly necessary, ultimately leave us feeling more and more as if we are "doing it all" for little return. Our own success in partnership rests first, as does the addict's recovery, on maintaining a sense of personal dignity. If we maintain the integrity of our-selves and our values, the "cost" of intimacy and partnership with a recovering sex and love addict will not be too high. On the contrary, it can bring wonderful rewards.

Even if it comes to be apparent that you and your addict cannot build a partnership, either because sobriety is too elusive or because communication somehow fails, you will still be able to move on in your life with self respect and confidence in yourself and your future.

For those of you who are still suffering the pains of suspicion or the agony of discovery, we reach out in love and compassion. We are still only a few, a testimony to the power of this addiction to destroy relationships with those who do not share the illness. We hope that you will find comfort in the experiences we have shared. Like the addict, you are powerless over this addiction. The only efforts that will bear fruit are those you direct toward understanding yourself and preserving your own dignity. Tremendous obstacles will confront those attempting to build partnerships with sex and love addicts, even in the best of circumstances. We do not know if your personal situation can be transformed in reconciliation or not. But our prayers are with you, and we offer the hope and the vision of a golden coin of wholeness that has come to be in our lives. You are not alone. There is hope.

Chapter 4

The Twelve Step Program:
A Path to Sexual and
Emotional Sobriety

The Twelve Steps were originally formulated by Bill W., a co-founder of Alcoholics Anonymous, in 1938. They grew out of the principles then espoused by the Oxford Groups (a religious fellowship which sponsored early A.A. in Akron, Ohio), tempered by the practical experiences which were a common denominator of recovery from alcoholism among A.A. members at that time. These steps were first published in *Alcoholics Anonymous* (1939) and received a more detailed treatment in *Twelve Steps and Twelve Traditions* (1953), both of which were written by Bill W.

In presenting the S.L.A.A. version of the Twelve Steps here, we wish to do what A.A. had in mind in presenting them initially in the book *Alcoholics Anonymous*. Enough of us have worked through these Twelve Steps that a common experience of recovery from sex and love addiction has emerged. The fellowship is still small, however, and there seem to be many people desperately in need of the hope the Twelve Step program offers. We earnestly hope that families and others suffering from the destruction caused by an active sex and love addict will stop blaming themselves after reading of our experiences in this book. However, our primary concern is that the suffering sex and love addict may find the way, through the Twelve Step program, to turn from the self-destruction of this disease, and lay the foundation for spiritual and emotional recovery.

Our presentation does not intend to be a complete treatment of the Twelve Steps from the S.L.A.A. perspective. Yet we are endeavoring to present them in enough detail to indicate the scope of recovery from sex and love addiction which we have experienced. If you are thinking as you read this book that S.L.A.A. may be a fellowship worth serious consideration for your own problems, we recommend that you also read the books *Alcoholics Anonymous* (especially chapters 5-7) and *Twelve Steps and Twelve Traditions*. We have found these books, in spite of their occasionally somewhat dated ideas and language, to be surprisingly appropriate and useful to us in applying the Twelve Steps to sex and love addiction. We substitute such words as "our addiction" or "sex and love addiction" for the direct references to alcoholism in those books.

Their timeliness after half a century, and their applicability to a different specific addiction such as ours, are tributes to their psychological and spiritual insight and to the high quality of their writing.

One thing is clear. The Twelve Steps, as originally set forth in *Alcoholics Anonymous,* do provide a comprehensive and thorough approach to the problem of dealing with addiction, including sex and love addiction. Our gratitude for the efforts of the early A.A. pioneers is very great. Our expression of it must necessarily fall far short of sufficiently honoring their tremendous achievement.

Here are the Twelve Steps of Sex and Love Addicts Anonymous: *

1. We admitted we were powerless over sex and love addiction—that our lives had become unmanageable.

2. Came to believe that a Power greater than ourselves could restore us to sanity.

3. Made a decision to turn our will and our lives over to the care of God as we understood God.

4. Made a searching and fearless moral inventory of ourselves.

5. Admitted to God, to ourselves, and to another human being the exact nature of our wrongs.

6. Were entirely ready to have God remove all these defects of character.

7. Humbly asked God to remove our shortcomings.

---

*The original Twelve Steps of Alcoholics Anonymous differ from this adapted version, used here with the permission of Alcoholics Anonymous World Services, Inc., in the following ways: We have substituted "sex and love addiction" and "sex and love addicts" for "alcohol" and "alcoholics" in Steps 1 and 12, respectively. We have also avoided using the pronoun "Him" in Steps 3, 7 and 11, and we have changed "in all our affairs" to "in all areas of our lives" in Step 12. This adapted version of the Twelve Steps (with the exception of the wording change in Step 12) was adopted by the S.L.A.A. Fellowship after extended debate on July 8th, 1981. The change in the wording of the Twelfth Step was approved by a Fellowship-Wide S.L.A.A. Group referendum on May 15th, 1984.

The Twelve Steps of Alcoholics Anonymous follow. (1) We admitted we were powerless over alcohol—that our lives had become unmanageable. (2) Came to believe that a Power greater than ourselves could restore us to sanity. (3) Made a decision to turn our will and our lives over to the care of God *as we understood Him.* (4) Made a searching and fearless moral inventory of ourselves. (5) Admitted to God, to ourselves, and to another human being the exact nature of our wrongs. (6) Were entirely ready to have God remove all these defects of character. (7) Humbly asked Him to remove our shortcomings. (8) Made a list of all persons we had harmed, and became willing to make amends to them all. (9) Made direct amends to such people wherever possible, except when to do so would injure them or others. (10) Continued to take personal inventory and when we were wrong promptly admitted it. (11) Sought through prayer and meditation to improve our conscious contact with God *as we understood Him,* praying only for knowledge of His will for us and the power to carry that out. (12) Having had a spiritual awakening as the result of these steps, we tried to carry this message to alcoholics, and to practice these principles in all our affairs. Twelve Steps Copyright © 1976 by A.A. World Services, Inc.

8. Made a list of all persons we had harmed, and became willing to make amends to them all.

9. Made direct amends to such people wherever possible, except when to do so would injure them or others.

10. Continued to take personal inventory, and when we were wrong promptly admitted it.

11. Sought through prayer and meditation to improve our conscious contact with a Power greater than ourselves, praying only for knowledge of God's will for us and the power to carry that out.

12. Having had a spiritual awakening as the result of these steps, we tried to carry this message to sex and love addicts, and to practice these principles in all areas of our lives.

The First Step

Step 1.

We admitted we were powerless over sex and love addiction—that our lives had become unmanageable.

The word "powerless" summons up for us several related ideas. First, it means that whatever power is usually involved in making sound choices in our sexual and emotional behavior did not reside with us. We were enslaved to sex and love (which we experienced as emotional dependency or romantic intrigue). The fact that we became captives of these things shows that there was something extremely important and powerful in our sexual and emotional patterns which gave us some kind of "payoff" that we thought we needed.

Sometimes we were seeking to screen the world, with all its demands and responsibilities, out of our awareness by mesmerizing ourselves with sexual activity. Sometimes we were trying to deaden a load of guilt and frustration by taking romantic or sexual holidays. Sometimes we sought to fill the emptiness within us with another person. Or perhaps we masked the fear of commitment by thinking of ourselves as living out new standards of morality based on "guilt-free sex," "free love," or "recreational sex." But all of us were using our sexual powers and emotional investments to either lessen pain or augment pleasure. These pervasive motives governed our sexual and romantic intentions and actions.

At some time in our lives our behavior began to take on the compulsive hallmarks of addiction. The once rare liaisons became monthly, then weekly. They happened when inconvenient, or when they interfered with work or family obligations. The occasional pleasurable daydream grew into a constant obsession that destroyed our ability to concentrate on more ordinary and more important things. One by one such things as satisfaction in our work, friends and social activities dropped away as we found more and more of our time and our thoughts absorbed by one person. The occasional relief of sexual tension with masturbation became a need for which the opportunity had to be created. We had lost control over the rate or frequency (or both) at which we would seek the romantic or sexual "solution" to life's ills.

Some of us were caught up in the hypnotic intensity of sexual and romantic encounters or relationships, merging ourselves into our lovers or spouses. These experiences became overwhelmingly compelling, carrying us along with them, exuberantly at first, and then less and less willingly. Unrelenting, the imperiousness with which our sexual and romantic interludes or absorption in a relationship now forced themselves upon us led to prolonged bondage to our sexual and emotional needs: a real, undeniable craving.

The original quest for distraction from life's tensions and responsibilities, for relief from past guilt and present frustration, now led us into oblivion. The brave new worlds of morality where "anything goes" because "nothing matters" boomeranged, leaving us grasping for some residual sense of meaning or reality in life. Obsession and compulsion, now our masters, meant that control over our sexual and emotional lives no longer resided with us, or within us. We had lost control, regardless of whether we admitted it to ourselves or not.

From the standpoint of "anything goes, who cares?" loss of control didn't seem so bad. In fact, the addiction itself often held us spellbound, convinced that *it* was what we wanted. Many of us were so numbed that only a blast of physical and emotional intensity from a sexual or romantic "hit" could penetrate and animate our progressively deadened, dissipated beings. Like a cattle prod jabbed into someone who is exhausted and dazed, an addictive hit jolted us into a temporary illusion that we were alive and really living. It was as though we had a voice in our heads which said, "If you get more, then everything will fall into place."

If our addiction took the form of dependency on one person, again, loss of control did not always seem so bad. We could tell ourselves that our bondage was really the sign of a "match made in heaven," that since we would sacrifice anything for this love, we would surely be rewarded for our unselfishness. Alone, life was drab and empty; if we could only become more a part of our lover, become ONE, everything would be alright.

Yet a vague but persistent nagging within our deepest self continued to bear witness that all was not well. Despite all the cultural and rational camouflage behind which our addiction could hide, it was impossible, short of suicide, to kill that innermost voice that whispered to us of life's opportunities for growth and wholeness that we were helplessly letting slip by. The guilt of prior deeds and passions or missed opportunities gave way to the deepest, most pervasive guilt of all: that of having left life unlived, of having turned our backs on the possibility of fulfilling a meaningful destiny.

These existential pangs were not welcomed into our awareness. Yet they found their way in, whatever we did. The heat of addictive passion was less and less able to blot them out. The addiction itself could no longer deliver that formerly reliable, thoroughly engrossing sexual and emotional return. The utter futility of going on under the sway of our sex and love addiction was finally becoming clear.

It mattered little whether our patterns were primarily those of unbridled promiscuity, or excessive emotional dependency on one person, or some combination of these. Each of us, in his or her own time, finally experienced a sense of real desperation. To continue to live out our addictive patterns, or to be controlled by them, brought us in touch with the terror of irrevocably losing sanity, of slipping over the edge of an abyss beyond which any stability and life purpose would be forever out of reach. We found *this* prospect to be more terrifying even than the thought of physical death. This loss of one's soul could only be all the more poignant if the body in which it lived continued to exist, unanimated spiritually from within, and monstrously driven by imperious instinctual drives which would now have become its masters.

Yet for a few of us the terror of being further devoured by our sex and love addiction brought us to the point of unconditional surrender. We decided we HAD to stop. Now we began to confront the second aspect of powerlessness: the paradox that surrender to the impossibility of control is the beginning of recovery.

Most of us had attempted at various times a wide range of strategies to control our behavior so that our lives as addicts would somehow blend in with our "other" lives as members of society. We would break up with a particular lover, or find another lover, often in rapid succession. We stopped masturbating—or started masturbating (as a substitute for getting sex from others). We changed gender preference, seeking relationships with those less sexually attractive to us. We moved to another town, made inner resolves, took oaths before friends or loved ones. We married jealous, suspicious lovers, or got divorced so that we would be free to find a more satisfying mate. We had religious conversions, sometimes choosing a monastic life where sex would not be available. We sought deep emotional involvement, trying to balance the intensity of one relationship by starting another somewhere else. And on and on.

These strategies, no matter how strong the conviction with which they were adopted, always turned out to be like "going on the wagon." If we had some initial success in curbing our addictive behavior, we would quickly take on an air of smug confidence, wholly unwarranted, and conclude that we would now be able to "manage things." This merely lowered our defenses, so that we sank back into the quicksand of our patterns again, sometimes within months or weeks, more often within days or hours.

Our lack of success in managing our addiction, our loss of control, had become an established fact. We had experienced over and over the mind-altering effect which had sapped the strength of our resolve to free ourselves from sex and love addiction. Thus we approached the prospect of surrendering our sex and love addiction with real humility, for we had no way of knowing if such a surrender was even possible.

The addiction itself made our willingness to attempt freeing ourselves of the disease highly questionable. But at least we were becoming desperate enough, once again, to try to extricate ourselves. We began to recognize that *we were powerless, not* merely to change *some* specific sex partner, lover, or situation. We were powerless over an addictive *pattern*, of which any current, specific circumstance was just the most recent example.

The whole trouble in our previous attempts to manage the addiction was that we had underestimated the desperate seriousness of our condition. In flailing about, trying to be free of a particularly painful situation, we had failed to comprehend the scope of the pattern towards which our current disaster was pointing, and of which it was a result. True surrender of our sex and love addiction meant not only being willing to take ourselves out of the painful situation at hand. It meant, most importantly, being ready to be free of our whole life strategy of obsession with and pursuit of love and sex. The resolve only to be rid of a specific painful situation, without the readiness to break the whole addictive pattern, amounted to "going on the wagon."

In coming to terms with our individual patterns of addiction, we may have felt somewhat buoyed initially by the fact that in S.L.A.A. each person defines his or her own particular manifestation of sex and love addiction. This led many of us to the private conclusion that we could "define" our patterns in ways that would let us enjoy our addiction in another form. It would be sufficient, we thought, to label only the obviously troublesome behavior as addictive, and unnecessary to include other "courses on the menu."

If, for example, we claimed that our "bottom line" addiction was engaging in exhibitionistic behavior, then in defining our pattern only as this specific practice we might kid ourselves that new, paid-for sexual liaisons actually were not part of our addictive pattern. We would claim that such novelty actually was a step forward, because we were no longer engaging in purely solitary acts. The opposite was true for those of us who labeled only blatant promiscuous behavior as addictive. We would engage in such solitary activities as masturbation, voyeurism, or exhibitionism, and claim that they were improvements because we were no longer involving others directly in our disease.

Such attempts were as futile as for an alcoholic to switch from beer to wine, or wine to beer, claiming either as an "improvement" over the other. Those of us who tried to deceive ourselves in the way we defined our sex and love addiction either found ourselves slipping back into the old behavior, or getting into real trouble with our new "steps forward." We learned the hard way that there was no such thing as half-surrender. The "freedom" to define our own addictive pattern could not be used in a self-serving way. Our addictions are a reality that persists regardless of any short-sighted, convenient definition. If we were leaving out of our personal definition some behavior that was addictive, it would certainly pull us back into the pattern again.

The certain pain of continuing our sex and love addiction brought us to the admission of Step 1, that "we were powerless over our sex and love addiction" and that we could not manage our lives unless we were free of it. Finally, we reached a point of surrendering unconditionally. The proof that our surrender was indeed unconditional was that we now refrained, one day at a time, from every form of bottom-line behavior we saw as part of our own addictive pattern. If our primary addictive problem was obsessive love dependency, we separated from or severed ties with our "partners." This was not done to punish ourselves or others, but out of a recognition that these were no-win situations. Many of us suspected or realized that we would need an indefinite period alone in which to learn to understand and deal with our disease. Distractions through some form of sex or love relationship could only abort our own recovery. If we had just been jilted by someone we felt was "indispensable," surrender meant that we accepted our loss, and refused to take revenge or recriminate. It also meant that, perhaps for the first time in our lives, we were not going to relieve our wounded feelings in some new person's arms!

Each of us, regardless of individual circumstances, was now willing to go to any lengths, a day at a time, to stay unhooked. This decision was unilateral. It did not depend on the cooperation or lack of cooperation of our spouses, lovers, or sex objects. We were willing to be available *not* to the next lover or new sexual fantasy, but to whatever might happen next *within* ourselves. Paradoxically, this was not willingness that came from strength, but from the certainty of the dire consequences of continuing on in our addiction. As we turned from the old patterns, the painful emotions we had always tried to evade brought us to a series of insights which were the gift of the Second Step.

The Second Step

Step 2:

Came to believe that a Power greater than ourselves could restore us to sanity.

We endured the early phases of withdrawal, sometimes achingly putting one twenty-four stretch together after another. As this continued, we faced a real dilemma concerning our personal identity. While actively involved in sex and love addiction we had found it impossible (if we had thought about it at all) to assess just how great an investment we had been making in our addiction throughout the course of it. We began to recognize that our disease, far from being just a way to stop the clock with pleasure and intensity, had molded our personalities in ways that would maximize our ability to get the addictive returns! Our physical appearance, our mannerisms, the way we went about our careers or other activities, many of the traits we thought of as our identifying trademarks, as *who* we were, had been designed to serve our sex and love addiction. Even if we seemed to possess some positive traits, such as authentic concern for others, we could see that these had been perverted by our addiction, leaving us full of conflict and working at cross-purposes. The line between compassion and passion had never been clear to us.

Indeed, our sex and love addiction, dictating who and what we had striven to be in the world, had supplied our principal source of identity, our entire self-concept. We had felt so self-assured, surveying a crowded room, advertising or broadcasting our availability. We knew we would be met with similar energy from others, a never-ending source of "rainchecks." What security we had derived, knowing we could foster insecurity in others, making them all the more needy and dependent on us, thus insuring our own sense of well-being. We enjoyed the power our sex appeal gave us in enforcing our dominance over others by hinting that they could be replaced. We felt safe in knowing that physically, emotionally, and mentally we could continue to attract new people to us, or further bind those already in our web.

Yet, whether we were aware of it or not, our entire being had been molded by our failure, or refusal, to solve from within the problems of our real lives: insecurity, loneliness, and lack of any abiding sense of personal worth and dignity. Through sex, charm, emotional appeal, or persuasive intellect, we had used other people as "drugs," to avoid facing our own personal inadequacy. Once we saw this, we realized that in surrendering our addictive behavior we would inevitably have to question the whole foundation of our self-image, our personal identity.

This task was staggering, implying as it did that our former selves would have to die, or at least risk dying, so that a new self, free of the addiction, could live. Nor could we get much relief from this dilemma by bravely making declarations of some set values we were NOW prepared to live by! We came to realize that this disease of sex and love addiction so subtly and thoroughly permeated our best-intentioned and most fervid plans to reform ourselves, that even our ability to think clearly was undermined. There could be no such thing as a self-powered cure. Too many of us had tried this and had failed repeatedly. It was not that our logic, motives or intents were wrong. Rather, our very ability to see the problem clearly, and our wishes to change ourselves, were themselves systematically distorted by the addiction. That part of our mind which at least intermittently recognized our sickness was *itself* not immune, and could not be solely relied upon to guide us to health.

As we came to appreciate the magnitude and mind-altering

nature of sex and love addiction, and the extent to which it had perverted our value system, we had to admit that we could not reshape our whole identity unaided. In the stark recognition of our profound frailty, we experienced the *need* to find a Power greater than ourselves—something that would be at least one step ahead of our diseased intentions, and give us the consistent guidance we could not provide for ourselves. The possibility of finding some form of faith, based not on any specific conception of "God" but rather on a *need* to find such a faith, was the beginning of spiritual healing.

Nevertheless, the fact that we needed faith in some Power, since we could not trust ourselves to be consistent in either behavior or motive, left some of us feeling even more shaken. Where would we find even the rudiments of a faith that could carry us through this dissolving and reconstruction of our whole personality? If there WAS no Power greater than ourselves, it would be impossible!

The most elementary solution to this problem of faith was found through contact with sober people at our regular S.L.A.A. meetings who had surmounted the need-for-faith barrier themselves. As we listened to their stories of sickness and recovery, we could identify at depth with their patterns of addiction and diseased values. And we could clearly see that they were now leading more positive and healthy lives. As living examples, they offered us the hope that whatever sources of spiritual aid they credited as helping them might be available to us as well. We could not question the insanity of their past addictive histories which they shared with us. It was *so* apparent. Nor, when we contrasted the quality of the lives these people were now living with our own addiction-rooted struggles and dilemmas, could we really doubt that they had been delivered over into a form of redemption.

Contact with those already recovering from sex and love addiction was also a source of practical help in sustaining our day-to-day sobriety. Suggestions on how to avoid addictive situations were given, and the simple act of explaining a current temptation or situation to someone else who understood seemed to help us stay honest with ourselves. As we realized how helpful this network of support was, we sensed that a belief in any specific God or divinity was unnecessary. Our need for *faith* could be answered with an affirming *hope,* a sense of the possibility for spiritual guidance that was already apparent in the experience of the S.L.A.A. members who preceded us.

This shift in our attitude from *need* to *hope* brought us to another fundamental milestone in our recovery. We had laid the first foundation stone for the acquisition of faith. We had seen that it was possible for us to live through the pain of withdrawal without returning to our old patterns, and we sensed that the Power to do this was coming from outside ourselves. Now we were ready to consider just how we might turn this faith into a practical, working asset. We began to examine the implications for our lives of the Third Step.

Step 3:
Made a decision to turn our will and our lives over to the care of God as we understood God.

The situation was roughly this: if our sex and love addiction was such a fundamental part of our personality—if it had developed long ago and had shaped or deformed many of our other personality traits, our relationships, and our value system—then we had to ask whether all our prior ideas about who and what we were might be incorrect or ill-founded. This is not to say that on a practical level everything we thought we knew about ourselves was wrong. But if we really wanted to change ourselves and lead new and sane lives, we had to at least pose the question, if only on the abstract level. We had to admit to the *possibility* that anything, if not everything, we believed could be faulty.

To use the Biblical expression of the "cup that runneth over," we were like cups that had run over with obsession—with neediness, lust, and intrigue. Step 3, as a spiritual exercise, suggested that we could choose to tip our own cup over and let the sickness run out of it. We knew that having done this, we could not refill the cup through our unaided will, because we had become convinced that any solitary attempt to do so would inevitably take on the obsessive/compulsive character of our personalities. We could not outwit our own addictive natures. The enemy was US.

We could see that if we were ever to be as cups running over with redeemed, non-addictive lives, then some Power greater than ourselves, the need for which we had already affirmed, would have to do the refilling. Such a Power (He, She, It, or They) would do that in Its own time, according to *Its* scheme of things, not our own.

What would our lives be like, we wondered, if we were really to empty our chalice of disease and refrain from refilling it again ourselves, and instead let it be filled eventually through God's grace?

We simply could not know. There were no guarantees. All we knew was that we did not want to go back into our active sex and love addiction again. The certain hopelessness of *that* condition, were we to go back, compelled us to move forward into the unknown. With no guarantees, and with much apprehension, but with at least the rudiments of faith, we came to understand that if we were unable to prescribe our own treatment for sex and love addiction, then we would be better off turning "our will and our lives over" to the God of our understanding, even if we did not know what might happen as a result. We made the decision to do this, however abstract the idea seemed.

Having made this decision, how could we now commence our new relationship with God? The answer, like all good answers, was simple. We had already been staying clear of addictive entanglements and episodes day by day for some time. What we added to this outward change in behavior was prayer. We now began each day in communion with the God of our understanding by asking for help that day in staying free of addictive behavior. We asked also that God help us in the immense undertaking on which we had embarked, that of undergoing the death of our former, addiction-riddled self, and the rebirth of a redeemed, affirming *person*. And if we were successful in not acting out addictively by day's end, we thanked God, whatever we understood God to be, for having helped us live another twenty-four hours free from bottom-line sex and love addiction.

The time-honored Serenity Prayer became a part of our daily repertoire for handling challenging and potentially dangerous situations:

> God, grant me the serenity to accept the things I cannot change, courage to change the things I can, and wisdom to know the difference. Thy will, not mine, be done. *

As we looked at the remaining steps, we saw that they were structured on the principle of Step 3. Our cup of diseased behavior would be emptied out, and we would cleanse it as best we could, making it ready for God's Grace to refill it, in accordance with God's plan, not our own.

---

* *Twelve Steps and Twelve Traditions*, A.A. World Services, Inc., New York, 1980.

The "decision" had been made, and we were now trying to open our lives to God's influence through the use of daily prayer. Yet much of what was to come still seemed like wishful thinking, and very far-fetched indeed. We were still plagued by sometimes prolonged bouts of obsessive thinking or emotional yearning for intrigue and romance, for sexual oblivion. These could be set off by accidental encounters with our former addictive lovers, which seemed almost fiendishly psychic in the uncanny way they happened just when we were most vulnerable. At other times we would fantasize about all the people in the world who, we fancied, were blissfully unaware of anything called "sex and love addiction," and who were, we imagined, indulging themselves with great exuberance. Or we would remember with longing the "good times" in a past marriage or addictive relationship, forgetting all the awful experiences.

Such musings would leave us in a very foul frame of mind, indeed! How deprived we were! When these clouds descended on us, any vision of the process in which we were engaged was obscured. Disregarding how much better off we really were now, we yearned for our former ignorance. And yet we found that the door to awareness, once opened, could not be closed. We had seen—we had even felt—occasional hints of what a healthy existence could be like. We knew it was open-ended: there was no apparent upper limit to the spiritual, emotional and mental well-being toward which we were now moving, even though sometimes grudgingly.

What would often serve to break a spell of bad weather was getting a new insight into ourselves, through sharing at an S.L.A.A. meeting, or during a time of reflective solitude, or perhaps in a dream. These insights seemed to stem directly from the fact that we had not squandered our energy in addictive acting out, in spite of severe temptations to do so. They put us in touch with deeper levels of our inner nature, bit by bit. Sometimes these "delivering" insights seemed to be a kind of reward for not having abandoned our sobriety, and from the vantage point of these oases, we felt grateful that we had not acted out again.

In this phase of recovery we found that much of the emotional energy which had been spent on our addiction was now surfacing as feelings and memories that were charged with meaning. More and more of our past pattern of sex and love addiction was being revealed or becoming clearer to us. Some of us kept journals, or a dream log, or entered into counseling or psychotherapy. We found that, almost in spite of ourselves, we were becoming formally engaged in the spirit of the Fourth Step.

Step 4:
Made a searching and fearless moral inventory of ourselves.

When we first saw the words "moral inventory," we had recoiled in alarm. Surely such a task would be too massive or too unnerving! However, to our surprise we found that there came a point when we approached this task without fear, because we had come to terms with Step 3. As we surrendered to the God of our understanding, we found ourselves having "intuitions": stay away from here, call this friend, go here instead of there, and so on. We came to trust the guidance that was helping us navigate away from the old addictive patterns. If God was helping us manage our external lives, it was easier to become open to clearing out the inner debris, to trust God's guidance for the inward journey.

But how were we to accomplish this inventory? Our shared experiences showed us that no two people would do it exactly alike; there was no one, single "right way" to go about it. What we were really after was not just the relief of confession, of having completed a specific checklist or narrative of our lives. What we needed was to achieve some real understanding about ourselves, as much as possible without fear, pride, or reservations. We needed to find some bedrock from which to assay, without illusion, who and what we had been in the world, what we had held ourselves up to be to others and to ourselves. Furthermore, we needed to see the motives behind the roles we played and the image we presented, to understand the payoffs we had derived from our addiction.

Most of us found that writing down our inventory was very helpful. Looking at what we had done in black and white was a valuable aid to honesty and objectivity. The very qualities that helped us to build the addiction—pride, resentment, and self-justification (among others)—were the things that could prevent us from seeing it for what it was. As we read our own version of what had happened, we could often see through our excuses and our need to blame others; we clearly saw the progression of our spiritual malady, and how "convenient" our memories could be in seeking to minimize our roles in our more painful debacles. (What was "between the lines" of our written inventory was often more important than the lines themselves.)

As we looked at our current lives and at our past, we saw that virtually everything we did and everyone we knew was exploited to satisfy our addictive needs. We may have started our inventory with the relationships that were particularly troublesome in our lives. But we soon began to see the patterns: we gave away our lives to blondes, or to successful people; we sought out people we could rescue, or who would rescue us; we dressed to attract the kind of person we said we did not want; we seduced those who had some power over us through work or friendship; we drove away our families with verbal or emotional abuse when we really needed them the most, and on and on.

The process was something akin to peeling an onion. We could only do it one layer at a time, and there were often many bitter tears at the cutting of each layer. As we looked deeper, we found that many aspects of our relationships that we had labeled as "healthy" or at least "harmless" were in fact less obvious expressions of our addiction. Thus, as we looked at our non-sexual relationships with friends, family, co-workers, and so on, we often found the same motives and character defects driving us there as well.

At first we saw only the events and the patterns that repeated themselves. Then we began to identify the emotions and motives that flowed underneath in a vile current. We now saw how dishonesty had prevented us from really seeing the progression of our disease. We had not let ourselves think about the money we had wasted on sex, about the risks of disease to others and ourselves, about the signs of powerlessness over being sexually driven, about the many lies we had told to cover up our activities. Self-centeredness and pride seemed to be at the root of our difficulties. We had dressed and acted seductively, craving attention and more than our share of sexual intrigue. We spent money to impress people, and verbally abused those who did not give us the attention we thought we deserved, or tried to hurt those who would not give us our own way. We proved our power by seducing our friends' lovers or spouses, and responded with anger when the satiation of our self-centered needs was thwarted.

As this exhaustive inventory of ourselves continued, we came to understand why we were sex and love addicts. This was not abstract psychological theorizing about whatever influences might have "made" us this way. It was an honest look at some of the payoffs we had derived from our addiction: the comfort of self-pity, the luxury of self-justifying resentment, the apparent insulation from having to take authentic emotional risks and assume real responsibility to others. The shoddy misdeeds and happenstances of our past lives were revealed as manifestations of our persistent dis-ease. We were not merely people who had done "bad" things; we were what we had done.

Yet even as we realized how dishonest and self-centered we were, and had been, we also saw that we ourselves had often been done *in*. We had not consciously chosen to be sex and love addicts. Often our normal, right-sized human needs had somehow never been met during the formative period of our lives. We realized that there was a basic loneliness which had made us afraid to be alone. So we had made lovers feel guilty over leaving us, or we had slept with strangers. The fear that we were not or could not be deserving of real love led us to make excessive sacrifices to parents or lovers, to flirt with everyone to prove we were attractive, and to lie to impress others. Our fear of facing pain or making commitments drove us into relationships with people we did not like, or to stay in destructive or empty relationships. Through the Fourth Step process, we realized that pride and willfulness had hidden the yearning of a lonely and fearful child, an emptiness that cried out to be filled. We did not cause it, and we could not control it. In this realization was the beginning of compassion, our first glimpse of self-forgiveness.

The Fifth Step
We began to feel the inner pressure to release, rather than to sexualize away, what we had learned about ourselves. We found ourselves ready for the Fifth Step.

Step 5:
Admitted to God, to ourselves, and to another human being the exact nature of our wrongs.

Many of us recognized that a characteristic of our sex and love addiction was that our lives were divided into carefully segregated compartments, underscored by secrecy and confidentiality. This was so, regardless of whether we had been promiscuous, or had maintained addictive romantic or emotional ties with more than one person at a time, or had been hooked into dependency on one person. Indeed, we even took pride in our ability to keep a secret, to keep our stories straight, to keep our feelings hidden, to go it alone. This brave, solitary strategy had an important payoff. If we were able to manage the maze of intrigue without discovery, or could keep the one we were dependent on from knowing our true feelings, then we *apparently* never had to deal with the consequences of our actions. We could even deny to ourselves that there were such things as "consequences." What a tremendous incentive this was to stay closed and not reveal our true selves to anyone!

But in continuing to "go it alone" we were suffering from emotional and spiritual constipation, unable to make constructive use of our experiences and emotions. Our inner condition resembled a trash compactor rather than a recycler. We were mired in our own sludge.

Step 5 was the way in which we began to allow our lives to become open. It had been difficult enough, through the lengthy process of Step 4, to become open to ourselves. Nevertheless, if we did not go further and share with another person what we had discovered about ourselves, our sobriety was in real danger. It was of no use to identify our powerlessness to manage our own lives without a return to addictive patterns, if we were now to attempt a solitary reconstruction. The loneliness and isolation, which was both the root of the disease and a consequence of it, would not be eased until we began reconciliation with God and with other human beings.

Here, as everywhere else on this road to wholeness, we had to be willing to take a risk. In the steps that had already become a part of our lives we had learned to trust God at least a little. We were now quite aware that the God of our understanding had known all along what we were doing, and seemed to care about us regardless. Now we had to risk revealing these terrible truths about ourselves to another human being, to face the exact nature of the difficulties that now filled us with such shame, guilt, and remorse. While this prospect seemed quite terrifying, we had to do this if we were to make a sincere commitment to turn away, at depth, from our past pattern of addictive behavior and the underlying motives which drove it.

How were we to choose the person with whom to take this step? While some people felt they would be more comfortable sharing bits and pieces with several people, most of us felt we needed to find one person with whom to be totally honest for this first inventory. Too many of us had addictive patterns that included being only partially honest with different people. Forging a link of total honesty with one human being was an important step in humility. More importantly, in finally telling all, we could break the terrible, lonely isolation that had kept us from getting what we craved all along—unconditional love and acceptance for what and who we really were, both good and bad.

This confidant was sometimes an experienced member of S.L.A.A. Or sometimes we chose to talk with a therapist or member of the clergy. It was most important that whoever we chose would keep our disclosures completely confidential, and understand that we were not seeking penance or moral judgement. This person needed to have a good understanding of human nature, and a good sense of balance and control in his/her own sexual and romantic life.

Two cautions were in order. Confessions build intimacy, and healthy intimacy is one important step toward wholeness. However, we needed always to be on our guard against emotional intrigue. We needed to choose someone for whom we had no problematic sexual attraction, which meant s/he could not be a former or potential lover or mate. Also, while it was tempting to seek forgiveness from those we had hurt by making *them* wholesale recipients of our "Fifth Step," the goal of making amends was not an immediate objective of this step, and could not be a hidden agenda in taking it.

The second caution was not to confuse the Fifth Step with an "X-rated" tale of every sordid event in our lives, nor with the object of much therapy which seeks the "cause" of our disturbances. While we could not hesitate to disclose any details that were relevant, it was the motives within ourselves, the payoffs which we extracted, which really had to be revealed. While it was not wholly appropriate to blame either our early experiences or ourselves for our behavior as sex and love addicts, we *had to* accept some personal responsibility for it. We needed not to hide our true motives behind cosmetic rationalization or blame.

Our lives had been rigorously closed for years, and this initial experience of sharing ourselves in full honesty with another sometimes took a physical toll. The migraine-prone suffered headaches. Others suffered real physical exhaustion or nausea from the effort. This whole exercise of revealing ourselves to another was just *so* uncharacteristic! For a few of us the positive effects, which we all experienced eventually, came almost immediately. For these few the first unbundling of their self-constructed straight-jackets resulted not only in a feeling of relief, but of emotional release as well. But no matter what our reactions were to this first thorough sharing of ourselves with another human being, *all* of us found over time that we had turned another corner in recovery. We could belong to the human race, and our shared vulnerability was our membership card to unconditional acceptance by others. We would never have to live closed or divided lives again.

The Sixth Step

We had now come a long way along our new path. Ceasing the addictive behavior had led us to the tentative acquisition of faith. Under the protective mantle of our new faith we had taken a hard look at ourselves, unearthing in the process some basic patterns we had unwittingly lived out. We had been carried along by the excitement of self-discovery to share what we had uncovered with another person, another risk ventured and survived.

Now another problem gradually revealed itself. We discovered that while we had gained perspective on ourselves and espoused God's guidance in our lives, we were nevertheless continuing to live in self-destructive or self-defeating ways in many areas of our lives, often in the very same areas our inventories had flagged as being problematical. There was no doubt about it: a big discrepancy existed between what we had come to realize was beneficial for our lives, and how we were actually still going about living them.

We had been hopeful, of course, that all our troubles and character defects would dissipate as a by-product of the labors we had taken in doing an inventory and sharing it with another. But as evidence accumulated that some of our "old friends" were still with us, in spite of our best efforts to take stock of them, discouragement mounted. It was frustrating to have to acknowledge that becoming aware of our defects was not the same thing as having them removed. This dilemma brought us into contact with the Sixth Step.

Step 6:

Were entirely ready to have God remove all these defects of character.

The idea of surrendering our entire identity to whatever process of change was necessary was only an abstract concept in Steps 2 and 3. Now we were facing the reality of what that meant. Summoning the willingness to let go of every defect we had uncovered in Step 4 was much easier to think about than to accomplish. What was it that was blocking this willingness?

One problem was that it was easy to find ourselves feeling "deprived" once again. Hadn't we given up enough when we stopped all forms of bottom-line addictive behavior? Wasn't our real problem the active addiction itself, and now that we were sober, didn't we have the right to relax and "be human," to go through life guilt-free? Weren't we at least better off than most people we saw around us? Did we have to be perfect to be acceptable? Besides, who wanted to be a saint!

This attitude was easy enough to justify to ourselves; however, we were actually at a very critical point in our sobriety. In the first five steps we were walking away from the active disease; now we needed to make that first real step toward rebuilding. While it might be true that not every part of us needed wholesale remodeling, it *was* true that we could not trust ourselves to direct the project solely on the basis of our unaided will. Our twisted motives, often hidden, could far too easily turn qualities that were quite harmless, in others, into a source of addictive return for us.

Once again, we had to grapple with humility. It would have been a serious error to attribute all of our troubles to the addiction alone, for our character defects affected all other areas of our lives as well. This was not time to relax, for we needed to continue our vigilance against the constant sexual and romantic temptations and the illusion of "the perfect romance." In becoming ready to give up our character defects, we were deciding to give up that part of ourselves which was capable of "putting on a con," the devices we used to attract lovers or deceive others. Giving up these defects meant not only that we would be stripped of our addictive hooks for others, but that we would have only ourselves to present to friends and potential partners. Addicts that we were, most of us were riddled with insecurity and feelings of inferiority. We were terrified that if we gave up the "con," and the defects which gave rise to and supported it, we would be viewed with contempt and would never find anyone to "love" us again.

Another problem was that as addicts we had become accustomed to pain. More often than not, pain was a central characteristic of our romantic involvements and even many of our sexual pursuits. Some of us even equated pain with love, so that in the absence of love we would at least be comforted by the presence of pain. But in sobriety, having gone through surrender, withdrawal, and an inventory, what did we still have of ourselves? Couldn't we at least be left with our pain? If we let go of all of our character defects (the source of our pain), what would be left of us? Did we have no choice about what we would be at all? Such was our diseased thinking.

The old emotional habits which were still so much a part of us had subtle payoffs which made them difficult to surrender. Many of us, ourselves victims of emotional deprivation in our early years, had learned to survive by cultivating hatred, anger, and resentment as motivating forces, seeking to insulate ourselves from hurt and fear. Now we discovered that we had crippled ourselves by using this monotonous strategy of distrust and isolation in all relationships, whether they were inherently hostile or not. In the extreme, we had become incapable of trust and authentic intimacy with anyone, even people who now seemed in our recovery to be more willing to trust us and to work towards partnership.

But we still seemed unable to respond in kind, often coming up against our own inner blocks, which kept experiences of genuine trust and caring at arm's length. These blocks were painful to recognize, especially since we now knew that we wanted to trust and take risks in sharing ourselves with others. This was all the more painful because we could see that the barriers were within us, and we didn't see how they could be dismantled. The end result of being weighed down by these internal blocks seemed to be the fear of being emotionally steam-rollered by anyone else we let get close to us, or of winding up in inescapable isolation.

As we continued to have to live with ourselves, however, we found the consequences of indulging in our character defects increasingly uncomfortable to endure. Anger could seize us unexpectedly and fill us with murderous rage, or emotional binges would leave us despairing and suicidal, or depression would sap our will to go on, our hope for any future at all. We began to see the fallacy of that logic which said we could be guilt-free since everything we had done was caused by our sex and love addiction. We saw the spiritual bankruptcy behind the cosmetic humility of not wanting to be perfect. It became apparent that it would not work for us to specify just exactly what God could and could not do with us.

Our attitude towards our defects and underlying problems began to change. With new eyes we could see the serious consequences in the lives of others when they could not voluntarily surrender these difficulties. With growing maturity we realized that healthy relationships could only exist if we were human rather than superhuman. We came to understand that sex and love addiction appears to be a disease of actions when viewed from without, but is really a perversion of moral and ethical values *as experienced from within*. The spiritual dimensions of our dis-ease were now clear.

We now moved from a limited surrender of a specific addiction toward surrender to a life-long process which would refine the qualities we carried within and contributed to life. Underlying this whole shift in our attitude was increasing reliance on the God of our understanding. Indeed, it seemed that we were being given still another invitation to deepen our partnership with God. It was enough that we be willing to do the legwork, and be open-minded about what the result would be. God's grace would give us freedom from the burden of our old self. In humility, we understood that we were only being asked to get out of God's way, so that, with our cooperation, God's work could be done in our lives.

The
Seventh
Step

Step 7:
Humbly asked God to remove our shortcomings.

The nature of humility—which had once been so elusive, complicated, or undesirable to us—was now clearly apparent. We no longer confused it with humiliation, being forced to swallow unpalatable truths. We had come to see that our struggle with character defects and underlying conflicts was a crucible in which our relationship with God was being further refined. A lot of what we thought we were, and thought we couldn't live without, was being boiled away. As this became clearer to us, our attitudes changed profoundly. We felt a deep desire to experience God's will in all areas of our lives *for its own sake,* rather than for some limited, self-defined objective. We were becoming vessels more suited to God's purpose. Our capacity to experience fulfillment in our own lives was directly tied to being more available to God's will for us.

Although we had come a long way in our recovery, we were, however, still unable, by our unaided will, to shape our lives in a consistently positive manner. The reality of this estimation of ourselves was a truth we could now accept, if not gratefully, at least without struggle. This acceptance of truth, and willingness to allow a Power outside ourselves to continue to do what we could not do for ourselves, WAS humility.

When we continued to ask God daily to remove the shortcomings that were all too apparent in every area of our lives, we began exercising spiritual muscles that had been very flabby indeed. It was easier to accept God's help with the defects that had already caused us to suffer extreme consequences. It was far more difficult to come to terms with patterns which were still giving us short-term payoffs, even though they might be costing us longer-term peace of mind.

As our consciousness of these things continued to sharpen, we sometimes resented God. After all, we had already achieved what had, at an earlier time, seemed utterly impossible—freedom from acting out on our sex and love addiction—yet despite our success, we still seemed to be left on the hook with our unresolved conflicts and frailties. However, even if we held a grudge against God, we realized that this Power was still the only force we could rely on, overall, to be on our side. Even in the midst of deep discouragement, disillusionment, and pessimism, we knew that there was really no other game in town with odds as favorable for a positive outcome. No matter how many failures we had each day in the intention NOT to act on a particular defect, there was no way to go but forward. Like it or not, we belonged to God by default.

With time, we began to take a wider view of our predicament. We had been expecting God to remove these defects of character by skirting them out a side exit so that we would not really have to confront them! We had hoped they were surface blemishes, and as easily and painlessly removable. Now we began to feel that God was indeed a great "allower." Rather than taking us off the hook with minimal effort on our part, our higher Power seemed to require our active participation.

Apparently God was not interested in relating to us as a parent might to some helpless child who was always getting into scrapes. God seemed to want to form some kind of partnership. Perhaps we were supposed to develop our full human capacities, including those involving sharing and cooperation, instead of passively turning ourselves over to God as a wholesale protector or a punitive, omnipotent dictator. This new and open communication with God about our shortcomings was not to be the kind of hypocritical bargaining, or desperate pleas and demands, that we were prone to during our active addiction. God did not owe us anything, and was not going to take instruction about what we required.

This new partnership with God, in which we accepted direction about just what part of our spiritual being needed exercise, had amazing results. We might have asked to have the shortcoming of impatience removed, only to find that we did not need to practice patience. Instead, we had to get honest about our self-centered willfulness. As we practiced thoughtfulness towards others, really giving without holding onto the expectation of reward, impatience slipped away. The quick temper we asked God to remove was checked momentarily; we could suddenly feel the defensive fear that was hidden behind the anger, and find the courage to act on faith, rather than fear. We asked to have our longing for a person or a particular sexual hunting ground removed, and found ourselves given a choice. When we voluntarily chose to avoid those places and those people, the longing eased. The feelings of inferiority and insecurity, which we petitioned God to replace with confidence, were openly admitted, and as we accepted the support or the confessions of similar insecurity from others, we felt comforted.

Even our failures to make noticeable headway on some troublesome defects could be used for spiritual nourishment. For instance, two prevailing character defects which many of us experienced were perfectionism and pride. Even as we failed to control our petty selfishness or chronic procrastination day after day—were less than "perfect"—we saw that we were learning how to accept progress, rather than perfection! If we could not always be proud of the results of our efforts to change, at least we had earned the right to respect ourselves for the efforts themselves.

The Eighth Step   As we continued to experience this evolving relationship with God, it came as no surprise that more housecleaning was needed. From the surrender to our powerlessness over sex and love addiction and then over ourselves, we had come to know ourselves more as we really were, and had entered into partnership with a Power that could free us from the addiction and lead us into a new life. We had begun to develop spiritual qualities which we had never had, or had allowed to go unused during our active addiction. Working hand in hand with our new partner, God, it was time to begin making our peace with other human beings.

Step 8:
Made a list of all persons we had harmed, and became willing to make amends to them all.

In Step 8, we returned to a process of self-examination and housecleaning similar to that in Step 4. This time we were dealing with the more difficult and emotionally charged problems of our relationships with others. The list we made was often a long one, since we now realized that our defects had affected virtually every relationship we had ever had. Each one was examined carefully, even those going back into childhood.

Like other people, we had been life's victims in many respects. Many of us had memories of emotional deprivation or of being physically or even sexually abused. It mattered little whether this abuse was objectively true in every detail or merely perceived as such. The point was that our *feelings* about these events had hardened into a great bitterness which we held for those people who had mistreated us. We had also turned this hatred inward, redirecting it against ourselves, using our self-loathing to justify our unworthiness to be loved by others, letting *them* off the hook! As we examined these old relationships, we could not see why we owed *them* amends. Surely *we* were the ones who had been harmed in those relationships.

In many other relationships we also had difficulty in seeing ourselves as wrong-doers. Much of our experience seemed to say that the real power in our addictive relationships was with those others: "They preyed upon me in bars. They sought *me* . . . I tried to get out of the relationship, but s/he begged me to stay. . . S/he used me, took my money, hurt me."

But the Steps we had already taken had brought about an important change in attitude. The inventory had helped us see that the root of our problems was in our own self-centered motives and uncontrolled passions. Whether we were victims or victimizers (and most of us were both), we had used the disturbed relationships about us for our own purposes, for obtaining the addictive payoff. Regardless of what others had done or failed to do, our own part in these relationships was riddled with dishonesty and manipulation of others, with willfulness and pride. We realized that we needed to forgive others for essentially the same qualities and deeds for which we ourselves were also seeking forgiveness. For our own sake, we had to extend to those we thought we hated the compassionate understanding we needed in order to experience forgiveness ourselves. We could not make our forgiveness of others conditional on their having redeemed themselves, or righted their wrongs. We had to forgive them because, like us, they were sick and afflicted, and presumably had not set out in life to be so.

The problem now was that we had to examine the nature of the harm *we* had done to others, and see if there was a way to make it right. It was not a simple willingness to apologize we needed, but the capacity to see exactly how we had harmed others and how we could set the record straight. The prospect of going to those at whose hands we had experienced humiliation, or admitting our own

wrongdoings to those who had suffered as a result of them, was intimidating, to say the least. But even if we could not see how we could find the courage to carry out these amends, the willingness to try to do so was vital to our progress. If fear and pride kept us from addressing this important step in our spiritual journey, we might go through life still trying to avoid the host of those with whom we had been involved in mutually destructive relationships. We sensed that there could be little freedom of choice for us in future relationships if we were not willing to take full responsibility for the part we had played in the destructiveness of past relationships.

We stopped looking only at the harm that had been done to us. While it was human to want justice and equity—to be "even" with the world, neither a ravisher nor a victim—in practice we had generally concentrated on what we felt was owed to us rather than on what we owed to others. It was important now to get out of the emotional accounting business, to stop trying to "balance the books," or "even the score." Regardless of the damage done to us, we could not change another person; it was only our own contribution to a problem that was within our power to control. The Serenity Prayer took on great significance as we asked over and over again for the serenity to accept those people and events which we could not change, and for the courage to change what we could—with Grace and luck, ourselves.

As we considered our wrongdoings towards others, closing the books on the side of the ledger that said "owed to us," we saw that we owed a great deal to others in the amends department. Even as victims we had done much harm, cluttering the lives of those around us with our own sickness, sometimes crowding out the possibility of their finding more honest relationships elsewhere. We saw that we had made something trivial of "love," with our long lists of those whose names we didn't even know, cheating them and ourselves of anything authentic or genuine. We saw especially how our dishonesty and deception had led everyone in our lives to expect from us what we could not or would not deliver. We had been masters of false advertising.

Now it was becoming easier to forgive others for the harm done us, as we saw ourselves in need of forgiveness for the harm we had done to them and others. We felt new depths of humility, as we saw how much damage had been done, and how much of it could never be undone. As we concentrated on our own part in this, we came to a new understanding of our motives, so often a poignant mix of

normal human needs for love and a meaningful life, twisted by the addiction into something ugly and harmful to ourselves and others.

Humbly, we turned to God. "I am not responsible for the conditions which created me, but I am willing to try to be responsible for myself," we prayed. "Help me to be willing to make right what I have done to each and every person in my life." We had closed "their" side of the books, and audited ours unsparingly. In the god-consciousness called love, we found compassion for ourselves and a new awareness of our responsibility to others as sober people. During our active addiction, we had been the embodiment of sickness, tainting reality for all those who came in contact with us. Our spiritual, emotional, mental, and sometimes physical disease had contaminated even those relationships which could otherwise have been healthy.

The Ninth Step   Our commitment to recovery had now moved beyond the self-interest of survival. We wanted to act on the humble knowledge of the suffering that others had experienced at our hands, and make amends to those we had harmed.

Step 9:
Made direct amends to such people wherever possible, except when to do so would injure them or others.

The practical application of our willingness to make amends, as in other steps of our recovery where action was necessary, had some inherent pitfalls. It was our experience that we had to be very cautious when it came to making amends. When we were new to S.L.A.A. and first learning about the Steps, some of us were quite anxious to "make amends," especially to former addictive lovers. We imagined ourselves beating our breasts with dramatic confessions and soulful remorse, seeking both relief from painful guilt and the chance to start with a clean slate. This wish to clean up the messy, incomplete feelings which were so common in our addictive relationships, however, could only result in "falling under the ether" of our addiction once again. Of course, it was often necessary to break off some relationships, or otherwise set some situations involving others right, early in sobriety. In such cases we found that writing a simple letter to these people was safest. *However that messy, "incomplete" feeling which was so often a part of the aftermath of an addictive relationship had to be faced in the new context*

of withdrawal, and not evaded through the inappropriate use of this Step. Amends-making, as we experienced it in Step 9, was quite a different thing from the early desire to "fix" damaged relationships. The solid foundation built with the preceding eight steps was vital to insure that we could make amends with the right spiritual intent. If we had not yet put our lives and will into the hands of a Power beyond ourselves, worked diligently on our personal inventories, and allowed God to work with us in removing our shortcomings, then we could not reliably distinguish compassion from passion. Without this kind of clarity, it could only be best to stay clear of those who were a part of our past addictive lives.

In Step 8, we had examined all of our relationships and, closing the books on whatever wrongs had been done to us, we had faced the many wrongs we had done others. It was not hard to see just how we should go about making direct amends in some cases. We could burn the letters from ex-lovers that could be used as blackmail, return their family heirlooms and possessions. We could write letters to those we had kept on the hook, uncertain when and if romance might be renewed. Sometimes we shared these letters with another S.L.A.A. member before sending them. This helped us censor any subtle or overt sexual or romantic innuendos, and to keep the hint of accusation out. Without a return address, these letters could serve to free others, once and for all, from bonds of uncertainty and expectation.

However, the most important amends were those which we needed to make face to face, requiring considerable courage, humility and preparation. It was important to be accountable for the effect our amends could create, as well as for the wrongs which made them necessary. Especially in these cases we found that it was wise to consult with other sober members of S.L.A.A. about exactly when and what kinds of amends would be made, and under what conditions. More than one of us went off with good intent, only to find ourselves in situations of seductive solitude, being solicited once again by a person who seemed determined to misunderstand our purpose. We came to expect that in amends-making, as in all areas of our lives, God would give us willingness and the intuition to know what settings and words would be appropriate for our purpose. But it was also true that, in these matters, God often spoke most clearly through the very human voices of experienced S.L.A.A. members!

Now we understood that guidance from both conscience and the experience of others would help us find the appropriate circumstances for this Step. But it was clear that much more was needed than eloquent apologies. As we looked at what we had done, it seemed clear that many of those persons on our list had continued on in their lives with their reality persistently distorted by their past interactions with us when we were actively sick people. Our amends were thus to provide them with the reality-checks which could set the record straight. The full admission of our contribution to these destructive relationships, and honesty about how we had been living as sex and love addicts, could justify—make just—for others much of what they had assumed had been their fault. Perhaps, too, we could offer enough perspective to others that they might release themselves from their load of unresolved feelings concerning their past history with us. We realized that it would be up to them to draw their own conclusions from what we presented. All we could do was try to be helpful by setting the record straight, admitting *our* faults and wrongs in the light of our addictive illness.

Obviously, we had to consider carefully whether we were justified at all in gaining entrance to other people's lives after what was sometimes a long absence. We had to weigh the nature of our disclosures just as carefully. We could not put others at risk by revealing information to them that might jeopardize their peace of mind or their current circumstances. Our own progress could not be built on the new wounds of another. We had to keep in mind that very important difference between leveling *with* someone and simply "leveling" someone!

If we still burned inside with guilt, or a sense of unfinished business we could not resolve because there was a possibility of inflicting some fresh injury on another person, we just had to live with it. We could gain release as best we could by sharing these predicaments with others in S.L.A.A. Sometimes these situations in which amends could not be made were actually of benefit, because they kept us humble. We could not easily assume a condescending attitude toward others in and out of S.L.A.A. on the grounds of just how spotless our own lives and consciences were, if we knew that in our darkest past there were things for which we could never make amends. In certain respects we would forever remain about as "pure as the driven ash."

In some cases our sense of vulnerability to certain people continued for a long time. While we certainly felt ready to be freed from the pain our past relationships had caused us, in practice we often had to return to the preceding steps over and over. There was no freedom or dignity to be gained from attempting amends to any particular person until we were truly ready. We found that prayer was a vital part of the process, especially in coping with relationships that had been part of our lives during the addiction, and were still with us in our sobriety. We asked daily for God's help in making our contribution to each relationship what God would have it be. We prayed to be freed from the bondage of self, so that we could honestly and without reservation do whatever was possible to free each person in our lives from whatever pain and deception we had caused. We tried above all to be scrupulous in monitoring ourselves, while causing others no further grief.

In working Step 9 as best we could, we completed the clean-up of our past at our current level of understanding. We could never do an absolutely perfect job, nor was this expected of us. As our sobriety became longer and our awareness continued to expand, we would periodically find more things to do, new or better amends to make. In going through the first nine steps, we surrendered our illusion of power over our sex and love addiction, acquired at least the rudiments of faith, decided to live a day at a time on the basis of this faith, explored ourselves, and fully shared what we found with another. We did our honest best to recognize our character defects and allow God to remove them, and we made what amends we could to people we had harmed.

We could not rush the process, because we found that at any given moment we could not be more honest with ourselves than we were ready to be. Our willingness often ran ahead of our readiness. Willful efforts to speed up recovery sometimes brought us into painful contact with our own limitations in being able to heal ourselves, and this itself was part of our recovery and growth. However we meandered, we were still on the path of recovery as long as we did not act out in bottom-line behavior.

The Tenth Step

Now we were truly feeling some sense of deep release from the past! We were free of much guilt for our misdeeds, from the shame of having fallen short of our inner values. In many instances the values we had thought were ours had turned out to be someone else's, and we had shed or changed these to allow the seeds of our own personal wholeness to take root and grow.

We were indeed living new, positive, unfolding lives. Whether in partnership with others or in solitude, we had truly been granted a spiritual release from our sex and love addiction. While vigilance was still important, the choices we had to make now seemed easier. We felt increasing confidence in our developing partnership with God, and were full participants in the Fellowship of S.L.A.A. We enjoyed solitude and were unafraid of honesty and openness with others. We could comprehend what it means to have dignity of self.

Step 10:
Continued to take personal inventory and when we were wrong, promptly admitted it.

We found that we now felt remarkably free of the burdens of guilt and longings for the past. However, if we were to continue the lifetime process of reconciliation and intimacy with ourselves and others, we would need to learn how to process life as it was happening, day by day. The blockage which had kept the poison of our undigested past buried within had been cleared, but we needed to stay current with our emotions and needs, or the same poisonous stagnation would soon build up again.

We still had many troublesome feelings and reactions to people or circumstances in our lives. Sudden anger could still sweep through us, triggered by something someone said or did, and it often seemed to us that others were even trying to cause this response. Or people with whom we had casual contact sometimes seemed to be offering subtle or not-so-subtle signals of romantic or sexual interest which could leave us feeling quite off-balance. In groups of people, or even at S.L.A.A. meetings, we occasionally could be struck suddenly tongue-tied, unable to communicate on even the most basic level.

Whenever we were troubled by things other people said or did, or by what we *feared* they might say or do, we needed to make a quick assessment of our own spiritual condition in order to gain perspective on ourselves and the other person. We found that one easy way to do this was to ask ourselves, "If *I* were doing to someone else what I think is being done to me, would it be a symptom of *my own* illness?" and "If I saw someone else reacting to this situation as *I* am, would I take it a sign of *his* or *her* illness?"

Whether or not the answer was "yes" to either of these questions (and it was often "yes" to both), we found that what we saw in others was generally a reflection of our own vulnerability. The emotional demands others made on us, their apparent interest in

causing our downfall, and their insensitivity to our needs were like echoes of our own demands and neediness. To our further discomfort, we often found ourselves feeling entitled to being treated in a particular way, and trying to coerce others to meet our own exalted standards. Or we were aroused by what seemed to be the machinations of others, feeling that we were being victimized.

The simple truth was that when our own spiritual condition was less than solid, everyone around us seemed to be "sick" with a malaise which, upon reflection, was remarkably like our own! Regardless, we had to conclude that it was silly and futile to let ourselves be upset at what we saw as diseased actions by others, especially if we hoped that others would continue to be tolerant of our own frequent lapses into dishonesty or manipulative behavior. When we found ourselves getting bound up, we strove hard to flag our *own* frailty, to label it, understand it, and forgive ourselves for having it. And it was important not to entertain the idea that we could save face with others by keeping our knowledge of these day-to-day struggles going on within ourselves a secret.

One area in which we often experienced difficulty was in continuing to be open and forthright about our feelings and motives, and our expectations of others. We would hide disappointment, hurt, fear, or anger under a facade of acceptance. We would keep silent about the mild fantasies that came to mind over some person with whom we had repeated contact, assuring ourselves privately that of course we would do nothing about it. We found that it was not enough to have the intention to avoid wrongs. We had to put into action on a continuous basis the principles we had used in our inventories and amends-making. We had to concentrate on making frequent appraisals throughout the day of our own intentions and short-comings, and to do as much as we could to make these right as they happened.

Then, too, we continued to learn about how the defects we had already identified could emerge in milder but still troublesome forms. Sometimes a new defect in our character was discovered, such as selfishness that had been lurking under dependence, or the fear of intimacy that hid behind absorption in solitary activity and geographical restlessness.

Many of us found that both daily and on a periodic basis we needed to set aside times for solitude and reflection. These times of self-overhaul provided an opportunity to touch base with ourselves and our progress, and keep perspective on our spiritual develop-

ment. We often sought out people who could help us with this perspective: friends in S.L.A.A., or perhaps spiritual advisors or therapists. The portion of S.L.A.A. meetings set aside for "getting current" was another place where we could process our emotional reactions to situations in our lives and our relationships as they occurred. Setting aside time to "get current" with those individuals with whom we had committed relationships was also needed, whether these were spouses, close friends, or others. We could not achieve partnership with anyone by our own solitary efforts! It took practice and cooperation to learn how to respond to the needs of others without fearing sacrifice of our own dignity, and to be open and honest without defensiveness or destructiveness.

In all of this we concentrated on our own faults and failures. We were coming to know that our own attitudes and actions were the only aspects of our lives which we stood any real chance of influencing. We had always been, were now, and forever would be, powerless over the deeds and motives of others.

The Eleventh Step

As we continued on in our new way of life, growing more accustomed to living in the present with real emotional consistency, we found ourselves pondering our relationship with God. Our journey into the realm of spiritual healing had begun long before. It had started with a provisional concept of reliance on God as a Power greater than ourselves, in the absence of any assurance that there would be anything left of us, or worth living for, if we withdrew from the grasp of sex and love addiction and surrendered the personal identity we had derived from it. Yet even with our painful surrender and withdrawal behind us, we had found that desire for power and prestige could still motivate us into striving for goals that turned out to be very inappropriate. Deep-seated fear still lurked behind the scenes, prodding us into making unreasonable demands and attempts to extract absolute security from our personal relationships and endeavors. Only slowly and sometimes grudgingly had our provisional use of a Power greater than ourselves given way to a more regular reliance on this Power for guidance.

As our recovery progressed, we had begun to feel less and less sure that our old values, even some of our former life-goals that seemed far removed from our activities as sex and love addicts, were really worth pursuing. Some of us were able to bring a new spirit and fresh energy to an otherwise satisfying career or relationship which our addictive behavior had only marred or temporarily suspended.

But for others, the advantages which many a particular career or life-strategy had seemed to promise were turning out to be illusory, or not worth the price we had to pay for them. As our game plan continued to fall short on delivering either worldly security or inner peace of mind, we were inevitably led to ask ourselves just what could be worth living for. In the absence of any workable, purely self-determined value system or strategy for living, we found that we had to examine our lives more or less continuously in the light of God's plan. What were the implications of our relationship with God? This question brought us to the Eleventh Step.

Step 11:
Sought through prayer and meditation to improve our conscious contact with a power greater than ourselves, praying only for knowledge of God's will for us and the power to carry that out.

Our personal conceptions of God had changed radically. From someone or something to bail us out of scrapes or to pray to only amidst crisis, we had progressed beyond an overseeing caretaker or parent-like God to the sense of being in conscious partnership with this Power. We had been apprehensive about this. Some of us suspected that God had been the architect of many a painful, growth-fostering situation we had encountered along the course of our sobriety, or at least had allowed these to occur. Only gradually did we see that in God's scheme of things, these difficulties might have been permitted in order to spur our awareness of our own finite nature, thereby rendering us more ready to further our relationship with God. This relationship appeared to be structured more along the lines of a conscious adult partnership centered on mutual sharing and cooperation. It seemed that through our pain and growth, we might come to participate as conscious partners with God in living out our new lives—as conscious partners in God's creation.

We could no longer separate our worldly security from the feelings we had inside. We knew that feeling right with ourselves was a direct result of participating in this relationship with God, and of accepting this Power's grace and guidance. This kind of "security" was not necessarily based on having specific goals in the world, nor did it necessarily mean renouncing all that we had aspired to be or do. It was, rather, a matter of priorities. Spiritual reliance on God

as the prerequisite for having relationships with other individuals, and for committing ourselves to careers and other endeavors in the world, had to underlie our attempts to accomplish personal, social, or professional goals.

We found ourselves increasingly praying for God's guidance in all matters, both major and minor, spiritual and mundane. As we did so on a daily basis, we made a number of discoveries. The first was that God's grace was, indeed, available to us in all matters, whether critically important or trivially commonplace. Apparently we could experience a sense of being connected with God even in such detailed, routine matters as planning our day, carrying out daily chores and responsibilities, or taking part in our everyday dealings with others.

This discovery of God's presence at these seemingly insignificant levels of our existence led to a second discovery. We found that our efforts in meditation and prayer were resulting in greater emotional evenness as we proceeded in our lives, day in, day out. It did not seem to matter if our prayers were very informal, or taken from the inspiring words of great writers. Meditation could be a formal time set aside for that purpose, or simply a moment of quiet listening, stilling our own thoughts to allow God's ideas to slip into awareness. The style or amount of time devoted to this was unimportant, as long as it was frequent enough to be a regular part of our day.

Our growing relationship with God was like a stabilizing keel beneath us. No matter how stormy the winds above the surface of life's waters, or how much sail we sometimes hoisted into the gale in the form of commitments beyond the scope of our limited strength and energy, we found that the keel beneath us, meditation and prayer, guaranteed that we *would not capsize*. We would retain our buoyancy on the ocean of life. We could survive whatever life might throw at us.

Another discovery was a gradual awareness that our relationship with God was indeed a personal one. It did not need to be consistent with the definition of any religious institution or the experience of any other person. In fact, we didn't have to define our higher Power even for ourselves. For many of us, awakening to an omnipresent God-sense led us to explore other spiritual avenues, such as the practice or study of meditation or theology, formal or informal. We began to see that our partnership with God was an open-ended relationship, a rich tapestry which had barely begun to be woven. It offered that ultimate possibility for self-transcendence

which so many of us had sought through the addictive experiences of our past. And miracle of miracles, here we were now, experiencing the mystery of spiritual reality as a fruit of participating in "everyday" reality, rather than as a prize for escaping it.

One other discovery which arose from regular use of meditation and prayer was a dawning sense that a basic need in our lives was being filled. Especially for us as sex and love addicts, the need for love had seemed insatiable. The active addiction hadn't really touched it, and the support network that we built for ourselves in sobriety, while life-sustaining, didn't quite touch that intense need either. We might say that, during the addictive period, it was as though we were trying to quench a terrible thirst by drinking salt water. The more we drank, the more dehydrated we got, until our very lives were threatened. In new sobriety we tried to alleviate our thirst by busying ourselves with S.L.A.A. and with emotional nourishment, something like eating oranges. But in order for our real thirst to be satisfied fully, eventually we would need pure water.

We found that this thirst—the need for love—was a spiritual thirst, and the water was the God of our understanding. Although some of us did not believe in or had turned away from God when we came into S.L.A.A., we came to find a way of life that involved a loving partnership with that Power. As we developed that closeness with God, we found that our need for love was mysteriously satisfied. It *had* been love we needed all along. And love was of God. Most wonderful of all, when we walked through each day with the sense of being hand in hand with God, as a spring of love seemed to flow from within, available to help us quench the thirst for love of ourselves and others. Thus we came to find intimacy with ourselves, intimacy with God, and the intimacy with others.

The Twelfth Step

We had sought full partnership with God, and knowledge of God's purpose for us. By seeking to live with honesty and integrity, and to be of service to others, we had discovered that the source of love, which was of God, had begun to flow from within us. We had lived our way into step 12.

Step 12.
Having had a spiritual awakening as the result of these steps, we tried to carry this message to sex and love addicts and to practice these principles in all areas of our lives.

As we read over this Step, we recognized its experientially based wisdom: the effectiveness of our efforts to help others would be directly related to the level of our own "spiritual awakening" which preceded these efforts. This spiritual awakening was itself the product of having hit bottom and surrendered, having acquired a faith, having accomplished a practical examination of our past and our character, having developed a deepening relationship with God, having accepted responsibility for the impact our sex and love addiction had on others, becoming aware of problem areas in our lives and resolving to deal with these constructively, making amends, and reaching into the spiritual domain through regular prayer and meditation to place ourselves in closer communion with the source of guidance and grace.

We discovered that we could continue to affirm our recovery by working with other sex and love addicts. Minus the guilt, our experiences in addiction had been transformed into lessons for living of profound depth and durability. We shared our experiences freely and openly with others, establishing a healing bond through that language of the heart which could move others to recognize their own straits, and point them towards the source for their own healing. No experience in living was more meaningful for us than letting ourselves become channels through which healing and redeeming grace could flow. The paradox was that our usefulness as channels for healing was a direct result of our experiences in sickness, as well as in recovery.

We discovered that we needed to continue to live out the values which emerged in us through our recovery in S.L.A.A. in all areas of our lives. We had learned to work toward a high standard of honesty, openness, sharing, and responsibility, and to treasure the feeling of purpose and sense of belonging which accompanied these values. We found that personal or professional situations in which we could not affirm these spiritual values were expendable. These values were not just "window dressing." Careers that had been exploited mainly for material security at the expense of self-fulfillment no longer appealed to us. We either changed our way of going about them, or let them go.

In relationships with others we let go of self-serving power and prestige as driving motives. This left us open to the discovery of just what it is that makes *any* relationship between people, whether professional, personal, or social, worthwhile. We found that in relationships with others we had only as much to gain as we had to share.

In domestic partnerships we discovered a whole new experience of sexuality as a non-addictive medium. We discovered that sexuality could not be considered unto itself. Its realization was actually a by-product of sharing and cooperation. In our addiction we had leaned on sexuality and romantic or dependency strategies to yield nearly all of what we considered to be our identity. Now, however, in full possession of our own personal sense of dignity, and living our way into intimate partnership with another, we found that we no longer needed to rely solely on sexual expression to provide our sense of security and identity. Our growing ability to trust, to share, and to live openly in a partnership was already helping to provide these things. Freed from this burden, our sexuality was becoming more like a barometer—*an expression of what was, already, in the partnership.* It could be no more, or less, than this. Discovering new freedom and joy in the experience of sexuality, however, was a potential which was realized only gradually. We had held so many illusions about the relationship between sex and "love," that we had to do much living in sobriety before these illusions became truly tempered. Gaining sober perspectives in the areas of trust, sex and intimacy was difficult. True intimacy, we found, can not exist independent of commitment.

We know, as we continue to live out our recoveries in S.L.A.A., that we are indeed engaged in the great adventure of discovering true freedom of the human spirit. We have received, and continue to receive, many blessings we would not have known how to ask for. Life is open-ended, and wonderful. New chapters in well-being await us.

Chapter 5
The Withdrawal Experience

If you have read this far, and have, however reluctantly, come to the conclusion that sex and love addiction is the problem you are facing, you are probably feeling very scared and apprehensive. Perhaps you are still trying to shake off the awareness of sex and love addiction even as we have been sharing our experiences with you. Maybe, you tell yourself, these people are crackpots or extremists, or at the very least, party-poopers!

Yet some of you, despite efforts to deny the truth of what we have been laboring to share, can hear the bell tolling, and know that it tolls for you. We are with you. We recall only too well how terrifying the unknown was, looming before us as we ran from the grips of active addiction into the apparent void of ceasing it. How intensely we resisted the idea that our sexual and emotional lives were addicted!

What now? If, for instance, your pattern of sex and love addiction involves masturbating, how can you be sure that, if you stop, you won't find yourself climbing the walls with horniness? How do you know that stopping won't bring on premature senility, with atrophying sexual powers (or organs!), along with encroaching death? If you cease initiating, responding to, or otherwise feeding force-field energy from others (that near-psychic communication advertising that one is "AVAILABLE!"), how can you be sure that you won't just become an emotional and sexual eunuch, vitality gone? And how can you be sure, if you try to withdraw from a prolonged and sickening dependency on another person, one to whom you have long since given over control of your life, that you can find the necessary inner resources to stabilize on your own?

The answer to these wrenching questions is twofold. First, in terms of what your feelings are likely to tell you, the answer is that you *can't* be sure of any of the above. Second, however, is the possibility that our experience, as shared through this book, may serve to give you hope of being able to go through, and survive, withdrawal. Perhaps you will get the sense, as you read this book, that withdrawal has left those of us in S.L.A.A. much better off than we were when we entered it. Be assured this is true, and that we share in common the experience of transformation to which it has led in each of us.

We can not go through your withdrawal for you, nor would we, if we could. Who would ever knowingly volunteer to go through it again? Certainly none of us! Yet the pain of each withdrawal is unique and special, even precious (although you probably don't now think so). In a sense, the experience *is* you, a part of you which has been trying to surface for a long time. You have been avoiding or postponing this pain for a long time now, yet you have never been able to lastingly outrun it. You need to go through withdrawal in order to become a whole person. You need to meet yourself. Behind the terror of what you fear, withdrawal contains the seeds for your own personal wholeness. It must be experienced for you to realize, or make real, that potential for you and your life which has been stored there for so long.

There are different ways sex and love addicts have started this process. The end result is the same: addictive sexual and emotional behavior, on a daily basis, *stops.*

It also does not matter what the specifics of your own pattern of sex and love addiction have been, although it *is* important that you do identify your own pattern. Some of our patterns have included "one night stands," frantic sexual liaisons with no emotional ties, or manic masturbation, exhibitionism and/or voyeurism. Others have involved obsessive intrigue with, or dependency on, one or many people (serially or concurrently) with the conviction that without an "other" we would be at death's door. Regardless of which pattern is yours, *it has to stop.* No matter how powerfully your thoughts and feelings are tugging at you to continue indulging, you cease acting on them. It is this point when you finally stop that really signals the start of your recovery in S.L.A.A., and the day on which it starts is your personal sobriety date.

Those of us in S.L.A.A. arrived at this point of complete cessation by different routes, and they are worth noting.

First, some of us maintained our addiction on full doses of whatever "did it" for us right up to the day we hit bottom and surrendered. Then we threw in the towel and went "cold turkey" from the whole pattern at once. This was the most brutal way of doing it, the most black-and-white. Stopping cold provided the strongest, immediate shock to our emotional and mental system, and the onset of withdrawal was hard and fast. Withdrawal entered into in this way was *not,* however, necessarily of shorter duration or of any higher "quality" than withdrawal which was arrived at more gradually. Our collective experience suggests that the scope and outcome of withdrawal is, within certain limits, the same for each of us. Here we are only referring to the various ways we used to start the process.

Some of us approached withdrawal gradually, chipping away at obvious problem areas. Even marginal success in doing so increased our awareness of *other* aspects of the addictive pattern that we really hadn't known were there. This process of increasing awareness led inevitably to a final surrender of the whole addictive pattern, and thus we were launched into withdrawal, and sexual and emotional sobriety.

To those who are familiar with concepts of addiction, such a "gradual" approach to surrender might seem like wishful thinking. There is no such thing as "half pregnant," and "one drink begets a drunk" is part of the conventional wisdom of A.A. Besides, the addictive experience has been so mind-altering for most of us that, once enmeshed in it, we have lost track of ever wanting to be out of it!

There is great truth to this. Usually, however, by the time we let the concept of withdrawal into our thinking, the addiction was not reliably delivering the oblivion or pleasure we sought so ardently. More and more energy had to be poured into the emotional and sexual activities just to break even, let alone "go to the moon." It was as though an inner voice was saying, as we embarked on each new sexual or romantic episode, "Wherever I'm 'going' with this new face, or body, or mind, I've already 'been there' a thousand times before!"

The novelty of each new romance or "reconciliation" no longer screened the truth from view: each new situation was just another hopeless episode, holding about as much promise of fulfillment as swapping bubble-gum cards. As this jaded feeling broke through, the addictive "high" was becoming harder and harder to achieve and maintain. As we approached withdrawal, the sense of futility about continuing on was felt acutely. Although many of us tried more experimentation with just how much we could "handle," we finally encountered a mandate to withdraw just as surely as a steam locomotive driven on a one-way trip into a glacier is ultimately faced with the prospect of cooling off.

Still others of us tried to use "external constraints" as a means of entering withdrawal. As the energy necessary to manage the addiction became greater than what we had at our disposal, the dam broke and the truth flooded out, as we revealed wholesale to spouses or lovers just what exactly was going on in our lives. The act of "vomiting up" the unpalatable truths had become an involuntary response. Some force within us was going for broke, forcing us to expunge the poison from our system. In becoming "open" in this way we still may have had little concept of "withdrawal" or "addiction." But as we witnessed the impact that these long-delayed revelations had on the important people in our lives, we experienced for the first time the consequences of our actions, both past and present. Nor, when our guts had split wide open, did we dare stitch them up again, or let them heal over superficially. Not only were we too exhausted emotionally, we were deeply afraid of what the infection still in the wound could do to us. Therefore, by default as much as through courage, we maintained a standard of sharing and openness that was nearly absolute. In any realistic terms we were probably not yet really sober, or even necessarily aware that we were in the throes of an addiction. This meant that addictive experiences and episodes were probably still ongoing. Yet, whenever one of these addictive experiences occurred or threatened to occur, we sensed that there was some safeguard against further loss of control if we revealed to *all concerned parties* what was happening. For instance, we might make long-distance telephone calls in order to tell a spouse or mate that we were on the brink of plunging into some tantalizing situation. The dismay or disappointment which came from these people was a *consequence* of our behavior, and by *choosing* to be open and face this consequence, we were cutting ourselves off from acting out further on the tempting situation.

In "going public" with those whom we had routinely deceived about our activities, the motive was not to punish. We were relying on these people, and their reactions to the disclosures of our shoddiness, in order to guarantee that we would encounter the consequences of our actions right away. We were choosing to pull the rug out from under our inclinations to cover up, segregate, or manage our intrigues and liaisons. It was often the cumulative result of these consequences in our relationships with those people who mattered to us which finally forced us to an awareness of the lack of control in our behavior, and the need to label it as addictive. This inner commitment to sustain a stringent standard of honesty with others about our sexual and emotional behavior seemed to be sufficient, *in itself,* to start the inner process of self-honesty which finally delivered us over into unconditional surrender and withdrawal.

Of course, to speak of "ways" of entering withdrawal from active sex and love addiction is a bit misleading, because we are not really the conscious architects of how we get there. Most of us can identify with some parts of each of these paths into withdrawal. Finally, it is important to emphasize, again, that however honest we became through any last-ditch efforts at "control," our sobriety did not really begin until the last reservation had been let go, and we gave up the right, for one day (or one hour) at a time, to have "one more" liaison with our addiction.

And now you are there, and withdrawal is upon you. What are some of the dangers involved in going through it? What is the experience likely to bring you? How can you survive the inevitable temptations to slide back into old patterns?

The dangers can be described as being of two types. The first type involves the dangers inherent in the inner process itself. The second involves dangers stemming from outside yourself which can make it seem impossible for you to go through withdrawal, and can influence you to abort it.

Perhaps the greatest inner danger comes from finding yourself face-to-face with the unknown. It is one thing to make a decision to withdraw when the painful stimulus of a recent addictive episode is still fresh. It is quite another thing to be open to withdrawal, not as a reaction to a specific addictive situation, but *as a response to a recognizable life-pattern of addiction. Yet this larger perspective on the withdrawal experience is crucial if it is to be endured.* What we have found is that once we have recognized certain bottom-line behavior which we *know* is addictive for us, and refrain from acting out in these "bottom-line" ways on a daily basis, we then discover numerous habits and traits of behavior and personality that have been addiction-related.

Discovering this whole range of underlying behavior which is also tied in with sex and love addiction can feel very, very discouraging. A chronic hand-shaker, for instance, may find that this trait has been serving an addiction-related purpose. A person who dresses in a certain way may discover that the purpose of this is to attract certain kinds of attention. The person who "loves to hug" may be checking our responsiveness for later pursuit. Or one who "gives great back rubs or massages" can be subtly (or not so subtly) seducing the objects of this attention. These are just the barest examples of a very wide range of behaviors.

In the past these milder accessory behaviors had never been seen for what they were because they existed alongside the much more powerful, bottom-line payoff behaviors which were so obviously addictive. Minus the "big-payoff," however, we were able to see that these other behavioral manifestations were really procurement strategies. In withdrawal, we found that whenever we engaged in these accessory behaviors, regardless of how innocent or unaware we were of doing so, we had unwittingly set up the potential for sexual and emotional intrigue—just what we were trying so desperately to avoid!

Our habits of thought also needed changing. We were not accustomed to having our lives restricted. We found ourselves wandering freely "where angels fear to tread."

Our justifications generally sounded very convincing to us: "I can't help seeing him; he works in the same building as I do." "If my partner were more sexual with me, I wouldn't have to go outside our relationship for sex." "It feels crazy not to be talking to this person that I care about." "I have as much right to be at a certain location or function as s/he does. Why do *I* have to be the one who has to stay away?"

Some of our excuses were not so convincing, but we held onto them anyway: "I haven't seen this person for several days/weeks/months; that must mean I'm not addicted and can start seeing him/her again." "I only want to engage in this particular sexual practice *sometimes*. I know I have a problem, but I don't think I ever had any trouble with *this*." "If I don't tell anyone what I'm doing, then it doesn't count."

The dilemma was that we didn't realize that we were culling "intrigue" from these behaviors, and when we finally did realize it, we didn't know what else to do. Our personalities could not be separated from these characteristic ways of rationalizing, of making eye contact, of "hugging" and handshaking, and on and on. We found, however, as the addiction-serving motives for these behaviors and personality characteristics became clearer to us, that battling our addictive cravings with every minor "set up" was becoming too exhausting. It was becoming necessary for us to grapple with the ache of wondering just who "we" really were without our addictive trappings.

This unraveling was wrenching. We found it necessary to live through withdrawal in day-at-a-time, twenty-four hour compartments. We would awaken in the morning, sometimes very early, and inwardly exclaim, "Oh God! Another day of THIS!" Sometimes we found ourselves wishing that we had died in our sleep. Regardless of how we felt, however, we asked in prayer for God's help in facing the day at hand. If we had any grievances with God, we threw those in, too. No one was trying to force us to trump up gratitude! We were striving to be "honest," not "good."

We would then embark on our day. Living alone, as many of us were at this time, even the daily rituals of bathing, clothing and feeding ourselves became very important. Just going through these ordinary tasks was an affirmation of our caring for ourselves.

We then surveyed the day. There probably were tasks we needed to attend to, whether paying the rent, doing the laundry, shopping, or going to work. Physical activity, even as basic as taking a long walk, could get us out into the day a bit. Some took up jogging, or other exercises that required greater physical effort. These helped to provide a physical sensation of tiredness which could fill the void left by the absence of sexual release, or even replace it. Contact with other S.L.A.A. members or trusted friends, perhaps members of other Twelve-Step fellowships, was helpful. Attending open A.A. or Al-Anon meetings was likely to be possible, or perhaps we were fortunate enough to have an S.L.A.A. meeting in our area. Maybe we were trying to start such a meeting, and had tasks to attend to there.

The purpose of all this was not to clutter our day with activity. Most of us needed rest and solitude just as much as we needed other tasks, personal contacts and responsibilities. We were, within ourselves, expending as much energy as most people do who hold full-time jobs and maintain active family lives. In fact, most of us were "working" far harder than we ever had before. After all, we were working at standing still, at freeing ourselves from the tentacled clasp of a frightful addiction which had driven us to such a pitch of self-destroying activity. Simply *not* doing it took tremendous effort. We were suspending, for the moment, our very real fears concerning the *outcome* of all this by attending to those tasks immediately at hand. We were living in the immediate present, and discovering that we could indeed make it through an hour, or a morning (mourning!), or a day. And we were discovering that there was a joy to be had in successfully negotiating our way through each twenty-four hour period.

We found that the most healing antidote to the gnawing pain of our struggles and doubts was to turn over any questions concerning the outcome of our withdrawal to God, or to whatever Power we felt was helping us to abstain from our old patterns.

Through all of this we became, one day at a time, available to *ourselves.* By the simple act of "standing still," we inaugurated a relationship with ourselves based on growing self-honesty, trust, and intimacy. Now we knew that our goal in withdrawal was to lay the foundation for personal wholeness. How this would translate into personal relationships or careers, we did not know. But what we did know was that the externals would eventually develop around this inner foundation of wholeness, and come to reflect our inner state. We were able to embrace this feeling of our growing capacity for wholeness, and leave specific outcomes to God. This shift in our attitude eased the sense of existential crisis.

The other kind of danger encountered in withdrawal consisted of external threats. Here the risk was not so much in facing an unknown self, a "self" minus the addiction-derived self-image. Rather, the "threat" came in the form of situations which contrived to abort the withdrawal process itself and force us to resume the addictive pattern. Locked in once again, we risked being prevented from ever facing those existential questions which would have to be dealt with for recovery to develop.

The range and nature of external threats varied greatly, but many of them were incredibly "coincidental." With seemingly diabolic accuracy, they tended to occur when we were most vulnerable to them. For example, if we had severed (or been severed from) a clearly addictive relationship, and were still having a lot of mixed feelings about this (as is always the case), we could count on "running into" this person in places where we would least expect it. More subtle, but equally dangerous, was the "chance" meeting of mutual friends and acquaintances who took it upon themselves to "enlighten" us about the emotional condition of our former addictive lover(s). Hearing that our former lovers were depressed and suicidal, or that they were courting or being courted by others, was compelling for us.

Many of us have found, in S.L.A.A., that we needed to accept the possibility that psychic occurrences can happen, in order to make sense of some of these situations which seemed so uncanny. Even when we felt far removed from actual contact with a former addictive lover, such things happened as unexpected letters, or finding ourselves in settings with special meaning in the past relationship. These things could serve to catalyze, or charge up, a feeling of being psychically connected to our former addictive lover. Eventually we came to expect that we would continue to encounter a barrage of such experiences! This was equally as true in those cases where we had been "dumped" by a former addictive lover, and ambiguity still persisted. We have found that *wherever* ambiguity is present, the potential for reactivating sex and love addiction is present also.

All of us, without exception, went through periods during which we were extremely vulnerable to mental and emotional shocks. Often these seemed to occur as a result of coincidental meetings or contact, direct or indirect, with old addictive situations. Yet just as frequently we discovered that our vulnerability had already flared up *prior* to one of these external tests. It was, in such cases, as if our own vulnerability and susceptibility to addictive sexual and emotional experiences—either romantic or sexual intrigue, or emotional dependency born of personal neediness—were sufficient *in themselves* to set in motion the makings of a "coincidence"!

When external challenges, especially those with psychic overtones, did occur, and we felt ourselves thrown back into having to devote all our energy, once again, to abstaining from addictive behavior at a "bottom line" level, we once again felt the extent to which the roots of our sex and love addiction had infiltrated our very souls. It seemed, sometimes, that the forces which chained us ran far deeper than did our abilities to counter them.

It was, and is, humbling indeed to have to entertain the possibility that we are possessed at such great depth. Even for those of us who have been sober in S.L.A.A. for a long time, this possession-at-depth can still assert itself with great force, and hold on to us with a fiendish tenacity. Yet we must say that, tenacious as the psychic hold may appear, *it, too, does respond to the withdrawal process.* In these matters, time and daily consistency of action are the tools with which we fashion our release, under God's guidance, from the tyranny of the psychic realm. This may be the last domain of the addiction to relinquish its power, but it *does happen.*

What are some of the tools we have found which can help us hold up and behave with consistency in spite of external challenges? Clearly we needed some ways to counterbalance the erosion of our awareness and resolve by these psychic coincidences.

Perhaps the most important principle here was *not* to deny to ourselves that we were, indeed, being severely tested. In light of the fact that these external invasions of our personal resolve seemed to be unavoidable, they were better dealt with if recognized for what they were right away.

Another defense against these unnerving onslaughts was sustaining awareness by starting and keeping a list of very short observations of exactly how we were feeling in withdrawal. Many of us didn't wait until being tested to start keeping a list like this: it could have been too late by then. In our list we did not edit out any negative sentiments. Despite the pains of withdrawal, the positive results of early sobriety were very evident to those of us who had truly encountered terror while in the active phase of the illness. Even the difficult feelings of early withdrawal were better than the alternative. So we "listed" away! There was no such thing as a feeling or an observation that was not germane.

Here is a small sample of some of the observations we came up with. Perhaps some of them may apply to you, too:

> "I'm feeling acute pain of withdrawal and loss today, but I am not feeling self-disgust."
>
> "...anxiety and neediness, clawing at my guts..."
>
> "Sex and love addiction: I don't 'have' it; I *am* it."
>
> "Seeing a squirrel eating a nut, so systematically devouring it layer by layer, the way I felt devoured by X."
>
> "Three hours today without thinking of X. Can I believe it!"
>
> "'Chance' encounter..., that needy hunger calling me back. How I crave it."
>
> "Maybe X is healthy and I am the sick one. Regardless, in combination *we* are sick."

In addition to daily prayer and S.L.A.A. related activities, maintaining such a list was a major bulwark against acting-out on the addiction whenever particularly disconcerting possibilities presented themselves. Every item was a feeling we had had about our sex and love addiction and withdrawal, and in writing them down, we crystallized them—*Made them stand still.* When a challenge came along with all its emotional turbulence, we consulted the list. It helped us stay centered, almost in spite of ourselves. Even as we felt ourselves being swayed, reading this list could reconvince us that "It really *was that* bad," and that the current "possibility," were we to follow through on it, would be an extension of our addictive pattern, not an exemption from it. However bruising these clashes seemed between the addictive, tantalizing forces and the forces for maintaining emotional, mental and behavioral consistency, we knew what we had to do—and avoid doing.

Of course, regular contact with other members of S.L.A.A., or others who were trustworthy and knew what we were trying to accomplish, was also very steadying. In fact, every way we found that had awareness-sustaining power was important; they were all true anchors to windward. However, devices such as list-keeping were especially helpful because they could be used at *all* times and in *all* places, regardless of the availability, or lack thereof, of support from other S.L.A.A. members.

How do we know when we are approaching the end of this stage of recovery? After all, withdrawal does not go on forever (although it may *feel* interminable). What signposts do we have to indicate to us that we are ready for a new chapter in our sober lives? We would like to share some of these signposts with you, as we have experienced them.

The first signpost was a growing awareness that we were now quite seasoned at dealing with temptations on a regular basis. Those situations which had been so transfixing in the earlier phases of withdrawal were now easily, if not always comfortably, handled. We had developed a capacity to assess these varied threats, and to deal with them with real consistency. In withdrawal we had found our "sea legs;" we had become "street-wise." We had been granted freedom of choice over becoming sexually or emotionally involved.

The second signpost that we were ready to leave the withdrawal phase was that we were no longer concerned with how much longer we would have to abstain from sexual or romantic entanglements. Early on, many of us had exclaimed, "How long do I have to *wait* before I can have a relationship, or have sex?" "I want to get this over with, get through this so I can *have* a relationship." But now these concerns did not plague us in the same way, or with the same intensity. In fact, we could laugh, retrospectively, at concerns like these. We could see that they really consisted of this underlying thought: "How long do I have to refrain from acting out before I can begin to act out again?" Well . . . !

What came to pass is that as we refrained from seeking to escape from ourselves through acting out on our sex and love addiction, we began to become *intimate* to ourselves. Such an experience is difficult to describe. However, essentially we were inaugurating a new, inner relationship. Despite the grueling qualities of dealing with outer temptations and inner insecurities, we began to experience withdrawal *not* as deprivation, but as self-enrichment. It was not simply a matter of having something taken out of our lives. *We* were doing the "withdrawing;" *we* were choosing to take *back,* or withdraw, the energy which we had been squandering on futile pursuits. This very energy, now back within us, was helping us to become whole people.

This deepening awareness of our own inner change buoyed us up. As long as we were on the road to growth, time didn't matter so much. The paradox is that once we accepted that we simply could not know how long withdrawal would last, and felt prepared to go on with the process regardless of how long it took, we discovered that we had triumphed! The fear of being deprived of our addiction was the real fear behind our concerns about time. In coming to terms with this fear, the chances were great that we were becoming ready for the withdrawal phase to wind down.

A third signpost that we had come through withdrawal was that we became more aware of personal relationships with children, spouses (or lovers or partners), friends, siblings, and parents. The time of contemplation during withdrawal had brought with it awareness of how our sex and love addiction patterns had permeated our relationships with most of the important persons in our lives. We were now ready to put some of our new-found energy into the tasks of reassessing these relationships, repairing them when warranted.

Often, withdrawal brought with it the need to make some difficult decisions. We had built some relationships on false illusions or premises. In others we had been using the term "friendship" very loosely indeed. In the absence of much personal dignity, we had "settled for less." "A little of a bad thing" had seemed preferable to "nothing of anything." We had never stopped to really question what our needs were in these relationships. We began to notice those daily telephone calls, or other overtures which we habitually made to those who never responded in kind. We came to regard the energy needed to maintain these meager relationships as an unacceptable expenditure.

There were other situations in which a person who had seemed so "indispensable" (and convenient) during our past turned out to be unable to accept our awarenesses about sex and love addiction and our need to grow via S.L.A.A. Sometimes these people seemed threatened by our awareness. They wanted us the "old" way. We had to face the sometimes painful truth that we had outgrown relationships like these. We were, indeed, beginning to feel more worthy of reciprocity!

Those of us who had separated from spouses or former partners (individuals who had been in our lives and involved with us, but were not necessarily sex and love addicts themselves) began to question the healthy and unhealthy aspects of these relationships. In early withdrawal, we had been quite ready to write off all prior relationships in which sex and commitment had played any part as "sick." Now we were "coming around" to a more perceptive and accurate understanding. We realized that we had never been emotionally available on a consistent basis to these people. Until we had given these relationships a chance *in sobriety,* we would not know what potential was there to build on. With the perspectives of other S.L.A.A. members to help us maintain our clarity, we began to explore the possibility of reconciliation.

A fourth signpost of being ready to move beyond withdrawal was closely related to the third. We began to have new energy available to invest in new, or once abandoned interests. The possibility for personal growth led us to explore new careers, schooling, new hobbies, new circles of friends. Perhaps a new partnership was beginning to unfold. In many areas we found ourselves ready and able to address these new opportunities.

Nor was this energy the kind which had once driven us so obsessively and compulsively. It was as if in the process of having encountered, and *passed through,* our own inner turmoil and suffering, the rite of passage had changed the very obsessive/compulsive character of our past "energy" into something that was now much more smooth and even. In the spirit of this basic change, we felt that whatever new, real-life possibilities were now awaiting us were direct extensions of our inner growth, not diversions or escapes from it.

We were beginning to be able to feel a sense of direction which was now pointing beyond the withdrawal process toward what our lives might come to look and feel like as our inner experiences were translated into partnership, activity in a community, and career. The energy which had been devoted to the inner experiences of withdrawal was now freed up, the better to enable us to address what life offered. This represented another major signpost that the withdrawal phase was drawing to a close. Strangely, we often found that events or circumstances which provided either motivation or opportunity for us to live out more of our potential as sober people would just "happen." These situations or events seemed to appear providentially at just about the point when we felt our own readiness to explore and respond to these opportunities. Where we once seemed to be swimming upstream against the currents of Fate, we now felt ourselves moving *with* the flow. Fate was starting to work with us, and a sense of having a personal destiny was starting to emerge.

And what can be said of the final signpost that withdrawal is ending? Well, this signpost was really after-the-fact. It showed itself at that time when we *knew* that our lives in sobriety and withdrawal were, in fact, due to change. Perhaps a marital reconciliation was scheduled to commence, or a new partnership was being explored, or a change in career status was imminent, entailing a major shift in personal responsibilites. Life tasks, whether personal, relational, occupational or academic, were due to be taken up again. No longer a mere possibility, the time had been specified: the date was set.

As we approached the point of enacting this change in our life circumstances, we usually became aware of a range of surprising feelings. We realized that the time we had spent in withdrawal—and the whole withdrawal experience itself—had been a precious, singular period in our lives. With all the pain and ache of the early going, with all the difficult and dangerous challenges to our new and vulnerable sobriety which we had faced, and throughout all the gut-wrenching we had undergone over our crisis of personal identity and meaning, we somehow *knew* that we would miss this period once it was behind us.

Amidst all difficulties and uncertainties, a simple intimacy had come into being for us: we had met ourselves, and found ourselves worthy. We had become "beloved" to ourselves. We had discovered a whole new relationship with God and life. As we contemplated our changing lives, we actually felt longing for a future time in which we might once again come to experience the magnificence of our own solitude, and come again to know directly that well-spring of inner dignity and wholeness which was filling us, and which was now to flow, through us, on into our lives in the world outside.

We knew we had experienced a Grace.

Chapter 6

Finding, and Starting to Work With, Other Sex and Love Addicts

One of the ironies of being in withdrawal was the difference in our reactions when we happened to run into someone who would have been a suitable object for our addictive intents only weeks or days earlier. Now, instead of looking for "rainchecks," we found ourselves sizing these people up for the signposts of sex and love addiction. Sometimes we would attempt to "carry the message" to these ·individuals, quite a change in our old pattern! Often, however, this disclosure of our identity as a sex and love addict to another was impulsive, and born of self-defense. Our awkwardness around those to whom we felt susceptible *forced* us to talk about these things openly, in spite of the likelihood that doing so would end any further opportunity for an addictive indulgence. In fact, this outcome was *desirable*.

Early in S.L.A.A. we coined an expression, "In order to maintain sobriety, we have the right to be a jerk." Self-disclosure shattered romantic and sexual illusions and was, as well, a continuing affirmation of our new life-direction. In spite of embarrassment and self-consciousness, this affirmation resulted in more positive feelings for ourselves.

Occasionally we found that "going on the record" concerning our addiction seemed to *attract* addictive persons who sensed in us the possibility for intrigue. These situations, although enticing, gradually became less difficult to handle. We could clearly see that the inability of others to take us at our word gave evidence of how distorted their perceptions were. In truth, we could see, in their reactions, much of our own former, addiction-serving "misreading" of the intentions of others.

The sense of deprivation which would accompany this intentional "screwing up" of a possible addictive episode was severe. But slowly we became accustomed to dealing with these temptations on an ongoing basis. The titillating or potentially entrancing sexual and emotional overtures,.which once would have led us into months or years of emotional slavery, became more like common happenstances which we could deal with routinely.

Sooner or later, however, disclosure of our sex and love addiction, which began as an awkward defensive ploy, started to take on a decidedly different tone. We really *needed* to affirm the meaning of these events which had lowered us to such great depths and which were now forcing us into confrontation with our own values. As we saw people who were still locked into the addiction, perhaps struggling with the initial phase of coming to awareness about it, we were also seeing ourselves more clearly. Watching others experience the agonies we had been through, the awareness of our own sex and love addiction patterns stayed sharp. Feeling motivated to find others with whom to work, we were also responding to the need to find a non-sexualizing, non-physical "holding environment," in which we could feel at least relatively protected and could continue to grow. This imperative to find other possible sex and love addicts with whom to work came from deep within ourselves, and it could be denied only at great peril.

One early member's experience showed this peril graphically. Moving into a new region with a short six months of sexual sobriety, it seemed easier for her to avoid mention of her sex and love addiction. Allusions to the fact that she had had addictive sexual and dependency experiences in her past had been greeted sometimes with shock and disgust, and sometimes with laughter, derision or propositions, even at meetings of other Twelve Step fellowships which she attended.

It was all too easy to let the natural desire to be accepted and respected within this new circle of friends convince her of the merits of remaining silent. Within months, reference to her addiction was being made only in the privacy of prayer and meditation.

Almost without realizing it, the mind-altering character of the addiction began to subtly influence the values by which she was living. Six months later, a temptation suddenly became an episode-out-of-control. Fortunately for her, the other person chose to terminate the encounter with the hapless addict's sexual sobriety still intact—a technicality based solely on dumb luck, not on her own awareness and vigilance. A panicky letter to her S.L.A.A. sponsor left no question that the quality of her sobriety had slipped backwards nearly to the starting point! The importance of finding others with whom to work, for her as for us, was not just theory.

Where did we find these prospects with whom to work? In the early years of S.L.A.A., many of us had already established personal affiliations with other Twelve Step fellowships, notably Alchoholics Anonymous, Overeaters Anonymous, Al-Anon, and Gamblers Anonymous. While S.L.A.A. as such has never had (nor, according to our Traditions, can it ever have) any affiliation with any other organization, as *individuals* we maintained our personal memberships in these organizations. Many of us had discovered our sex and love addiction to be a further manifestation of an addictive pattern in other areas such as alcoholism, compulsive overeating, and gambling. Thus, it was natural for us to look for S.L.A.A. prospects among those people whom we already knew in these other fellowships to which we belonged.

We discovered, however, that it was extremely difficult to come up with real, live prospects. This seemed to be true whether we included a heavy allusion to our patterns of sex and love addiction as we related our histories of addiction at meetings of these other fellowships, or whether we sought out others on an individual basis with whom to share our awareness. What seemed so patently obvious to us—that when people stopped an addiction in one area, they might then abuse other substances or activities—seemed like "Greek" to others. We were so *sure* of our correctness about this! We could see others being eaten alive by destructive patterns which closely resembled what we had been through, and yet the spark of awareness could not be kindled in these people. We had thought that people in these other fellowships whom we could see had addictive problems in this area would flock to S.L.A.A. Yet it was not happening, even with those whom we regarded as having extreme problems.

What, then, could we do? First, we had to remember that even if our sex and love addiction stories fell on deaf ears, recounting them continued to put us in touch with our *own* experience, which in turn deepened our resolve. Second, the denial we saw in others was not necessarily any different than the ignorance concerning this topic which we had ourselves maintained so painstakingly for so many years. Third, we needed to realize that we, ourselves, were only in the very early stages of our own recovery. Our pains of withdrawal were undoubtedly very evident to those with whom we shared, and hardly served as an inducement for them to follow in our footsteps. Fourth, our own recoveries depended not so much on our success in finding others who would come into S.L.A.A. as on our *efforts* to find such people. Therefore, it was not important to promote our consciousness of these matters in any way, nor to try to "recruit" others into S.L.A.A. Our Fellowship's tradition of "attraction rather than promotion" (from Tradition Eleven) had to be observed, never more so than on the one-to-one level. All we could do was share our experience. Finally, we needed to rely on guidance from a higher Power that we would be shown how to find others, or that others who were in need of recovery and receptive to what we had to offer would be led, or attracted, to us.

This reaffirmation of our attitudes concerning working with others provided a healthy frame of mind with which to continue. Sooner or later a real prospect would come along, usually through circumstances that were too unlikely to have been merely "accidental." Perhaps a "friend of a friend" would call us. Or sometimes a person we did not know at all, but who had been observing *us* for some time, would initiate contact. These were far different circumstances than those in which we had gone about promoting our program of recovery. Here *we* were being sought out. What was the best way to handle this?

The first concern was to avoid diagnosing others. We had to concentrate on what we knew best, which was our own personal pattern. Yet within the details of our own patterns were the universal hallmarks of the experience of addiction: the motives of avoiding pain and/or enhancing pleasure, combined with loss of control over choosing or rejecting indulgence (i.e., giving one's power over to the addiction), and progression (the increasing damage to all areas of one's life fabric as loss of control continued). In working with others, we could hammer away at these concepts, using our own case histories as illustration. Perhaps progression was the key, driving home the fact that—once we had lost control over how often or how long we engaged in sexual and emotional indulgences—there was no way that we would avoid, over the long run, a critical threat to sanity, and even to life itself. Our condition was, indeed, one of powerlessness and hopelessness.

In describing our experiences with surrender and withdrawal, we found that it was wise not to minimize the pain involved by painting an unduly rosy picture of recovery. We knew that if a prospect was *really* entrapped by the illness, then whatever pain s/he was currently experiencing was already worse than anything we could describe about withdrawal. Withdrawal as the "lesser of the two pains" was just as effective an incentive for a prospect to stop the addiction as was "Withdrawal—the Avenue to True Bliss in Life!" And it was a lot more honest.

Another important stance for us, in working with others, was to admit that there were a lot of things we didn't know. We didn't know, for example, where our own recoveries were headed, or why we had been "chosen" to live them out. We didn't "know" another's pattern, or the duration of the pain someone else might encounter in withdrawal. We didn't "know" if there were those who could be promiscuous, or "romance" in safety, without becoming addicts, nor why, if others could, we could not. We didn't "know" a lot of things.

If, in fact, our recoveries had progressed to a point where we sensed a higher Power's design for our lives, we certainly *could* mention these new states of being, these new ways of experiencing ourselves. However, it was important to remember that this new landscape of the mind would probably be beyond the grasp of new prospects. In all likelihood they would be so caught up in the prospect of feeling deprived of sexual or romantic indulgences that personal and spiritual wholeness could only appear as a pallid substitute, or rude self-delusion.

We learned not to worry about the inability of the blind to comprehend the concept of "color." Our affirming experiences in sobriety would later fall on more receptive and appreciative ears, once the new prospects had themselves faced and lived through the rigors of withdrawal and apparent deprivation.

One additional note: we could never tell (and still can't) who would actually "get" sobriety, and who wouldn't. Since practically everyone coming to

S.L.A.A. for the first time was (and is) facing acute pain, it was tempting to conclude that everyone was hurting enough to get sober. Yet often those individuals who seemed to experience the most desperate pain and turmoil, and who expressed the greatest immediate relief in coming into S.L.A.A., turned out to be the ones who *forgot* their pain most quickly after the immediate crisis had passed, and then disavowed any further interest in S.L.A.A. Often such people found some grievance to serve as an apparent justification for leaving S.L.A.A. Some other S.L.A.A. member's personality traits, or some perceived S.L.A.A. "line" on a topic relating to sobriety, was often used as an excuse to have nothing further to do with the Fellowship. (In fact, our group experiences seem to indicate that our difficulties with open, honest relationships with other human beings make us especially vulnerable to this kind of excuse to isolate ourselves from the Fellowship.)

We have seen this happen countless times. We have neither resisted this type of strategy, nor have we encouraged it. After all, such individuals ultimately answer, as do we all, not to the S.L.A.A. Fellowship, but to the personal addictive pattern itself. Sometimes letting someone go without rancor, and even with honest cordiality, further prepared the way for such an individual to come back into S.L.A.A. at a time when s/he was more capable of hitting bottom and surrendering the addiction. Several times we have seen an attitude of benign farewell yield gold in terms of a prospect later returning to S.L.A.A. to get sober. Actually, we have found that those people who came into S.L.A.A. and thoroughly *resented* having to be there in the beginning, were often the ones who turned out to be in S.L.A.A. for the long haul!

Chapter 7

Starting an S.L.A.A. Group

According to S.L.A.A.'s Third Tradition, "...Any two or more persons gathered for mutual aid in recovering from sex and love addiction may call themselves an S.L.A.A. group, provided that as a group they have no other affiliation." Within the spirit of this Tradition, once you have found a real, live prospect who is entering withdrawal and with whom you are meeting informally, you actually do have an S.L.A.A. group (provided that, as a group, no other affiliation exists).

Nevertheless, at some point it will probably be desirable to establish a more regular time and setting. The formality of having a regularly scheduled S.L.A.A. meeting, even if only two are present, can lead to a deepening sense of personal commitment in furthering the recognition of sex and love addiction by others who need to withdraw from it. A meeting can also serve as a focal point for sharing experience, strength and hope concerning recovery from sex and love addiction, a place to which new people can be directed.

Early in the history of S.L.A.A., we encountered several potentially divisive pitfalls which we faced and surmounted constructively. Our experience may be helpful, if you become involved in starting, or participating in, an S.L.A.A. group.

In the beginning, conceiving of a group was very exciting. A group seemed the logical extension of the informal but intense sharing among a few of us which had been going on sporadically for a few months. Although S.L.A.A., as such, dates from the establishment of the first regular S.L.A.A. meeting, over nine months elapsed before this meeting witnessed a second recovery. When the second person made a real beginning on recovery and became sober, this early group really became a fellowship, and a new phase began.

About all those first S.L.A.A. members knew, as they wrestled with the early stages of recovery, was that they needed to find others with whom to work in order to continue to keep their own awareness of the addiction sharp. Working with others was the best way to thwart that erosion of consciousness which they knew was such a characteristic of the disease itself. The commitment that there was now to be a regular meeting, regardless of whether there were other prospects or not, helped to provide continuity, to stabilize the exhilaration or disappointment stemming from the erratic participation of those on whom we had already devoted a lot of time and attention.

Meetings were monthly at first, then became semi-monthly. From the beginning, there was no attempt to seek publicity for this meeting. There were several reasons for not seeking public notice. First, there was never a doubt, not even at the very beginning, that the principles which had been worked out on the hard anvil of A.A. experience were to be our guiding principles. These principles* had safeguarded the A.A. fellowship during a time when alcoholism was thoroughly stigmatized in society's view. We believed that these same traditions would serve us equally well if we observed them. We knew that our "condition" of sex and love addiction was no less stigmatizable, in contemporary society, than alcoholism had been in the 1930's and 40's. Nor were we, as individuals, any less ego-driven than the early A.A. pioneers had been. We needed to be protected both from adverse attention from the outside, and from that destructive inner demon: self-serving personal willfulness.

Our fellowship could survive only if we successfully negotiated both these external and internal threats. If we failed to recognize and meet these challenges, and our Fellowship collapsed, we knew that we, as individuals, would probably not survive. Although we were in no mood to re-invent the wheel, we knew we had to take responsibility for the guidelines we would follow. In fact, it was our own early experiences as a Fellowship, in addition to the examples from A.A.'s history, which continued to convince us that each and every one of these principles was necessary. Sometimes heatedly, we discussed each one, modifying them wherever necessary to fit the needs of our own Fellowship.

Here are the Twelve Traditions of Sex and Love Addicts Anonymous: †

1. Our common welfare should come first; personal recovery depends upon S.L.A.A. unity.

2. For our group purpose there is but one ultimate authority—a loving God as this Power may be expressed through our group conscience. Our leaders are but trusted servants; they do not govern.

---

*For an overview of A.A.'s Twelve Traditions and the formative experiences which resulted in their codification, see *Twelve Steps and Twelve Traditions.* (New York: Alcoholics Anonymous World Services, Inc., 1976).

†Reprinted for adaptation with permission of Alcoholics Anonymous World Services, Inc. The Twelve Traditions of Alcoholics Anonymous follow.

(1) Our common welfare should come first; personal recovery depends upon A.A. unity. (2) For our group purpose there is but one ultimate authority—a loving God as He may express Himself in our group conscience. Our leaders are but trusted servants; they do not govern. (3) The only requirement for A.A. membership is a desire to stop drinking. (4) Each group should be autonomous except in matters affecting other groups or A.A. as a whole. (5) Each group has but one primary purpose—to carry its message to the alcoholic who still suffers. (6) An A.A. group ought never endorse, finance, or lend the A.A. name to any related facility or outside enterprise, lest problems of money, property

3. The only requirement for S.L.A.A. membership is the desire to stop living out a pattern of sex and love addiction. Any two or more persons gathered together for mutual aid in recovering from sex and love addiction may call themselves an S.L.A.A. group, provided that as a group they have no other affiliation.

4. Each group should be autonomous except in matters affecting other groups or S.L.A.A. as a whole.

5. Each group has but one primary purpose—to carry its message to the sex and love addict who still suffers.

6. An S.L.A.A. group or S.L.A.A. as a whole ought never to endorse, finance, or lend the S.L.A.A. name to any related facility or outside enterprise, lest problems of money, property, or prestige divert us from our primary purpose.

7. Every S.L.A.A. group ought to be fully self-supporting, declining outside contributions.

8. S.L.A.A. should remain forever nonprofessional, but our service centers may employ special workers.

9. S.L.A.A. as such ought never to be organized; but we may create service boards or committees directly responsible to those they serve.

10. S.L.A.A. has no opinion on outside issues; hence the S.L.A.A. name ought never be drawn into public controversy.

11. Our public relations policy is based on attraction rather than promotion; we need always maintain personal anonymity at the level of press, radio, TV, film, and other public media. We need guard with special care the anonymity of all fellow S.L.A.A. members.

12. Anonymity is the spiritual foundation of all our traditions, ever reminding us to place principles before personalities.

We knew that, in accordance with these Traditions, no one who needed S.L.A.A. could, or should, be denied access to the Fellowship. However we also knew, especially in the beginning, that if we were not very circumspect about tending to business as a meeting/fellowship devoted to recovery from sex

---

and prestige divert us from our primary purpose. (7) Every A.A. group ought to be fully self-supporting, declining outside contributions. (8) Alcoholics Anonymous should remain forever nonprofessional, but our service centers may employ special workers. (9) A.A., as such, ought never be organized; but we may create service boards or committees directly responsible to those they serve. (10) Alcoholics Anonymous has no opinion on outside issues; hence the A.A. name ought never be drawn into public controversy. (11) Our public relations policy is based on attraction rather than promotion; we need always maintain personal anonymity at the level of press, radio, and films. (12) Anonymity is the spiritual foundation of all our traditions, ever reminding us to place principles before personalities. Twelve Traditions Copyright © 1976 by A.A. World Services, Inc.

and love addiction, we might have many difficulties. That is, if we were to go out and proclaim our Fellowship's existence wholesale we could be overrun by vicarious thrill-seekers, contented voyeurs, and those who might be addicted, but were primarily looking for action. If we were overrun by those who were not serious about recovery, our original group purpose, which according to our traditions was to be maintained through the exercise of "group conscience," would be irrevocably altered. With the undermining of a group conscience committed to individual recovery, we would be destroyed.

If we were really to adhere to the principle of group conscience, we had to go about "carrying the message" prudently and selectively. While S.L.A.A. could not be denied to any sex and love addict in search of recovery, we could not trump up a national manifesto or vision for S.L.A.A. at the expense of neglecting to tend· to our own back yard. We could not stress getting great numbers of people to attend our meetings at the expense of diluting the quality of our message of recovery. There could be no short-cuts.

Even with this resolve clearly established, we had, unavoidably, some early challenges to our group's primary purpose. One example of this occurred during a brief period when the original S.L.A.A. meeting was held at the home of a person who was not sober. This person was obsessed with trying to be less inhibited about expressing his tactile desires, and during one meeting he solicited a back rub from one of the women. There were several newcomers at this particular meeting, and a stable S.L.A.A. member expressed alarm at this incident, firmly restating our group purpose. The person in search of the back rub got very angry and claimed we could not order him around in his own home. Needless to say, the meeting never met there again, and the member in question, shortly thereafter, went his own way in search of a more permissive environment.

We had learned a very important lesson. If S.L.A.A. meetings were to be held in individual members' homes, as they usually were in the beginning, then those individuals needed to have shown sustained sobriety in S.L.A.A. over a considerable length of time: they had to be *credible*. If they were not both sober and credible, then the very fabric of safety which had to form the background for each and every S.L.A.A. meeting would be threatened. We needed to be constantly on guard that what happened within our Fellowship was consistent with our Fifth Tradition: "Each group has but one primary purpose—to carry its message to the sex and love addict who still suffers."

Suggestions for Meeting Format

As our first regular meeting became more established, it began to meet on a weekly basis, and a standard format evolved.

The "chairing" function of the meeting would rotate among the regular members, week by week. In the early months, the initial requirement for chairing the S.L.A.A. meeting was self-defined sobriety, and no time qualification existed. Over a period of time, however, the emerging group conscience moved to establish a time qualification of six weeks of continuously maintained (and self-defined) sobriety *in* S.L.A.A. as the benchmark for chairing a meeting. This has been observed in established S.L.A.A. groups for a number of years now. The feeling is that early withdrawal from sex and love addiction is such a full-time endeavor that it takes quite a while for a new person to settle in to S.L.A.A. and to be sufficiently acclimated to lead a meeting. Persons entering withdrawal usually change radically in the first six weeks, and this is followed by an even greater self-perceived change during the next three to six months. However, while the six weeks of sobriety has worked well for chair persons, there is not, nor has there ever been, any time qualification for sharing personal experiences at a regular S.L.A.A. meeting.

Here is the format which developed in our first regular meeting, and which has worked successfully in other groups which have arisen since.

The chairperson announces: "This is the regular _____ meeting of Sex and Love Addicts Anonymous; we'll open the meeting with a moment of silence followed by the preamble of S.L.A.A."

The Preamble is then read:

S.L.A.A. Preamble

Sex and Love Addicts Anonymous is a Twelve Step, Twelve Tradition-oriented fellowship based on the model pioneered by Alcoholics Anonymous.

The only qualification for S.L.A.A. membership is a desire to stop living out a pattern of sex and love addiction. S.L.A.A. is supported entirely through contributions of its membership, and is free to all who need it.

To counter the destructive consequences of sex and love addiction we draw on five major resources:

(1) Sobriety. Our willingness to stop acting out in our own personal bottom-line addictive behavior on a daily basis.

(2) Sponsorship / Meetings. Our capacity to reach out for the supportive fellowship within S.L.A.A.

(3) Steps. Our practice of the Twelve Step program of recovery to achieve sexual and emotional sobriety.

(4) Service. Our giving back to the S.L.A.A. community what we continue to freely receive.

(5) Spirituality. Our developing a relationship with a Power greater than ourselves which can guide and sustain us in recovery.

As a fellowship S.L.A.A. has no opinion on outside issues and seeks no controversy. S.L.A.A. is not affiliated with any other organizations, movements or causes, either religious or secular.

We are, however, united in a common focus: dealing with our addictive sexual and emotional behavior. We find a *common denominator* in our obsessive/compulsive patterns which renders any personal differences of sexual or gender orientation irrelevant.

We need protect with special care the anonymity of every S.L.A.A. member. Additionally, we try to avoid drawing undue attention to S.L.A.A. as a whole from the public media.

After the Preamble is read, the chairperson then identifies him/herself, saying, "My name is _____, and I am a sex and love addict."

The chairperson then qualifies, meaning that a fairly detailed version of his/her own sex and love addiction story is related. A "story" consists, basically, of some description of the pattern that the person's sex and love addiction assumed, what the person was like when s/he reached S.L.A.A., and what has happened since. The general guidelines for any story is that it be told in such a way that it reflects experience both of the active addiction and of the recovery process of the person who has lived it.

After the qualification, a topic is usually selected by the chairperson. At new meetings, or meetings where newcomers are present, the meeting topic is usually selected with these new arrivals in mind, so that discussion, based on it, may provide new people with the opportunity to identify with our sex and love addiction patterns. Good topics revolve around several basic addiction and recovery themes: What brought me to S.L.A.A.? How did I discover my sex and love addiction? What does powerlessness over sex and love addiction mean to me? What is bottom-line behavior? Other good topics include: going through withdrawal; obsession and the sex and love addict; compulsion and the sex and love addict; emotional dependency; loss of choice.

Of course, there are many other topics equally good. Sometimes a chairperson may ask that, in lieu of a formal topic, each person share an abbreviated version of his/her sex and love addiction story.

When the topic or subject has been arrived at, the usual practice is to proceed around the room, in order, so that each and every person has an opportunity to share. This can take quite a while, and sometimes a time limit per person can become necessary.

When this sharing is completed, we then have a portion of the meeting devoted to what we call "getting current." Getting current means that each person has the opportunity to share what is currently happening in his/her life.

Particular emphasis is placed on sharing the stimulating or intriguing sexual and emotional situations which appear to pose the major threats, here and now, to maintaining sobriety in S.L.A.A.

We have found that this "getting current" portion of the meeting is indispensable. The mind-altering aspects of sex and love addiction are subtle yet incessant. Circumstances which can trigger this erosion of our awareness of our sex and love addiction are so frequent and numerous that we need to be able to "ground" any sexual and emotional ambiguity which has started to undermine our stable functioning. In practical terms, only through this ongoing sharing of our "current" trials can our lives be maintained as "open." From meeting to meeting, almost all of us, including those of us with relatively long-term sobriety, need to get current on a regular basis. No matter how far we have evolved in sobriety, we are never beyond reach of temptation's siren song.

The "getting current" sharing continues around the room, in order, until all who need to get current have done so. Again, sometimes time limits per person need to be specified and observed.

After the "getting current" phase of the meeting, a collection is taken (in accordance with the Seventh Tradition), and the chairperson announces: "This has been a regular meeting of the _____ group of Sex and Love Addicts Anonymous. We will end the meeting with the _____ prayer (often the Serenity Prayer), for all those who may care to join me, and during the closing prayer hand-holding is optional only, not mandatory."

This last statement about hand-holding being optional may seem trivial. However, a number of us discovered, through our own personal histories as sex and love addicts, the tremendous ambiguity with which supposedly non-sexual or non-erotic contact could fill us. In fact, many of us used to utilize just such innocent-seeming contact to continuously cull through a crowd, looking for an addictive response. Since we do not wish to cultivate unnecessary intrigue and ambiguity—mixed-message confusions—within S.L.A.A., those of us with this kind of susceptibility respect the vulnerability which our personal histories have shown us that we have. Therefore, no ritualized physical contact is mandatory within S.L.A.A.

With the conclusion of the closing prayer, our meeting is concluded.

This format for conducting an S.L.A.A. meeting is meant only as suggestion. There is no single "approved" or "official" format. Alterations of the one suggested can prove useful, as, for instance, deciding to split into two or more smaller discussion groups as the regular meeting gains a consistently large attendance.

One thing we have tried hard to avoid, within the guidelines already set forth, is over-ritualization. If a firm blueprint is laid down about how to conduct a meeting, "party lines" may develop concerning what is admissible and what isn't. Such attempts to launder a meeting might take the form of imposing "language codes," or "reinterpreting" comments so as to make them seem to conform to a certain viewpoint. An outcome of this kind of meddling is that the common denominator of sharing is reduced to low-grade homogenization, or sludge. Vital, individual sharing, which always involves *variation,* has been implicitly (or explicitly) discouraged, and therefore lost. Any group which falls into this trap will discover itself to have developed a pre-senile case of hardening of the arteries, with a prognosis to match.

Special Purpose Meetings

Over time, we discovered that our one S.L.A.A. meeting per week was being called upon to fill many functions. First and foremost, it provided newcomers with the environment in which sex and love addiction could be candidly discussed without pretense, and this has always been, and still is, paramount. Insofar as we are a Twelve Step fellowship, however, we experienced an additional need to have a forum where the process of recovery embodied in the Twelve Steps could be more fully explored and discussed. This led to a decision to make the first meeting of each month a "Twelve Step" meeting, at which we would read a step from the Chapter 4 material for this book, or from the A.A. book *Twelve Steps and Twelve Traditions,* and share our personal experiences which related to each step, from the sex and love addiction perspective. At this meeting, we also continued the practice of providing an opportunity to "get current."

As more people entered S.L.A.A. and started to go through withdrawal, the need for a regular Twelve Step meeting where the Steps could be taken up in regular order became more and more apparent. Shortly thereafter, a spin-off meeting began which could address itself exclusively to this need.

This period of our Fellowship's history was wonderfully harmonious. We had seen more individuals recover, and we had seen S.L.A.A. groups begin in some other states of the U.S. Now, however, the start of a regular Twelve Step group, the second group in our immediate area, lifted a burden from the first S.L.A.A. meeting, which could then return to doing what it did best: provide a place for newcomers to see examples of recovery and make a beginning.

With two local groups firmly established to fill different needs, the next major division of function occurred when attendance at both meetings grew to a level that the "getting current" portion of each meeting was being necessarily shortened, out of time considerations. This led to a special "getting current" meeting being established, at which getting current was to be the sole function. Our need for getting current was a constant one, so the establishment of a special meeting for this purpose was a desirable alternative to making do with the shorter time available at other meetings. At the original meetings, getting current was continued only on a "priority," or emergency, basis. Over time this has worked out very, very well.

A further aspect of S.L.A.A. group evolution should be mentioned. With three local groups in the Boston area, the need was recognized for a monthly "Fellowship-Wide" business meeting to deal with matters of Fellowship-wide relevance. Obviously, during the time when only one group and meeting existed, the individual group conscience and the "Fellowship" conscience were one and the same. However, this was no longer so as groups started to proliferate. There were sporadic challenges to our Fellowship's stated purpose and ways of functioning at the group level, and there were other matters concerning, for example, how we would work out the S.L.A.A. version of the Twelve Steps and Twelve Traditions.

The production of pamphlet literature, undertaking the project that has resulted in this book, incorporation of a non-profit service board (The Augustine Fellowship, Sex and Love Addicts Anonymous, Fellowship-Wide Services, Inc.) under which the book could be published and other service-oriented tasks coordinated, questions of how to deal with offers to give us wide-media exposure (they have typically been shunned*), and other issues were presenting themselves. The monthly Fellowship-wide business meeting tackled these problems, as well as the usual procedural ones such as qualifications for attendance and voting at the Fellowship-wide business meeting, how the traditions apply in terms of specific instances of group "growing pains," etc.

Eventually, the "Fellowship-wide" monthly meetings were supplanted by quarterly meetings of the Board of Trustees, the development of regional "Intergroups," and an annual Fellowship-Wide Service Conference, at which the concerns of the expanding Fellowship can be addressed. This Fellowship-Wide Service Conference, which convenes in mid-January of each year, will continue to be the future "Fellowship Conscience" for S.L.A.A., to keep S.L.A.A. forever responsive to its membership.

Perhaps S.L.A.A. will not always direct its own functioning as harmoniously as it has thus far. Nevertheless, the precedents set as the first group was established, leading to division of functioning into groups with varied formats and the development of a Fellowship-Wide service apparatus, seem to provide a structure within which S.L.A.A. can continue to evolve, both in the spirit of group autonomy and overall Fellowship cohesiveness.

Finding a Public Meeting Place

The first S.L.A.A. group met in private homes for several years, changing location on average about once a year. The time came, however, when we

---

*Twelve recommended guidelines now codify S.L.A.A.'s approach to the whole matter of media/public relations. These guidelines are reprinted in full on page 137.

needed to seek a public meeting place which could handle a greater number of people. This transition from a private home to a public meeting place was an important milestone for us, and we learned something from it which we wish to pass along.

We were aware of a church in our community which had a strong reputation for community service and outreach. Normally, when a group wanted to meet in this church, the liaison person of the group would simply see the person in charge of scheduling space in the church, and reserve the time. We decided not to go about it in this way. In view of the delicate nature of the subject around which our fellowship had formed, we decided to consult the pastor directly.

We met with him privately and explained who and what we were, holding back nothing. There could be nothing gained under false pretenses. At this time we had no printed literature, but the pastor listened to our presentation carefully. He said that he liked the idea of our meeting in the church, but that he would have to think about it some more and would contact us.

After several days we heard from him, and he said that our name, Sex and Love Addicts Anonymous, was a problem for him. He needed something which would not appear so "provocative" to his church board. After a cordial "Goodbye" and a forced "We'll see what we can come up with," resentment and defensiveness set in. We felt bitter. Who was this man to tell us to change our name! We felt a strong affinity and identification with the name "Sex and Love Addicts Anonymous." With a "milk-toast" name we could envision S.L.A.A. becoming a lonely-hearts society. Nor would this pastor tolerate any name with the word "sex" in it. (We had suggested several variations to him.) We pretty much concluded that this pastor didn't really want us in his church anyway, and had forwarded his complaint to sabotage our being able to meet there.

Still, after considering that this would be a problem wherever we went, we spoke to the pastor again. We told him how important the S.L.A.A. name and identification were for us. We expressed our reservations concerning how an altered name might really distort who we were and how we were going about recovery. He understood. He reiterated that he really *did* want our group, with our purpose intact, to meet in his church. He said that he was not trying to get us to change our name, only to come up with an alternate so that he could solve his political problems within the church. He had no reservations about our referring to ourselves as Sex and Love Addicts Anonymous at our own meetings. The question to us was, were we willing to help *him* with his considerations? The answer had to be "Yes."

A group/fellowship conscience meeting ensued, and out of it came a name which proved to be a galvanizing alternative: The Augustine Fellowship. Augustine of Hippo—as those who have read his autobiography, *Confessions,* know—was probably one of us. The fact that a church body later canonized him as a saint was not a formal concern for us, because as a fellowship we have "...no opinion on outside issues..." (Tenth Tradition). However, the dynamics of Augustine's story, the inner workings and struggles of the person himself, left us with little doubt that he would have understood, and felt welcome among us.

We returned to the pastor and asked if the name "The Augustine Fellowship" would solve his problem. He said it would, and it has. We have since seen fit to include "The Augustine Fellowship" as a part of the incorporated name for the non-profit service arm of S.L.A.A. (The Augustine Fellowship, Sex and Love Addicts Anonymous, Fellowship-Wide Services, Inc.).

Since the time when the first S.L.A.A. group moved to a public meeting place, a second has followed suit, finding space in a hospital. This second situation involved approaching the hospital administrator and showing him a pamphlet which included the name "Sex and Love Addicts Anonymous." The member making contact made a complete disclosure of who and what we were, and offered to use the name "The Augustine Fellowship" to appease the hospital. This administrator called the pastor of the church where the first group had met for well over a year. The pastor left no doubt as to the seriousness which we brought to our stated group purpose and the care which we had exercised in using the church premises. Soon thereafter, our local Twelve Step group was comfortably ensconced in its new meeting place in this hospital.

One final note to all this is that our pastor friend, a man of great conscience and sensitivity, became so supportive of our presence in the church that within eighteen months we were known within the church community by *both* names, and this good man, unsolicited, was placing S.L.A.A. literature in the pamphlet rack in the church vestibule!

Special Interest Groups

Now we want to address a matter which many of you, perhaps, have been wondering about. It may strike you as odd that in relating some of our formative group experiences, no mention has been made of the establishment of any "special interest" groups within S.L.A.A., such as "men's" groups, "women's" groups, "gay" groups, "lesbian" groups, and so on. The plain fact is that in over nine years of S.L.A.A. group development, none have come into being. From time to time, various individuals, both male and female, have made inquiries of the wider membership about starting "this" or "that" kind of group meeting, but support for such ventures has never been widespread, and such "special interest" group meetings have not occurred. We think there are a number of reasons why this has been so.

First, those individuals who have sought to establish an "all this" or "all that" meeting sometimes claim they have done so because they were seeking a "safer" environment in which to make their admissions of personal vulnerability. Yet the idea of a "safe group"—one in which group members would not be attracted to one another—can not really exist. For instance, a lesbian sex and love addict could clearly feel as much risk at a "women only" meeting as the founder of such a group might feel at a mixed meeting. Of course, the same concept holds true for gay men in attendance at "men only" meetings.

The simple fact is this: no S.L.A.A. meeting can be laundered of intrigue on the basis of limiting attendance to "such and such a group" on the theory that all members would be group-compatible by virtue of being sexually non-compatible. Our collective sexual behavior has been far too eclectic for that.

Secondly, there is another myth which could be all-too-easily fostered at "special interest" groups, regardless of the particular "special interest." Many persons with difficult sex and love addiction histories seek to blame "others" for them. These others can be labelled under such stereotypes as "emasculating feminists," "male chauvinists," "male dominated society," "female dominated society," "women's lib-ers," "male-sexist oppressors," "feminists," "masculinists," ad nauseam. To make polemical declarations about how various sub-groups (one's own, of course!) are victimized minorities suffering at the hands of would-be oppressors may make sense for a sociologist, but for sex and love addicts intent on recovering, such ruminations have no positive value. The truth seems to be that until we "own" our sex and love addiction as a personal condition about which we assume the responsibility to do something within ourselves, hostility directed outward towards some designated would-be "persecutor" is a waste of time. Therefore, we feel that special interest groups have *not* occurred because people in S.L.A.A. have generally been wary of any settings in which "external enemies" could be labelled, thus taking attention away from attending to sex and love addiction as a *personal affliction.*

A third reason why "special interest" groups have not caught on is that people in S.L.A.A. have realized that there is great therapeutic value to being around a wide spectrum of people which includes those who at one time might have provided opportunities for acting out. Being around very attractive people within S.L.A.A. has forced us, within this sanctuary, to begin to learn how to interact more humanly with those who would have been cast as "types," on the outside. Like us, these people are now, within S.L.A.A., also intent on getting sober and finding a stable recovery. We have discovered, at S.L.A.A. meetings where all sex and love addicts are present, that we have a common basis for identification of the illness regardless of any other factors. To a great extent, S.L.A.A. meetings have been a kind of training ground which we have needed in order to become more capable of dealing with others on the outside who might present real threats to our sobriety. We come to see through the addictive potential of individuals, breaking the illusion so that the human dimension can come into focus. Learned first in S.L.A.A., this capacity to see beyond the addictive potential has been carried over into our dealings with those on the outside who could still be available. The values developed in dealing with one another within S.L.A.A. have become the blueprints we apply in assessing the real value of relationships outside of S.L.A.A.

Clearly, "unisex" or "special interest" groups could, through attempts to exclude temptation, be ill-serving of those of us (all of us) who need to learn to deal with reality, rather than insulate ourselves from it. If we don't have opportunities to learn this within S.L.A.A. meetings which are open to *all* sex and love addicts, then we shall never come to terms with what can really thwart us on the outside. Our sobriety will be brittle, and probably not endure.

In drawing this section on "special interest" groups to a close, we want to observe that S.L.A.A., as such, can never prevent such groups from forming. However, if they are to form and serve a constructive purpose, they themselves will have to be based on a rationale other than the illusion of providing a "safer" environment in which intrigue and sexual attraction are supposedly laundered out. Such groups will have to coalesce for purposes other than labeling "external enemies," or otherwise justify their existence as havens for persecuted minorities.

The only real "safety" any S.L.A.A. group (and S.L.A.A. as a whole) can ever have is a desire to get well which is held in common by a majority of group members, and the availability of that Grace, bestowed by a Power greater than us all, which alone makes recovery possible.

Trusted Servants and Group Conscience

We now wish to address a very sensitive matter, aimed at those of you who will be starting, or have already started, an S.L.A.A. group. For all practical purposes, you are, especially in the beginning, the guiding light of S.L.A.A. in your area. Perhaps you have visited S.L.A.A. groups in other parts of the country, and have seen them function. Or perhaps, on the basis of this book alone, combined with your being in withdrawal from active sex and love addiction, you feel an inner imperative to start things off in your locale.

You will find, or have already found, a prospect for S.L.A.A. with whom to work. Perhaps you have started holding regular meetings in your home and have contacted a number of individuals who you feel are in obvious trouble. Maybe you have already worked with a succession of individuals, only to find each one drifting away after a short time. How discouraging this can be! Through your own perseverance and need for fellowship, you are keeping the hope of starting an S.L.A.A. group alive within yourself, waiting for this resolve to bear fruit. Sooner or later, it will.

When it does, you're likely to find that you are very much the kingpin (or queenpin). Even with regular attendees at meetings, and the joyful circumstance of one or a few others embarking on their own withdrawal and recovery, your own seasoned experience will make you pretty formidable in the young group. You are likely to experience very parental feelings towards it, and these can be complex. You have "brought the group forth," given birth to it, in a sense, through your steadfastness and dedication. The group members have, in return, validated your own recovery process through the very fact of replicating it.

If you are really careful and Twelve-Tradition-minded, as we have tried to be, the group conscience principle will be one that you will introduce early. Perhaps you will solicit group decisions on the relatively routine matters such as meeting place, time, who chairs, etc. At this early phase of group evolution, this expression of group conscience will be pretty much a formality. New people will be so wrapped up in the self-absorption of coping with their own withdrawal that they will tend to defer to you and your experience for guidance on most matters, whether personal or group.

Nevertheless, despite the apparent formality of this exercise of group conscience, DO NOT NEGLECT IT. The clock is ticking. Whether you know it or not, your days as "venerated regional founder" (or co-founder), as the one who always has the word which can reliably crystallize the group conscience, ARE NUMBERED. This is true *regardless* of whether you abuse the power which falls to you in the beginning, or whether you are the most careful, conscientious person on earth in trying to be evenhanded and responsible in group matters.

Let's consider two examples of "group founder" attitudes and explore why, regardless of intent, the founder's days as unquestioned leader are numbered.

We'll consider first the founder who abuses power. This is the one who generally has always been looking for a forum through which control can be exercised. S/he tends to take extreme positions on matters pertaining to S.L.A.A., withdrawal, sobriety, the way a meeting is conducted, and so on. Often this drive to control is partially (but never entirely) masked by the rationale that s/he is only trying to safeguard S.L.A.A. from influences that would make the meeting stray from its intended purpose. S/he does not really consult the group on much of anything: its voice is not to be trusted, or tolerated! Any questions concerning group procedures or questions of sobriety are met with rigidity and absolutism. This kind of "founder" must do this if s/he is to remain in control. Any questioning of the way group matters are conducted, or of his/her views on sex and love addiction, are taken as personal affronts, because such questions threaten his/her power.

People with this power-seeking disease can never really nurture anything or anybody. Typically, they seek to bind other individuals to themselves either through force of personal charisma or under the guise of conscientiousness, thus masking their own inflexible nature.

A group which forms under such heavy-handedness may tolerate it for quite a while, being much taken by the founder's charisma and compelling logic. Sooner or later, however, a revolt is inevitable as others become aware of the insatiable power-thirst of the once-revered founder. The sheep turn into wolves, and the group may self-destruct in a violent reaction to the "leader's" power. Other individuals who feel strong enough may try to usurp power themselves. Or the group may go through painful convulsions, but finally reorient itself around S.L.A.A. Traditions, with the founder cast out of the leadership role, and probably frozen out emotionally. The one who has abused power in this way sooner or later is served up this kind of recompense. If s/he can not deal with it constructively, the disease of sex and love addiction is likely to appear, once again, an attractive option.

In the case of the group founder or co-founder who proceeds carefully and conscientiously, similar risks are present, but they come about differently. In this situation the person is aware of the precedents incorporated in the Twelve Traditions, and has solicited group conscience on all regular matters. As s/he cultivates group input, people quite naturally defer to the experienced "shepherd" and do not feel rebellious under such benign leadership.

Yet the clock ticks for this "enlightened" group founder just as surely as it does for the abusive one. Here is why. A few years go by, perhaps, and our careful, conscientious friend is falling into a trap, although s/he may not see it in time. For the very reason that this person has never abused power, either openly or covertly, people have become accustomed to deferring to his/her open and careful manner of reflecting on group and fellowship issues. Indeed, this is the voice of seasoned experience in sobriety, often couched in genuinely felt humility and self-effacement. Yet it is easy for this group founder to become lulled into cultivating an expectation s/he may not even know s/he has. S/he comes to believe, on some level, that the position of "framer of the group conscience" is secure by virtue of the scrupulous exercise of personal conscience and good will. In a sense, this person comes to derive much the same sense of security from this seemingly assured influence as does the power monger. The expectation is that this will continue indefinitely. How unsettling it is for the founder when it doesn't!

Sooner or later someone comes into the S.L.A.A. meeting who may be in serious trouble with sex and love addiction, but who has a vested interest in finding and labelling an "external enemy" in the group rather than facing the fact of his/her illness. A newcomer reluctant to face the seriousness of the illness can find many compelling rationales which seem to justify labelling an "external enemy" as such. This newcomer will find other allies, just as sub-groups in society can find a cohesion with other groups, regardless of philosophical differences, by blaming their respective problems on a common external enemy.

Inevitably, regardless of how carefully they have conducted themselves, the founders of an S.L.A.A. group will find themselves cast as the external enemy. They will be so designated solely by virtue of the fact that they exert an obvious "authority," or influence, within the S.L.A.A. group. Whether the founders have arrived at this influence through abuse or by virtue makes not the slightest difference at this point. It is the *fact* of the "leadership" position that polarizes the external enemy seeker, and there is nothing a group founder can do about it.

Even more carefully worded, well intentioned "statements of conscience" on the founder's part only serve to further incense the external enemy seeker. The regional or group founder has been rendered profoundly powerless. Good intentions can avail nothing further in resolving the difficulty.

What happens then? This depends. If the founder has really been careful, the group conscience which s/he has continuously tried to invoke will resolve the problem. The group will sense the discord and, responding to the upheaval, move to assert itself, possibly for the first time. In the past the group members probably have deferred to the founder's judgements to such an extent that they have not really taken seriously just how essential their opinions are when acting in group conscience. Now, however, they rally. When they do, an irreversible shift of power and influence occurs.

The founder's reins (and reign) have been handed over to the group, whether s/he likes it or not. The external enemy seeker now no longer has a specific target in the form of "group founder" to aim at, and so confronts the source of real power within the group, a loving God, represented more or less well through the exercise of group conscience. Without a prominent target, this person may well calm down and get back to the business of dealing with his/her sex and love addiction. The founder suffers a very difficult loss through all of this, but one that is immensely healthy. His/her "child" has grown up—come of age. The experience of loss is not unlike that of a parent letting go of a child. If the parenting has been good, the group will still love and respect the founder(s) who still can have an important role to fill. But the relationship, henceforth, will be adult to adult, not parent to child.

If there is a basic lesson to be derived from this brief description of our experiences with group evolution in S.L.A.A., it is this: the perseverance, dedication and singleness of purpose which are such necessary traits, in the beginning, for a person to have who tries to start an S.L.A.A. group, are the very same traits which may later constrict or stunt the group's need, as a whole, to "come of age"—to assume responsibility for its own welfare. Things change, and, with time, so do the needs of an evolving fellowship.

The time for any group founders to introduce to a new group the S.L.A.A. Twelve Traditions and the concepts of power and service which are codified there, is while they still have the power and influence to do so. The clock ticks.

We have thus experienced the truth behind our Second Tradition: For our group purpose there is but one ultimate authority—a loving God as this Power may be expressed through our group conscience. Our leaders are but trusted servants; *they do not govern.*

In September, 1985, the Board of Trustees of The Augustine Fellowship, Sex and Love Addicts Anonymous, Fellowship-Wide Services, Inc. (S.L.A.A.'s incorporated service arm) formulated a series of guidelines regarding media/public relations which constitute S.L.A.A.'s current policy. These concepts are experientially rooted in our Fellowship's nine years of existence (to date). Here follow **The Twelve Recommended Guidelines for Dealing with Media/Public Relations Opportunities—for Use at All Levels of the S.L.A.A. Fellowship:**

(1) We try to avoid drawing undue attention to S.L.A.A. as a whole from the public media.
—from the S.L.A.A. Preamble

(2) S.L.A.A. has no opinion on outside issues, hence the S.L.A.A. name ought never be drawn into public controversy.
—S.L.A.A.'s Tenth Tradition

(3) Our Public Relations policy is based on attraction rather than promotion. (We do not court publicity.)
—from S.L.A.A.'s Eleventh Tradition

(4) Any unilateral action, by any S.L.A.A. member acting on his/her own, to place S.L.A.A. before the public media at any level is expressly discouraged.
—from Fellowship-Wide Business Meeting group conscience resolution of October 14, 1981

(5) Group conscience-based decisions need always be made regarding the appropriateness of accepting or declining any and all media or public relations opportunities, and, if an opportunity is accepted, regarding in what ways to respond, within the spirit of these guidelines.
—derived from S.L.A.A.'s Second Tradition

(6) All media or public relations offers which are extended to S.L.A.A. under condition of a "deadline," which, in order to accept such an offer, would make it necessary to circumvent or short- circuit appropriate group conscience decision-making regarding the offer, should be declined.
—from Fellowship-Wide Business Meeting group conscience resolution of October 14, 1981; observed by Bay Area S.L.A.A. Intergroup in media offer decision of August, 1985

(7) Public relations or media situations which are entered into need always be handled by at least *two* sober S.L.A.A. members. Participating S.L.A.A. members should make it clear that they speak only as individuals, and not for S.L.A.A. as a whole. No S.L.A.A. member should ever be in a position in which there is the appearance that s/he speaks for S.L.A.A. as a whole.
—guideline worked out by S.L.A.A. Fellowship-Wide Services, in consultation with S.L.A.A. New England Intergroup for Boston Phoenix *article of July, 1985*

(8) Any S.L.A.A. members involved in responding to media/public relations offers should utilize first name pseudonyms for this purpose. Visual anonymity is strongly recommended in all media situ- ations involving TV, film or video. We need always maintain personal anonymity at the level of press, radio, TV, film and other public media.

—first sentence worked out by S.L.A.A. New England Intergroup and S.L.A.A. Fellowship-Wide Services for Boston Phoenix *interview in March, 1985; second sentence adapted from A.A.'s policy regarding public media. Third sentence from S.L.A.A.'s Eleventh Tradition*

(9) We avoid participating in public forums, workshops or other media events in which there appears to be any possibility that S.L.A.A. would be pitted against opposing or adversarial view- points, or spokespersons representing other interests or causes.

—based on August, 1985 decision of San Diego S.L.A.A. group, in consultation with S.L.A.A. Fellowship-Wide Services

(10) The appropriate level of "group conscience" to be consulted in matters of media or public relations is that level which represents the geographical area of S.L.A.A. to be impacted, or affected, by the porspective publicity. Media/PR opportunities which would affect a larger level of the S.L.A.A. Fellowship should be referred to the "group conscience" body operative at that larger level of S.L.A.A. Each level of group conscience within S.L.A.A. may, if it chooses, appoint a Media/PR conscience committee, responsible directly to the group conscience which appoints it, to serve as the group conscience decision making body regarding media/PR offers, at each respective S.L.A.A. service level.

—derived from S.L.A.A.'s Fourth Tradition

(11) Any media/PR opportunities that have an aspect to them which could potentially affect S.L.A.A. as a whole should be referred to the "group conscience" decision making body operative at the Fellowship-Wide level, c/o the Board of Trustees.

—derived from S.L.A.A.'s Fourth Tradition

(12) It is recommended that media/PR decision making at any level of group conscience be preceded by one minute of silent group meditation, so as to clear a channel through which the guiding God-presence behind S.L.A.A. may make itself felt, helping to ensure that group conscience decisions will truly reflect this Power's design for S.L.A.A.

—derived from S.L.A.A.'s Eleventh Step and Second Tradition

(Approved by the Board of Trustees, The Augustine Fellowship, Sex and Love Addicts Anonymous, Fellowship-Wide Services.)

Chapter 8

Building Partnerships

As we came out of the withdrawal phase of recovery, many of us were encountering major changes in our life circumstances. The period of solitude and contemplation was ending as our attention now turned toward responsibilities and opportunities outside ourselves. Perhaps the most challenging and potentially fulfilling possibility in this new phase of our sobriety was in the area of partnership building. We knew that we wanted to translate our inner experiences of personal dignity, self-worth and self-intimacy into new guidelines within which we might explore partnership with another. We needed to learn how, and under what conditions, our sexual and emotional capacities could find a full and appropriate expression in such a partnership.

In S.L.A.A. our experience in partnership building has been a challenging adventure. Withdrawal from sex and love addiction consists to a great extent of learning how to get *uninvolved* from one's addictive partners, and how to *stay* uninvolved in spite of temptations. During this time a whole lot of attention is not given to what constitutes a healthy relationship, or to what the positive attributes of partnership really are. Nor can it be. Early withdrawal, in particular, highlights for us just what attributes are *not* a part of partnership. Any definition of a healthy relationship as one which exists solely in the absence of addictive attributes, however, leaves a lot of questions unanswered. The post-withdrawal period is when we started to learn something about our emotional, mental, and sexual capacities for partnership expressed as something other than just "minus the addiction." To a great extent, we learned through trial and error as we moved beyond focussing only on bottom-line sobriety from sex and love addiction and began to ponder partnership with another. Indeed, this is a kind of learning which we would never really finish. But before we share with you our experiences in partnership building, we would like to talk about another possibility which many of us explored: living alone.

Partnership? Or Living Alone?

If you are like most of us, the prospect of living alone is not particularly appealing. Most likely you have come into the S.L.A.A. fellowship wanting to learn how to have healthy relationships, not to learn how to live without them! In essence, you have been willing to clean house, but once cleansed, you certainly would expect to be able to invite visitors in! We would like to suggest the option of simply living in a clean house because it is pleasant, not because it is a prerequisite for having visitors. In S.L.A.A. terms, this translates into living alone because we have chosen that as a life style, not because we have been marking time to get "healthy" enough for our next relationship.

You may ask why anyone would want to live alone. The answer has several sides. For many of us, especially at first, it was simply a relief to be free of the obsessions and compulsions which had so driven us; we have been more than happy to luxuriate in this period in which we seem relatively safe from the day-to-day battle with our addiction. Some of us felt that we had had all we ever needed of sex and romance; once asleep, we saw no reason to waken the sleeping dog. Also, there was a new kind of vigor and excitement about life that we found when we were freed from our compulsive patterns. Here, especially, it was not a matter of seeking or avoiding relationships. We were simply not looking for romance because we were involved in many other things.

"Come on," you say. "Why would anybody who is capable of having a healthy relationship avoid having one?" Believe it or not, we actually got to a point where other things took precedence over even the opportunity for romance. We have not been avoiding them, it is just that relationships have taken a more realistic place in the vast arena of self-expression which is called life.

What happened was that in new sobriety we found that along with the task of staying away from addictive activities, we had the equally difficult task of filling up all that free time. We needed to have a lot of time alone, to give feelings a chance to surface, but we also needed to keep busy. Even in the midst of withdrawal, we turned to hobbies or new pursuits that were engrossing and would consume some time and energy. As the addictive cravings lessened, we often found ourselves actively enjoying these new activities and the discovery, or re-discovery, of talents. We have, among S.L.A.A. members, new Ph.D.'s, new musicians, new marathon runners, new artists.

By definition, our image of ourselves expanded to include these newly developed talents, and these lead to new and healthy roles in the world that could or could not include a "partner." This is not to say that we never had desires for a relationship. It is simply that this desire was not compelling enough to cause us to rearrange our lives in order to do something about it. Our consciences were clear, our lives were productive, and we were happy. Furthermore, we found that we were forming warmer relationships with friends, co-workers, and even casual acquaintances. Today we may live alone, but we have found rewarding friendships and companionship without sex, and we are not lonely.

However, it would be naive to suggest to a sex and love addict that simply finding an engrossing new direction in life is enough for a contented life alone. Our addiction served many purposes. It allowed at least a temporary escape from the pain of our lives, and it provided excitement and pleasure which we had seemed incapable of finding in any other way. But seeking to escape pain and to increase pleasure is what all human beings do, although most do not go to such extremes, or use addictive avenues to accomplish this. It is our belief that all along we were trying to derive something more meaningful from our addictive activities. Perhaps we confused sex and romantic intrigue with love, but in the final analysis it was authentic love we were, on a deeper level, seeking.

After we were sober a while, we began to name this need which drove us into more and more desperate and hopeless sexual/romantic situations: the need for our lives to have meaning. Having a steady income could be important, having a creative outlet was a pleasure, having mutually supportive friendships was essential. But none of these things gave our lives meaning in the way WE craved meaning.

We turned to philosophy and major religions to see how others, non-addicts, derived meaning for their lives. The answer seemed to be that the purpose of life is to love.

Perhaps our hungry search for "love" was not so far off base after all. While we were not able to extract lasting meaning from our addictive relationships, our *need* for meaning *was* real. We were right that a meaningful life is one filled with love, but we had distorted that meaning with selfishness, seeking only to "get" rather than to "give," to "rip off" rather than to contribute. There could be no enduring meaning in "love" that was a rapid consumption commodity on an open market. In S.L.A.A. the Eleventh and Twelfth Steps brought with them an idea that was a breath of fresh air; it could be a more complete expression of love to both give and receive. Each mode was the other's complement. Neither, unto itself, was complete.

For some of us, this spiritual wisdom of the ages has led to a life in which we have found satisfaction, happiness, and fulfillment in learning to be of service to others on a give and take basis. The spirit of service, both within S.L.A.A. and with the rest of humankind, has brought to us a deep sense of communion with our inner selves, with the human community, and with God. By expanding our definition of love beyond the sexual and romantic context, and aligning ourselves with this larger experience of love as we learn to give more freely of ourselves, we bring ourselves into the flow of divine Love, divine purpose. We may choose this way of life as an end in itself, seeking partnership with God-love through service, and finding that our needs for love are amply filled.

There is a danger, however, in choosing a life alone. It may be that, as we find intimacy with self and become involved in our new lives, we come to enjoy our own company to the exclusion of others. It is one thing to be comfortable and fulfilled by ourselves, it is quite another to become self-centered in our isolation. Just as we could temporarily retreat from the search for sexual adventure to fantasy and masturbation, in sobriety we can hide from the risks of human relationships in solitary pursuit of selfish pleasures. We have found that if we do not find balance *and* meaning in our lives, then we are all too easily drawn into *non*-sexual relationships that are *not unlike the addictive ones.* Our relationships with causes, with our heroes or gurus, and with ourselves must be subject to the same principles which keep our sexual lives sober. Real life is not without tensions, unhappiness, and conflict, if we are honest with ourselves and others. If we are to grow in sobriety, we must be willing to look for dishonesty and self-centeredness in all of our activities, lest we find ourselves seeking to escape from life once again. The basic principle is this: self-dignity and unselfish caring for other human beings are both part of a life committed to sobriety. The things we have learned about living in partnership, either in a marriage or in some other intimate, committed relationship, are equally as important in the whole array of non-sexual relationships with other human beings, regardless of whether we are choosing to "live alone" or not.

Partnership in a Committed Relationship

Even before we early S.L.A.A.'s had much practical experience with partnership building (since we were still up to our necks in withdrawal symptoms), we used to speculate about what a healthy relationship might be, and how it would feel. Reaching for ways to conceptualize what we might encounter, we stumbled onto a concept called "systems theory" that offered some startling insight.

It would be presumptuous of us to try to describe the complexity and subtlety of systems theory here. It is enough to point out the parallel between closed and open systems, and our experience in relationships before and after recovery.

The basic idea is that a "closed system" is one in which there is no energy exchanged with the environment outside the system. An "open system" is one in which energy IS exchanged, just as a living being takes in food, oxygen, and experiences, and transforms these into flesh, energy, and learning. Closed systems with living things cannot continue for long. Just as an astronaut in space will eventually run out of food and air, a closed system with living things must become "open," or die.

Addictive relationships, with their excessive neediness and demands on others for emotional or sexual salvation, are like closed energy systems. In such relationships, two individuals (who are really non-individuals) rely completely on their *relationship* to be the source for all personal identity, life-purpose and meaning. Each person has become totally dependent on the other for a sense of stability. Yet the "stability" derived in this way is not and cannot be stable. Like other closed systems, no external energy is allowed in, since this is perceived as being threatening to the system itself.

Let's look at one example of such a "closed" relationship, between Person A and Person B. Suppose that Person A starts to think about going back to school, or cultivating new friends, or exploring some activities that will not include the other. Person B, in the closed system, would *have* to see this as a threat to getting his or her own needs met in the relationship. After all, if Person A is spending time with other friends and activities, then Person B would no longer have unchallenged access to Person A. Forced into a time-sharing arrangement, Person B, especially if a sex and love addict, would sense that his needs might not be serviced if they had to fit in with Person A's schedule of availability. Even if Person A were to reserve special times to be devoted to Person B, the fact that new "possibilities" *could* occur would be a constant threat and source of anxiety for Person B. It would not matter whether these possibilities were for romance or for personal growth; they would both be seen as creating the possibility that Person A might not "be there" to meet the needs of Person B. Since contact-on-demand is the life-blood of the addict in a closed relationship, the potential for being cast involuntarily into the painful experience we now understand as withdrawal would be seen as the bleakest of prospects.

Confronted with this threat to the "closed system," Person B would *have to* try to sabotage Person A's initiative to try new life experiences. It would not be hard for Person B to accomplish this. Person A might well have been moving to expand horizons *because* of feeling relatively secure in the relationship with Person B. But this feeling of security, of "having it together" in an addictive relationship, usually comes about as a result of the other partner being more dependent on the relationship, however temporarily. In truth, the only "security" an addictive relationship *can* have is that "she needs me more than I need her."

Yet the roles of Person A and Person B, the one who feels "together" and the one who is "falling apart," are interchangeable. Each person, in a closed relationship, feels "together" to the degree that the other can be expected to "fall apart"! Person B, faced with the threat that Person A might not be available, threatens in turn to look elsewhere to have his or her needs met, needs that might emerge at any time. Person A, who is really just as dependent on the relationship for a sense of identity and meaning as Person B, will then scuttle his or her *own* life plans, in order to insure his or her own security.

So it is that in a closed system each person comes to expend more and more energy riding herd on the other, even as less and less energy is received from a wider experiencing of life. To maintain their security this energy *must* be expended in riding herd on each other, making sure that neither will stray, so that no possible shortage of supply from each other will follow.

Along with the increasing poverty of each person's range of life-experiences, each person, in the eyes of the other, is cast ever more passionately as "savior," despite occasional feelings that each is the other's jailer. Each person, leaning on the other, tries to be the whole life answer so that there will be no investment in openness to the outside. Each person uses the other to stunt his own need to grow.

Where does the energy come from to continue this closed relationship? Initially it comes from what each person brings to the relationship. But as the exclusiveness of each person as the source for meeting the other person's needs becomes more absolute, each person's individual reserves are rapidly depleted. Any perceived threat that the other might be lost or unavailable throws each of them back on their own individual resources, further depleting the energy available, and causing each in turn to demand still more returns from the relationship. The "lover as savior" is also the lover who must be held hostage if the addict is to survive, and this is usually true for both of them.

Such a closed-energy-system relationship is not at rest, because it demands more and more effort to create the illusion of stability. Each participant walks around feeling as if his or her nervous system is being consumed from within. A kind of half-alive stupor is punctuated with attacks of murderous rage or child-like deification of the other. Clearly the "crimes of passion" are an increasing possibility as this situation continues. Each person in the relationship needs to "live," *to have a life* of his/her own. Either consciously or unconsciously, each may hate the other for depriving him or her of that life. Yet the truest hatred is toward one's own being, for the truth is that each has defaulted on really living. Such a closed system, with sex and love addicts as participants, must inevitably collapse.

As we pondered this concept of a closed energy system, it was so terribly familiar to so many of us. Our personal histories supplied us with ample data of the inevitable decay and collapse which it postulated. Now, as we considered what real partnership might be in the light of "open systems," we realized that we were in new territory where we did *not* have direct experience. Here we had to make a leap of faith to believe that "open systems" might actually exist for us on the plane of human relationships.

As we thought about this, it seemed to us that if there was always new energy coming into the system to replenish and sustain it, the impoverished condition that resulted in the inevitable collapse of a closed system might not occur. Energy would flow in and out of a system, as well as within it. In human relationships two individuals could be nourished by each other and *also* exchange energy through experiences outside the relationship. Rather than being completely dependent on each other, individuals in open-energy-system relationships might have a degree of autonomy. Their ability to function would be only partially dependent on the other, and so they could adapt more easily to changes of all kinds. Very simply, we knew that, in a closed system, the total dependence of each person on the other meant serious consequences to *both* if anything prevented even *one* of them from functioning. In contrast, an open-energy relationship would tend to maintain itself even amid changing conditions affecting either person in the relationship.

This concept seemed to hold the possibility that there could be relationships in which the two partners' lives and activities would only partially overlap. There could be no contract of "life-exclusivity" between them, to shield each other from being exposed to other life experiences or interests. For each person, the relationship could represent an important source of stability, but *not one to the exclusion of all others*. The persons involved, either individually or as partners, would be available to a broader range of life experiences than what the relationship itself would offer either one.

Indeed, this only partial overlap of involvement might actually enhance the relationship. Each partner would be able to bring to the partnership the fruits of experiences in personal growth to which each was being exposed. A partnership might be *further* enriched as a result. Nor would there be a need to cling to each other out of fear of the system itself becoming depleted. No such possibility would exist as long as the relationship remained open, and each partner continued to have the capacity to grow. A plan to explore returning to school would *not* threaten such a system. Each partner would know that each could be content in the relationship for only as long as each would have the opportunity to realize the fulfillment of an intrinsic potential. Enrichment through the relationship, and intimacy within it, could be realized only as long as each partner was striving to be so enriched in all life areas, drawing on all appropriate resources.

In the closed, addictive relationship with emphasis on emotional dependency, the worst fear was that the relationship would fail. A failure of the relationship was tantamount to psychological death for both participants, breeding real panic over every minor tremor. In an open relationship, however, the failure of the relationship would not spell "death" to the individuals involved. The loss of the individual's own autonomy, and the forfeiture of personal dignity, would be seen as being far worse. The task of maintaining personal dignity and wholeness might therefore be experienced as a value transcending the potential end of a relationship. This lowered anxiety over personal survival if the relationship failed would serve, paradoxically, to reduce being so preoccupied with the possibility of there being such a failure. The sense of personal freedom for each of the partners in the relationship would be enhanced. Such a relationship might well stand a good chance of enduring.

The big question was: could we, in fact, given our past discouraging personal histories in addictive, "closed energy" relationships, become available to a positive relationship, the existence of which seemed to be suggested by systems theory? The big answer was: we didn't know, at least in the beginning.

What did we know? Well, we knew how to be open with others in S.L.A.A. about virtually everything we were thinking, feeling, and experiencing. Through this openness we had come to know something about personal honesty, and we had also learned something about being emotionally consistent. We had also experienced that warm inner feeling which stems from having a sense of belonging among people, based not on false pretense but on shared vulnerability.

We knew already something of what personal intimacy—becoming intimate to oneself—meant. Withdrawal had shown us this. We were aware, through our experience in S.L.A.A. meetings, that at least within these sanctuaries we were able to be around people who would have at one time been prime targets for our active addiction. Through mutual sharing, we had come to know these people as human beings, and their stories had exploded many a fantasy we could have trumped up about them. Myths about their addictive desirability had been dispelled before our very eyes. Our interactions with others were becoming more authentic and mutual. We even had moments when we were able to listen to another person's sharing of a story of sex and love addiction with complete neutrality on such issues as the person's gender, or gender preference. What we were increasingly "hearing" was the pulse of our common humanity, transcending all lines of gender, gender preference, or specific sexual aims. We were all fish in the same ocean.

This gradual but vital reorientiation towards others in S.L.A.A. contained many of the *same features which any prospective partnership would have to reflect,* on increasing levels of honesty, trust, intimacy and commitment. Indeed, S.L.A.A. as a whole was an open energy system, receiving much from what seemed to be a never-ending flow of God's grace. We were experiencing healing.

So it was that many of us began partnership building. As the current of withdrawal started to subside, we were ready to meet, and be met by, situations in life from which work on partnership could begin.

Obviously, our prospective partners fell into one of two general categories. Either we decided to try to resume a relationship with a person with whom we had previously been involved (however defectively) * or we embarked on the process of partnership-building with someone new. Whether picking up the

---

* Such a person was *seldom* a former addiction object. More often reconciliation was with one who did not exhibit all the symptoms of sex and love addiction, but who, in the past, had tolerated living with us for an extended period while we were actively ill.

pieces of a past relationship, or embarking anew, we were facing major tasks. Although the qualities in all successful partnerships hold much in common with one another, each circumstance—either reconciliation or starting anew—had its own specific tasks and problems.

The Reconciliation Project

Attempting reconciliation with an estranged spouse or former lover, we learned that the stresses of reconciliation were just as real as the stresses of splitting up had been. For one thing, many of us were only marginally sure that we could stay addiction-free. When these people who had been a part of our former lives rejoined us, we were really facing, firsthand, our own commitment to sobriety which we had made at the beginning of withdrawal. The concept of "one day at a time" became crucial during this period of new change and re-adjustment.

Most of us had been through lengthy talks with our former spouses or partners prior to their return. In spite of this effort, our feelings about these individuals often had taken on, during withdrawal, the rosy glow of sentimentality and idealism, especially in circumstances where the former spouse or lover had been living a considerable distance away from us. We were not thinking about the old, chronic, and perhaps only dimly recognized breakdowns in communication which had formerly crippled us. Unfortunately, if difficulties in communication had happened before, they were *certain* to occur again, regardless of our new found "sober" status.

Our attitudes towards reconciliation often carried a lot of unacknowledged expectations about what would happen. These expectations often included feeling entitled to some special notice from a renewed partner, in recognition of the fact that we were no longer screwing around, or on the market for romantic adventure. These self-centered expectations also showed up in our attitude toward sex with our partner. We often felt supremely entitled to be assertive about our sexual desires. This stridency was often in stark contrast to the reticence we had formerly cultivated within the relationship during the addiction years! During that period we often had had a vested interest in having *no candor* about sexual issues. In fact, many of us had had a lot invested in casting our former primary partners as sexually inadequate, unspontaneous, constricted, and dull, and in trying to guarantee that *that* assessment would never change. Now, "sober," we sometimes became willful and demanding that they learn to meet our self-styled sexual appetites.

These expectations, and many more like them, were unavoidable. The overall task in attempting reconciliation was nothing less than that of working through a lot of old sludge (sometimes there seemed to be an unending amount of it!) and laying an entirely new foundation for cooperation, trust and intimacy.

This task was, and is, massive. Were it not for "one day at a time," the discouragement during difficult periods would have been more than we could have borne. And if our surrender to sex and love addiction had not been unconditional, we might well have seized upon a momentary ugliness in our trying (full of trials) relationship-of-reconciliation, and gone out looking for addictive options.

Yet we *did* persist, and here is why. We knew that our difficulties in cooperation, trust and intimacy were within *us*. Regardless of external provocations (which, with our former partners, came rather frequently), we knew that these were our own *personal* issues. We could not blame them solely on another. We knew that if we ran from an exhaustive, honest effort to fully explore reconciliation with these individuals, we would only re-encounter these identical problems down the road, with whoever our "new" partner would be. If we ran, we could change the cast, but we could not revise the script.

Therefore, unless we really *knew* that partnership with a former spouse or lover was out of reach, we stayed. If the time came when we really did know that reconciliation was impossible, our feelings of having "unfinished business" left us. We could leave without regret, and with quiet candor. Throughout, we needed to remember that *the success of any venture into reconciliation was to be found in our sober capacity to be emotionally and mentally present to the relationship on something like a consistent basis.* Our striving for evenness, amidst all the cross-currents, *was* success, *regardless* of whether the relationship survived or not.

When reconciliation moved beyond refining out the old ways, and began to open up into a growing, new relationship, we experienced a state of grace, a sense of finding something we had always been looking for in a place where we had least expected to discover it. To pave the way to this possibility, we want to mention some aspects of our difficulties, and how these started to be resolved in partnership.

Emotionally, the largest single factor which had to be worked through was distrust. The obvious distrust or apprehension a former spouse or partner had concerning our apparent sobriety in S.L.A.A. was resolved relatively easily. Our main problem was with residual feelings of distrust and resentment which had received such strong reinforcement in the past. These feelings would be re-stimulated, or triggered, by any current circumstance that even remotely resembled the past. An occasional broken commitment to be home for dinner, or a scuttled plan to spend time away together—the kinds of circumstances which are entirely matter-of-fact and normal in all partnerships—could send our partners cascading into difficult, old feelings. This would serve to polarize us around the trust issue, and we reacted defiantly sometimes, proclaiming that we didn't intend to live the rest of our lives in a state of suspended credibility.

Perhaps even more trying was the situation when our partners seemed quite "removed" or "distanced" from us. These moods, sometimes, seemed to have a life of their own. They often could not be neatly tied to any specific current situation. When we encountered them, especially at times when we had been making a particular effort to communicate (often carrying within an unacknowledged need to be *recognized* for the effort we were making), global warfare could break out. This kind of conflict, flaring as it could seemingly out of nowhere, was the most discouraging development of all. It threw us back into wondering if our premise for reconciliation might not have been completely amiss? Did too much damage remain from the past to ever be healed? We ached with these questions, but we did not run from them.

In the area of sexuality, similar difficulties unfolded. Many of us could remember all too clearly specific addictive relationships which had featured explosive sex as part of the package. These intrigues had offered us a level of sexual intensity which we thought was impossible to have in our reconciliation partnership. Yet we still hoped to have it! Perhaps we could break down the barriers which had characterized our past relationship, and which we assumed was due to our partner's reticence. We secretly hungered to rekindle in our current reconciliation the excitement and sense of abandon which had been such a prized feature of addiction, and which had contributed such a large part of what we had defined as "love." This hope of rekindling sexual intensity with our partner-of-reconciliation was certainly an understandable wish. However, no such simple formula for creating "love" *or* sexual satisfaction was possible.

As we renewed sexual contact with our partner, it was all too familiar: too much self-consciousness, no spontaneity, not much spark, and so on. But now we were *sober,* and felt we had a right to register our complaints! Also, our lives were open, and had been for some time. Thus we could not hide our feelings. God, was this painful! Our acknowledged sexual dissatisfaction with our partner would bring intense sadness and feelings of loss over the lost passion and adrenalin of our former addictive lives. Our reconciliation partner was bewildered and much angered. S/he felt exasperated and forlorn, too.

However, in the atmosphere of these difficult yet complete disclosures, we started to *hear* what our partner's perspective was on all this, and our ability to "hear" was greatly improved when we were not so busy declaring our own sexual demands and our "right" to have them. This is some of what we heard: Even in instances when our partner had not "known" of our extra-curricular activities during the active addiction, we had *never* really disguised our emotional unavailability. We may have thought that we had hidden our feelings, but these had been intuitively perceived by our partner. The result was that our partner had automatically started to "shut down," regardless of whether s/he was consciously aware of this. It was automatic. As the intuitive message ran contrary to our loud (or silent) protestations, denying that we had other interests, our partner felt compelled to have sex with us out of fear that if s/he didn't, we might stray again! Yet with the motive being, "If I don't come across, I'm going to lose him/her further," any possibility of spark or spontaneity in sex, on the part of our partner, had been pre-empted. Sex was, instead, a form of extortion.

Nor was this all. Our former partner often felt that s/he was being compared with every other lover or sexual partner we had ever had. Our partner felt during sex that we were rating a performance. And, in truth, this perception was often accurate.

What a chilling effect these conditions had on our former partner's spontaneity! Again, we were able to perceive all this. It bears repeating that this drama of sexual crippling was equally true in those relationships where our former spouse or partner had had *no factual* knowledge of what we were doing as sex and love addicts. For so many years we thought we had been "getting away with it," when all the time we had been crippling any possibility of emotional and sexual fullness with our partner, the person with whom we were supposedly most closely connected. It was vital that we really listen to our reconciliation partner's perspective on these things. Only through careful listening and complete openness about these matters could we gain further insight into what the consequences of our addiction had been, and what our tasks were now.

At the end of a long road of alternately trying to enforce our sexual demands on our reconciliation partner, or trying to refrain out of "virtue" from making any such demands (usually a case of double entry bookkeeping: refrain now equals specific sexual payoff later), we had to surrender again. This surrender was the deep admission that we did not have within us, at this point, a *knowledge* of what constituted a sane standard for sexual expression. Our partner had felt bludgeoned and undone by our incessant expectations of sex. Our partner had never felt able to be in touch with his/her *own* sexual currents. There had never been a time free enough of our own sexual expectations for our partner to come to experience him/herself as a sexual being in his/her own right. Our partner felt like a loser, and said so.

The necessary surrender was this: Beyond all proclamations we had made about our rights and entitlements concerning sex, we *also* felt like losers. We had to admit that our fear of feeling sexually deprived was sometimes rampant. Sexual deprivation was, for us, experienced as global rejection. When victims of this fear, there was no middle ground for us, and this fear permeated everything! We also knew that what we needed in a relationship with our partner was a relationship of trust and intimacy. Our fear of sexual deprivation was really a fear based on basic distrust of another's willingness to take our needs, both emotional and sexual, seriously. Yet the very "needs" we were expressing, we *ourselves* didn't trust because they were (we were) so addictively rooted.

As we shared our deep, private feelings of being losers in the arena of sex and sexuality, we discovered with our partner the common ground on which communication —sending *and* receiving—could take place: We each felt like a loser—we were *both* losers.

We had both admitted to this now. We were losers for different reasons, perhaps, but the feeling of being a loser was the same. The stridency of accusations and denials, of good intentions and frustrations, lifted, and we found ourselves experiencing the commonality of our plight. Without expectations and hurt feelings, we were just two people struggling for some closeness and renewal. We were green shoots reaching for the sunlight, sprouting in some old battlefield from under a heap of spent artillery casings. As we met each other on this plane of shared vulnerability, utterly devoid of pretense, a warm inner radiance began to appear. We could cry, or we could laugh, or both at once. The sense of tyranny was gone. It was as if, having met on the level of shared anguish, we were already basking in the warm afterglow of a wondrous physical merger. We felt human, perhaps supremely human. We could reach out with love; we could let ourselves be loved. In this wonderful healing climate no one was guilty or innocent; these concepts were just not applicable. *We were just two people.*

From the vantage point of our mutual experience as "losers," we were released from casting each other as "the enemy." As sex and love addicts, we could let go of the myth of our partner's sexual inadequacy. Our partners found that they were able to be less critical, to feel less put-upon by our sexual persistence, even as we were able to admit that our own expectations were often out of line.

A new era of exploration and understanding began. We had much to learn together. For example, if our partner's sexual rhythm happened to be four days, and our own was two or three days, we saw that this discrepancy was sufficient, *if unrecognized,* to create great conflict and misunderstanding. The partner with the four-day cycle would perceive demands made after two or three days as "excessive." However, for those of us who "recycled" in two or three days, the reticence of our partner could only be construed as withholding sex. But from the standpoint of shared vulnerability it was no longer a matter of "Who's right?" or "Whose 'rhythm' is more reasonable?" but, rather, "How, given the unavoidable nature of this conflict, can we negotiate around it constructively?"

Negotiations in this matter, and many others, were lengthy. The old programming of expectations, distrust, and fear of deprivation ran very, very deep. Progress was *slow.* In some ways our lives as sober sex and love addicts had been simpler before partnership, because having *no* sex had been easier to handle than working this issue out with another. However, we *were* in a partnership now, and we continued to experiment with ways of handling sexual expectations. For instance, we tried alternating who would initiate sex, or sometimes we tried to go without it. Occasionally we tried an arrangement in which the person who was being approached could say "No," but would be obligated to come up with a raincheck for the person initiating. We tried many variations along these lines.

As sex and love addicts, one bind we got into was this: since our own "recycling time" (admittedly, a very unscientific concept!) was usually the shorter of the two (hardly a surprise!), we tended to get depressed and vengeful if our partner said "No." We felt that our partner had the best of both worlds. S/he could say "No" to *us*, yet whenever s/he *wanted* sex, s/he *knew* that it would be available. This seeming inequity, on occasion, made us want to withhold sex ourselves, in the hope that we could reduce our partner to being a blob of expectant horniness—the condition we thought we encountered when we were denied. Or, if we "submitted" to our partner's initiating sex after we had earlier been turned down, we sometimes felt as though we were selling out by having sex under those conditions. Sometimes, as a punitive measure, we felt we had to "prove" to our partner that we could "do without," too, even if we wondered whether we would rupture on the inside as a result.

At any rate, these mixed-motive confusions, and many others like them, were not unusual. The sometimes fragile foundations for trust and intimacy could give way to the old power struggles in a moment. Yet through all of this, we were learning that alternatives to the way things had always been between our partners and us *did* exist. Even an occasional, wonderful experience of genuine warmth and lovingness was enough to keep us working on the sexual and emotional issues within our partnership. We knew that gold was there to be found, and shared, if we could keep on working together.

As our learning progressed, we found that the quality of our sexual relationship was greatly affected by other family matters. Our partner's attitude towards sexual expression would often relate directly to the quality of our willingness to be available for childcare or domestic tasks. Our sex life was not something unto itself. It was a barometer of our emotional availability and the quality of communication in the relationship. As we improved the quality and consistency with which we shared in every aspect of our domestic lives, our experiences in shared sexuality also improved. Our spouses, whom we had so disparagingly cast as sexual losers in the past, evolved before our eyes into fully participating sexual partners. This change, though slow, was very marked, and extended into the realm of touch and body awareness. Sex was freed up to become what it could be. As an expression of our deepening love, it was wonderful, often playful, and wonderfully fulfilling.

At the same time, we were depending less on sex to hold us together. The tyranny of expectation lessened. We discovered that our partner could enjoy sex as much as we did! *And we, ourselves, were experiencing it in a new way.* Rigid scheduling of "sexual times" began to give way to a growing trust in our partner's (and our own) sexual and emotional rhythms, and in our mutual commitment to work these issues out constructively. We began to trust that we were "O.K." and that our partnership system was healthy and self-correcting. We could stop counting orgasms.

Emotional needs that had been dealt with previously only by sexualizing them, were now dealt with outside of sex. Often we set aside regular times to be with each other, such as "going out for tea," or an occasional dinner out. We found that it was very important to schedule non-sexual time together on a regular basis.

Gradually, the realization came to us that the whole past orientation of our lives together, which had become so strained under the impact of active sex and love addiction, had been transformed. No longer helplessly living out the destructive patterns of the past, we had undergone a total change in our relationship. Through the deep destructiveness of active sex and love addiction, through the foreboding uncertainties of a difficult reconciliation, through a prolonged period of learning how to cope with a maze of conflicts and irresolutions, our partners and ourselves emerged onto a plane of true expansive living, in loving partnership with each other. Our wealth of common experience, our deepening knowledge and understanding of each other, began to fulfill that promise of unfolding love which is what we had always been truly seeking in a relationship. We were now capable of loving, and of being immensely loved, redeemed, and filled with grace, and we *knew* this. Our appreciation of this new-found wealth continues to grow, to this day.

New Partnerships

There were those of us who were ready to start developing partnership, but did not feel bound by a sense of "unfinished business" with a past partner or spouse. This readiness for the possibility of a new partnership was evident in an apparently contradictory absence of feeling any particular urgency to enter a new relationship. With the rigors of withdrawal behind us, we had made our peace with the prospect of living within the behavioral limits necessary for our lives to be sober. Even without knowing what partnership would hold, or even what partnership *is,* we did know quite a few things about the way we *had* to live if we were to be comfortable, and reliably sober. These things we could do to help insure our sobriety and peace of mind would, we knew, *have to* be maintained in any new relationship.

In fact, the degree to which we could maintain honesty and openness, and our ongoing commitment to S.L.A.A., and the extent to which all this could be shared with another, would be the barometer of whether or not there was a possibility of developing a partnership with that person. A prospective partner's inability to accept us as we were would confront us with a choice. Either we would have to tailor ourselves to meet our prospective partner's expectations, or we would have to recognize that the raw material for partnership was not to be found with this particular person. If the latter were the case, we would have to let the relationship go.

In truth, the option to "tailor ourselves" to meet the expectations of another was untenable. Too much of our lives during the addiction had been built on just such a strategy, in the absence of possessing any real sense of who we were as people. We could not now, nor could we ever, sustain a relationship in which we had to destroy an essential part of ourselves in order to render ourselves more desirable to the eyes of another. No thanks.

Our increasing ability to size up more clearly the potential for partnership in various relationships sometimes left us in a pretty discouraged frame of mind. On the one hand, we were now really so awake and aware, so in touch with reality. On the other hand, this very level of awareness seemed a mixed blessing. The number of relationship possibilities which we were choosing to *avoid* made us wonder if we had such impossibly high standards that we were unwittingly relegating ourselves to lives of isolation. We mused over the possibility that with less awareness we could have already blissfully blundered down the road to involvement a number of times. When we were feeling lonely, we remembered only too well the excitement which the opening rounds of even impossible relationships could hold. Yet, for better or worse, our consciousness of the need to be sober was not to be scuttled by melancholic yearnings. And in fact, sooner or later, we *were* ready.

And other people were "ready" for us, also. Sometimes we found someone with whom a bond of friendship began to develop into something more. Perhaps a relatively recent acquaintance or "friend of a friend" came forth in our lives with whom a deeper exploration of interpersonal values could begin. No more need be said about the onset of such opportunities. Presumably the anonymous hand of a higher Power has an influence. In any event, when we were ready, things seemed to happen appropriately. And if we weren't, no amount of manipulation could contrive a fulfilling possibility.

In contrast to those of us who were faced with reconciliation projects, those of us who were starting anew felt that we were starting, relatively speaking, with a clean slate. Insofar as our current lives were not being directly affected by people from our addictive past, this was quite true. Yet this condition of being relatively unencumbered by the left-over repercussions of our active sex and love addiction meant that any new sexual or romantic situation could carry a lot of novelty along with it. We had to be careful not to get carried away with this. Beyond the unavoidable and exciting "newness" in any beginning relationship, especially those carrying the possibility of physical and emotional intimacy, we could not build a partnership on novelty.

This problem of novelty was closely related to another experience many of us had been through in the addiction period, specifically, the cultivation of an heroic self-image which we had assumed in relationships. For instance, if we had achieved any level of success or recognition in the world outside due to talent, we had often thought such accomplishments deserved continuous notice and praise from our partners. This was equally true in those instances where we felt we had been short-changed in worldly recognition, and expected those closest to us to make up the difference.

In fact, we really demanded this kind of homage because we secretly felt that without our heroic "currency" we would be unworthy of being loved. What we had cultivated was not a partnership. We had tried, literally, to cultivate these people, to make them members of our own *cult*. This all meant that in hiding behind the "press releases" the world had sometimes accorded us (or *should* have, according to our way of thinking), in trying to foist these upon the people nearest to us, we had barricaded ourselves away from genuine belongingness with these people. Our cries for recognition, for observance of our "stature" within the walls of our own house, were futile bleatings in a self-constructed mausoleum of loneliness and isolation.

How could we be "unheroic"? Would a prospective partner be attracted to us if we were to withdraw the basis for demanding homage? What we began to realize is that we had no real choice about this. To maintain ourselves as "heroic" or "exceptional" in a new partnership was to try to "command" love by remote control. Neither the "command" nor the "remote control" would work. The former killed spontaneity; the latter made openness and closeness in the relationship impossible. Collectively, they stood as two strikes against true partnership.

It was also clear that if our new partners were indeed persons in their own right, they could not let us get away with placing them in servitude as "on tap" worshippers. Whatever novelty we held for our partners in the beginning, it had to wear thin, and then wear off. For those who were getting more involved with us, our ability to take a suddenly sick cat to the vet's, or pick up a bag of groceries on the way home, or come through with some real childcare help, was worth a lot more than a professional reputation, or romantic dinners by candle-light in extravagant restaurants, or magnanimous gifts or gestures.

And we, ourselves, had to face the *real* self-image we had underneath our heroic visage, which was *not* one of heroic stature. Instead, we often felt essentially unlovable, incapable of loving, and un-love-worthy. We had found that our partners, on many occasions, seemed to appreciate us for traits we had which were beneath our contempt to acknowledge. In truth, we did not really know the "Why?" or the "For what?" of our being loved. It just had to be the surface gloss! After all, were *we* not also so taken with, and taken in by, our own heroic self-image?

Yet our partner's basis for loving us was *not* this. For us to gain a sense of inner love-worthiness and lovingness beneath the "promotional headlines"— the hype—was *very* difficult. Side by side with opening ourselves to another's "knowing" us ran the risk of being rejected, a deeply rooted and terrifying fear for *all* of us. We found sharing our vulnerability about being truly "known" by another the most difficult task of all. And the necessity for full disclosure never seemed to end! Temporary relapses into old patterns of demand, hurt, and accusation could occur. Mercifully, these emotional binges, or "dry drunks," were usually shortened by continued contact with S.L.A.A.

Sometimes the move into a deeper experience of shared vulnerability, trust and intimacy was accompanied by tears, a deep inner quaking, and sorrow. Yet even within the deepness of our old sorrow, we found that as we were met and received by our partners on this level, our fragility and terror could change into warmth and an abiding sense of belonging. We were loved as the frail beings we were. We *felt* our own love-worthiness as we experienced the courage to risk being known. We became even eager to jettison playing to heroic or exceptional standards. We *wanted* to release these shackles, and to be released from them. They were part of an armor which had constricted us. We now yearned for the capacity to know another as someone *real*, to be known for our innermost heart. We were soft and vulnerable, yet no longer stunted. We were human; we were growing. Our sense of Grace deepened.

In entering into sexual relations with our prospective partner after what was sometimes a lengthy absence from any sexual contact, we were really facing the unknown. The task was different than for those of us who were reconciling. Here we were not facing our past investment in casting a former partner as sexually inadequate, or in some other preconceived model. We were, instead, once again confronted with our own sexual attitudes. Not infrequently, during withdrawal, we had speculated about what renewal of sexual contact might be like. Our fantasies, naturally enough, had run the gamut from scenes of titillation and eager abandon, to detachment and cool indifference. Presented now with the reality of renewed sexual contact, many of us found ourselves strangely reticent. We discovered that we now had a lot invested in *not* getting carried away with these things!

Our early experiences in renewed sexual activity were very strange, indeed. If we found ourselves overly caught up in pursuit of sexual bliss, we reacted dubiously to the way we had conducted ourselves. This led us to share our reservations about our behavior with our friends in S.L.A.A., and perhaps more importantly, with our partner. If we were reticent (more often the case) due to fear of selling ourselves down the river should we become sexually enthralled, we needed to share this, too. Perhaps the common thread here is that *however* we experienced our initial sexual contact with our prospective partner, whether this contact was one of heightened sexual ecstasy or lowered, detached participation, *we were all bound to experience reactions of doubt and foreboding over the quality of our involvement.* We felt bound to hold ourselves to an unusually high standard of purity of motive in getting sexually involved. Yet we needed to know that motives are seldom "pure" in the sense of being unmixed. The most important aspect of all this was to keep our lives open by sharing as forthrightly as we could whatever reservations we had. This was so regardless of whether we felt we had abandoned ourselves once again to extracting a sexual return, or that sex had lost its spark and spontaneity and might never again regain these qualities.

By monitoring the quality of motive behind our sexual participation, and by revealing our feelings about this to another, we were starting to become responsible as sexual partners, whether we knew it or not. Our shared fears, doubts and insecurities all led to a deepening commitment. Sexual concerns, once they were articulated and shared, became emotional concerns to be worked through with our partner. The impossibility of maintaining a sexual oasis in the midst of an emotional desert was clearly confirmed.

Nor, we discovered, could we engage in sexual contact under false pretenses. Not only did we need to share, ex post facto, our reactions to the quality of our participation in sexual relations, we also had to be aware, *before* the fact, of whatever neediness we were carrying around which could be shunted into seeking a sexual escape. For instance, if our frustration level was up due to difficult circumstances in our work or our relationships with other people, these situations needed to be flagged. Flagging them meant disclosure of them and our frustration about them to our partner. We found that without trying to do this, true mutuality in sexual matters was not to be found. Without mutuality each person could only be "into it" for unacknowledged, private reasons. The other person would thereby be cast as a "function," the purpose of which was to supply relief. A residue of this kind of relief was a growing sense of loneliness and isolation.

We are *not* saying that disclosing to our partners the anxieties and frustrations stemming from non-sexual areas would thereby resolve those problems, or that all external difficulties had to be resolved before having sex. We are saying that we needed *always* to find a basis of mutuality, of sharing and respect, which could form a channel for authentic expression between *us,* and that this needed to be accomplished *prior* to love-making. "Love-making" could only be "love-showing."

If we were so distraught with external problems that an emotional channel could not be established as a basis for sexual intimacy, then we refrained from sex under these circumstances. Despite an occasional sharp pang of old deprivation, the net effect of abstaining in circumstances like this was *positive*. We had not tried to ditch our problems by screwing them away! We had affirmed, through correct action, our own dignity and intimacy with our own being. We experienced this as an inner tide of warmth, a resurgence of self-love. In possession of our dignity, we could be sure that future grounds for healthy sexual intimacy would come about.

Now it might well seem that the checks and balances provided by openness in our partnership (whether new or reconciliatory) and the almost wholesale emphasis on self-scrutiny and motive-monitoring would only serve to kill off genuine spontaneity and sexual excitement. Indeed, in the beginning these highly prized attributes tended to be forced to one side. Yet the cumulative effect of this continued questioning of our sexual myths and motivations was that a climate of trust and emotional intimacy began to evolve.

As this happened, our experiences in sex and sexuality began to undergo a profound change. The rightness of our beings began to nurture a deeper and more fulfilling sexual experience. Even as we relinquished our once unacknowledged, more inwardly held and entrenched expectations, a grand interplay of sexual and emotional themes emerged in our partnership. New experiences in intensity and sexual pleasure indeed became possible for us. This development finally put to rest the old belief that sexual satisfaction could only be found in the "highs" of novelty, intrigue, pursuit, and conquest. This discovery was all the more wonderful because we were no longer relying solely on sexual intensity to glue our relationship together. Sex was more fulfilling than we had ever previously experienced, even as it was no longer the source of tyranny which had constricted so many of us. In and of itself, it could not make a partnership "successful." Rather, it was a significant footnote to an already successful relationship in which openness, sharing, honesty, trust, and commitment were all indispensable, interrelated parts.

*   *   *

For those of us in S.L.A.A. who have approached partnership building, either as a reconciliation project or as a venture with someone new, what we are forced to admit, in conclusion, is that our experiences are still quite limited. Much of what we have tried to describe has involved the undoing of old patterns and attitudes. We have attested to having lived through this. We have also shared something of how we came to learn more and more ways of coping with an ongoing array of challenges and difficulties. Yet this chapter on partnership building, by necessity, must be left incomplete.

Those of us who have persisted along the partnership road can only add that we have emerged from the coping period onto a new plane of human experience which we had never previously known. This experience is, we suspect, the experience of authentic living, and loving. It is definitely beyond coping. The grounds on which we experience our relationship as "good" are not to be described simply as inverse functions of our former addictive lives. We feel that something new, indeed, is present. To describe these qualities in more detail is not possible, because they are difficult to comprehend and could easily be misconstrued. The descriptive capacities of language seem inadequate to the task.

The truth is, we feel we are "on to" something big. We don't know where it will lead us. We just don't know what the upper limits of healthy human functioning are. In any event, our hunch is that we are but newcomers to this larger experience of living, this wider arena of life. If all we are capable of doing here is to convey to you our sense of hope, and our conviction that a new life of fulfillment, richness and mystery surely awaits you as you move into sobriety, then we are meeting our task.

May each of you, as you embark on this adventure, discover your share of the golden braid: that unfolding wonder of which we are all a part. We are with you. We are all joint travelers on destiny's path, and we all have much to learn from each other.

Personal Stories of Addiction
and Recovery

Release Unto Hope

"What do you think?" he asked.

"I think I've been looking for an answer all my life," I answered, "And now I'm afraid I've found it." R. had just finished telling me his story of sex and love addiction, and I had seen myself in everything he said. But I left with a feeling of total rebelliousness. I *could not* face still another addiction! I was sober in A.A. for nearly four years, in Overeaters Anonymous for longer than that, with two years of abstinence. It wasn't fair. God was asking too much of me. I couldn't do it. I *wouldn't* do it!

But the door to honesty that had been opened could not be shut again. I could not remember the details of R.'s story—did not want to remember—but neither could I change the knowledge inside that what HE was, *I* was. My driving, lonely need for the arms of my lovers, the craving for more and more sex, this was a true addiction, and this awareness was now fully conscious.

I spent the next two weeks in steadily increasing pain. I wanted to drink. I wanted to die. I wanted ANYTHING except needing to start over at Step One with a new addiction. But I was already firmly into that step, aware of my powerlessness over the craving, unable to stop, my life totally out of control because of it. All that was needed was for me to open the door a bit wider with willingness, and a Power greater than myself would make possible that which I could not do alone.

Surrender did not come easily for me, but it didn't come easily for my addiction to food and alcohol, either. I had used food to fill loneliness and to comfort myself since I was thirteen. By the time I could get alcohol four years later, I was already full of self-hate and a belief that the world was to blame for being too unloving and hostile for me to deal with. I would diet and dream of being thin, as if thinness would suddenly make me witty, and confident, and beautiful. Yet I would binge, even while I dreamed of being thin ("just one more, and then I'll stop"), feeding the problem, even while the food eased the pain I felt.

Almost the first time I had a chance to drink, I got drunk, stayed out all night, slept with several men . . . and loved it. It somehow seemed as if that person who was suddenly the center of attention, who could get anyone into bed, was the REAL me. I knew I never really fit in that nice family with athletic brothers and parents who did not drink or "fool around," who went to church suppers and on family vacations. Here in the dim bars, surrounded by booze and men—THAT was where I belonged.

As I look back from sobriety, it seems to me my family was normal and loving. Why, then, did I feel so unloved and strangely out of place? Maybe there is no single answer; perhaps I was possibly an unfortunate combination of genes. But there was no question that I WAS different from my brothers. It was simply a fact, obvious from early adolescence, that I could not face any problem or pain in life without a drug of some kind, and I could not be happy without something to MAKE me that way. In spite of a family life that seemed very normal, the patterns were there that became interwoven with my addiction.

One pattern was a kind of underground defiance about doing "the right thing." No one in my family seemed to "sin." They didn't smoke or drink, they all went to church, no one ever swore, and my father never even raised his voice. Inside I came to feel incredible guilt over every little violation of morality, and I grew to hate the "churchy goody-goodies" I pretended to be like. Of course, the difference between my feelings and what seemed to be acceptable was so great that I learned to deny my feelings, and look for excuses so that I would not have to label myself a "bad person." I swore only because of what *you* said, I drank because of what *you* did, I slept with a hundred men because of what *they* did not give me.

I became so accustomed to denying my feelings and blaming my behavior on others that I truly did not know what anger or fear felt like, and I felt helpless to change my life. Normal sexual feelings were also unacceptable, since no one ever mentioned sex except in the context of immorality. There was very little expression of sexuality or sexual interest in my family, so even normal feelings seemed terrible to me. Since I could not even mention sex, much less deal with it, I quickly became obsessed with it. Before I was old enough to go to school, I already had elaborate masturbation fantasies, finding in the pleasure I gave myself a release for all the feelings I could not label, and did not know how to express. Later, in my early teens, I spent hours in fantasy and masturbation, the only means I had to express my feelings. That pattern of withdrawal from human contact and solitary concentration on sexual release, masturbating to climax several times a night, became a growing part of my active addiction.

Another pattern in my life came from the models of love available to me. From my mother I got a warm maternalism, and from my father an intellectual, achievement-oriented approval. Somehow I could not seem to integrate these two qualities, and so I came to separate the intellectual from the sexual-emotional. All my life I either seduced people with my intellect, or seduced them with my body. I never seemed to know what real emotional intimacy was. While I was too honest to steal, I was so emotionally dishonest I could not admit even to myself what I really felt. No wonder the pain I felt from needs that never seemed to be met. And the patterns of behavior that only added to my guilt and shame without filling those needs translated into a desperate search for relief. I found my magic pill, self-medication for loneliness and need, in food—and later in alcohol and drugs. When I got too fat, I would switch to alcohol. When I got too drunk, I would turn to food. And underneath it all was the secret, double life I led in the sexual arena.

Before I was twenty years old, I had slept with more than a hundred men, suffered from VD, had three suicide attempts, been sent to a psychiatrist by the police and my parents, and had a baby whom I gave up for adoption. It was time for my first marital cure.

Unfortunately my restless need for sexual release was already too great, and too many other feelings and problems were finding their outlet in sexual desire. My husband and I had sex every day, but it was never enough. I could not be happy or satisfied, and masturbated sometimes several times a day, attempting to relieve myself of the depression I felt. I drank more, and took lovers. The depression lifted, as the excitement and deception and intrigue took over my life. It was a rollercoaster of fear and lust, but the thrill of secret adventure and new lovers was somehow satisfying, and I did not want to stop. Sometimes I would become ashamed after some degrading episode like having sex with someone in the corner of a dark restaurant, and I would resolve to change. Then I'd let my weight balloon, as if to make myself ugly and undesirable. Then, driven by need, I would get thin and begin the cycle of seduction again. I would seduce friends, husbands of friends, the young college students my husband advised, anyone . . . .

Inevitably I was divorced, and just as inevitably the seduction cycle continued, only now more openly. Again filled with shame, I tried to find respectability by marrying it. I chose someone I met at a bar, and used the marriage as my excuse to be drunk (because he treated me so badly), to be fat (since he didn't love me anyway), and to get sex elsewhere (since I couldn't get it at home).

All three addictive patterns progressed and worsened. I would drink to relax so that I would not eat. When I ate, I would vomit up the food so I would not get fat. I tried to stay thin so I could get more men and more sex, and reassure myself that I would not have to be alone. I suffered from blackouts and deep depressions. I had suicide attempts and violent hangovers. I got fat and sick. I got VD. When I was in a pattern of overeating, I would get into dependent, masochistic relationships. When I was dieting and thin, I got very sexy and ran from bar to bar, and bed to bed, inhibitions released by the booze, drinking to forget, then waking with still more to regret.

Yet in those years of insane progression of my addiction, I managed to work as a professional in education, a "surrogate of middle-class morality"! No wonder I drank to forget, for oblivion.

Always, just at the fringes of awareness, was the troubling sense that something was wrong, that my sexual obsession was not just because of my bad marriage, or the liberal times in which I lived. I left behind me a trail of broken and abandoned friendships. I moved. And moved again. And again. I stopped trying to make friends since I was always "new in the area," or about to leave. And no one knew me well enough to realize that the self-imposed isolation hid a great emptiness and inability to love—or even to care. I played my role with skill—Great Seducer! Woman Who Needs No One! And I never let anyone get close enough to see what a sham I was.

By this time I could control my compulsion only with the help of rules (never seduce friends, or people you work with, or students), but my rules were being broken with greater frequency, and I was getting frightened. I resolved to stop masturbating, sensing that the hours I spent in bed with pornographic books were a kind of sickness. But I broke the resolution within hours. I began carrying a gun and thinking of suicide, an end to all pain.

It is another story how I got to Overeaters Anonymous and then Alcoholics Anonymous. It is enough to say that I got sober only when it seemed that the only other alternative was the gun. The withdrawal was terrible, because not only was I off food and alcohol, but staying out of the bars kept me from the sexual contacts that were filling *that* compulsion. I had a psychotic break and landed in the mental hospital. With surrender a simple necessity, I found three A.A. sponsors, went to meetings every night, and began recovery. I got sober, but I could not be alone. I found a sexual partner within three weeks of getting out of the hospital. My pain eased, and I managed to stay sober.

Like anyone else who gets sober in A.A. while holding on to another addiction, my progress was slow, and I did not get the release from pain that others seemed to get. In my first inventory I managed to rationalize that my sexual adventuring was caused by the drinking, and thus did not need any examination. So I continued in it, not in bars, but at A.A. meetings. There were many available men in A.A., and I availed myself of them. Again I tried the marital cure. Again I could not stay faithful. Again I could not live with the guilt and deception. Again I was divorced and back on the restless hunt for contentment, moving every few weeks, changing jobs, friends, and lovers. Again I made rules . . . and broke them.

Filled with self-disgust, I decided I MUST settle down. Considering my length of sobriety, my behavior was so bizarre (multiple lovers, affairs with married men, "thirteenth stepping" new men in A.A.) that I could not rationalize it any longer. I chose one lover, but he soon wanted to end the relationship. By then I had truly committed myself to not going back to my old promiscuous ways, and had gotten completely hooked on this new lover. I went into withdrawal.

It was while I was in that terrible forced withdrawal, wanting to drink, wanting to buy a gun and kill myself, that I met R. at a meeting of A.A. That "chance" encounter probably saved my life. Much as I did not want to hear about the hopelessness of my addiction, I now had only two alternatives: to die—or to try. Panicked and desperate, I still wanted to escape. Yet time was running out. I surrendered, for one day, one moment. And *that* was the beginning.

It was not easy, but it did turn out to be simple. The withdrawal from masturbation was very hard. Jogging worked better than cold showers, especially if I sang the Twelve Steps as I ran. I began a new moral inventory (my sixth!) with no rationalizing or excuses. After a couple of masturbation slips, I overcame my agonizing self-consciousness and read my inventory to a priest, every word of it. It was all in this one. All the pain was there, and the way I used that pain as an excuse. My betrayal of friends was there, and the self-pity and loneliness, along with the painful knowledge of how I had created these conditions. My rage against God, my fear of honesty, the rebellion over this new way I had to go, the self-centeredness that had ruled my life—I inventoried them all, and more. I lived through the next Steps, wrote goodbyes to former lovers, made amends to those I had hurt, as best I could.

And so the greatest adventure of all began. To my surprise the pain of my entire life seemed to lift; I felt like I had just been born. As I came to explore a new world of relationships in which I had some sense of dignity and the capacity for caring and commitment, I learned that old addictive patterns could slip back into my life in subtle ways. I learned the importance of contact with others who had the same addiction, and of the absolute necessity of rigorous *current* honesty.

Too much has happened in my sober life to share it all here. I feel that I have experienced so much—and only a little. Many of the lessons have been humbling, and I have not always lived through the pain of living and dealing with life's problems with either courage or acceptance. But I have lived through them sexually sober. I've learned to live in partnership with God, to practice humility in the Fellowship of S.L.A.A., to embrace dignity of self and the value of wholeness and honesty in human relationships. I have learned to love solitude, and to value companionship. I have learned to be watchful for the subtle addictive patterns that I can slip into so easily. I have come to feel part of the Fellowship, part of humanity, part of the world, part of God.

What is my experience? I had a life sentence to a hopeless search. I did not know why I should go on living such a painful life. An S.L.A.A. member brought me the message—and I was released into hope. I'm still there, one day at a time.

There's Everything To
Look Forward To

The day I admitted that I was a sex and love addict was the first day of a new life for me. I did not know it at the time. I was too vulnerable and frightened to understand that the trip out to an S.L.A.A. meeting in Newton, Massachusetts, was a beginning. It started a process that would irreversibly change the way I viewed my place in the world, the way I looked at relationships, and the way I felt about myself.

My road to that fateful October night was not unlike others who have told their stories at S.L.A.A. meetings in and around the Boston area. Our addiction is the same; only our individual baggage and circumstances are uniquely ours. My story started after World War II in Germany. My pending arrival was the catalyst for my parents' marriage. And in subtle ways, I was reminded of that fact for years to come. I don't think my parents would have married if my mother hadn't been pregnant. It was a forced marriage. My mother was a Catholic, my father Protestant. The marriage caused a stir in their small town. It became a source of friction between the in-laws. It was not a marriage made in heaven.

Looking back today with the help of therapy, I have come to realize that I was a physically and emotionally abused child. Much of what I remember of my early childhood revolves around memories of my parents fighting. The fights were frequent, and often my mother used me as a foil against my father. If there was love there, I rarely saw it.

I have vague memories of being a happy child outside the home, of being very happy with my grandmother, of being an open and hyperactive child. When I was four, my father left us for America, to find a job and save enough money to send for us. Everyone told me that I would see him again soon. It was more than a year before my mother and I travelled to America and were reunited with him.

While he was away, my mother fought with her in-laws, with whom we lived. So the house was filled with tension. I remember spending a lot of time out of doors with fantasy friends. From the beginning, I was different. Both sets of grandparents remarked on that. But it was my father's mother who saw into me and was a source of kindness for me for many years to come.

In America, life was no different. My parents fought a lot. My mother was unhappy about being there, away from her family. My father resented being married to a nag. Many times he came home to pick fights with my mother and me. He was always distant in my childhood and adolescence. He was an angry man who took out his frustrations and disappointments on his family.

Whatever I did, it was wrong. The way I spoke, the way I ate, my marks in school, the way I played, or who I played with. Encouragement was rarely offered; criticism came quickly.

Shortly after I came to America, I developed a severe stutter that did not go away until thirty years later. Often, my parents punished me because I stuttered. They wouldn't let me eat until I stopped. They constantly harped on me to improve. Yet, the more attention paid to my stuttering, the worse it got. Not surprisingly, I hated coming home. But I hated school also.

I went to a Catholic grammar school in New York City. Everyone there made fun of me because I stuttered, because I was German, and because I was different. There were few days when I was not bullied or beaten. The teachers joined in the fun by laughing when it was my turn to read a passage, or remained passive when kids were making fun of me in the schoolyard. My only defense was to laugh with my tormentors, to become a clown, and to develop a shield over my hurt that no one could penetrate.

When I was twelve, we moved from a Manhattan apartment to a house in Queens. We were becoming a successful middle class family. By now, we had grown to five, with a six year old and a six month old brother. The move brought no change to my family. The fights, the beatings from my father, and the alienation continued. The only change was in school. I had decided I was tired of getting beat up. So I beat up the schoolyard bully on the second day in my new school. It was not in my nature to be violent. But that little act kept the kids from bothering me from that point on.

Sexually, I was always an inquisitive person. I played the normal games with my peers. But from an early age, I sensed I was different. I would always go out of my way to take my clothes off or get into situations where I could see other boys naked. I remember purposefully leaving specific school books at home so I could sit together with boys in my class. And while sitting together we would feel each other up. Looking back, I could see that I was obsessed at an early age with male genitals.

Part of my curiosity was natural—what every young boy goes through as he drifts into puberty. But there was an intensity to my curiosity that was not normal.

I never liked being home. After we moved to Queens, I became a paperboy and spent a lot of time delivering papers. The paper route was a good cover for the time I spent with friends my own age "fooling around." And I could never get enough of it. Eventually, I got a reputation, and was either shunned or sought out, depending on the person's inclination.

High school didn't change me. I was accepted with a scholarship to a prestigious Catholic high school in Brooklyn. For the next four years, I commuted ninety minutes each way to school. Often, I would meet people on the subway or fool around with fellow students after work. I joined the track team because I wanted to see the other athletes naked.

It was about this time that I realized I was gay. It was not a discovery that I could reveal to my parents. Since even saying hello sometimes caused an angry reaction, I was sure that they would disown me or beat me silly if they found out.

Up to this time I was fairly religious. I went to church often. I was an altarboy. I made frequent novenas. Now, I turned against God. I was angry. How could he make me a stuttering sissy! I thought my life was ruined. I remember staying home one day after a fight with my parents and trying to commit suicide. I felt alone. I had no one to reach out to. My father always hit me. My mother always put me down. And my God had abandoned me.

Despite all the aspirin, I awoke again to face what I thought was hell. Little did I know that hell was yet to break loose. My relationship with my parents deteriorated. I could do nothing right. At fourteen, I ran away from home after spending two months planning my escape. One day in June, I took the subway to school with my father as I always did. Yet, this day was different. There was no school. And in my little gym bag, I had a new pair of jeans, underwear and socks, two shirts, and my coin collection. And $400. I got off at my usual stop, saw my train leave with my father, and took the next train to the bus terminal.

I ran away because I couldn't take my home life any more. I had become tired of the abuse. And I wanted to meet a man who would be nice to me and take care of me.

I had gotten a taste of "being taken care of." One of the pivotal points in the growth of my sexual addiction had happened the previous year. I went alone to see a movie in one of those old cavernous movie houses built in the 1920's. While I was sitting watching the movie, a well dressed older man sat down next to me. Before long he had his hand on my leg, then my groin. I remember clearly today, over twenty-five years later, that I was excited by his touch and by his attention.

He placed my hand on his crotch. From that moment on, I was hooked. I did not realize it then, but that afternoon was the first step in a quarter century of anonymous sexual episodes. Up to that point, most of the important people in my life abused me or were just not there when I needed them. My parents, my teachers, priests, friends, relatives, or my God.

Yet, here was a person who *liked me*—who was willing to accept me without conditions. I quickly realized that I had *something* that other people wanted. And what they wanted made me feel good.

When I ran away, I dreamed of meeting someone who would take care of me, love me, and make me feel good. I never did meet that person, even though

I spent nearly three weeks away, traveling to New Mexico, Colorado, Missouri, and Nebraska. I sometimes wonder what my life would have been like if I had met *my man* during that time.

I ended up in Boys Town in Nebraska. The priest asked me to reveal my real name and where I was from. He assured me that I could stay there. He just wanted to let my parents know where I was. As with other priests in my life, he was not entirely truthful. The next day my mother was there to take me home. And all the way home on the plane, she let me know how much money I had made her waste on the trip.

After that, I shored up my defenses and kept my distance from people. And I began the hunt for sexual gratification. I had some friends with whom I *fooled around*. But one by one, they became enamored with girls. And I realized they were no fun anyway. Like an alcoholic, I could sense a drink a mile away. I became astute at finding bathrooms in shopping centers, theaters, and bus stations where I could find what I wanted. I knew how to look at older men on the street to transmit my sexual availability. I had this wonderful sixth sense. Or so I thought.

Until I was seventeen, I never had sex in a bed. I remember working in a department store and cruising someone who returned the attention. I was a senior in high school and he was a freshman at a local college. We made a date for the next weekend and he brought me to his dorm. We took all our clothes off and got into his bed. I was totally freaked out. I thought that two people laying next to each other in bed was perverted. Up to that point I had never slept with anyone. All my sexual activity had been furtive, in strange places or dangerous situations.

Even though my parents wanted me to go to a local college while living at home, I knew I needed to escape from them. Against my parents' wishes and after turning down a scholarship to a local Catholic college, I enrolled at a state university noted for its liberalism. I remember the day my parents dropped me off. They were disappointed and angry. Yet, I felt such a surge of elation and happiness over finally being on my own.

I may have broken away from my parents, but I was now able to feed my addiction with a vengeance. Soon after arriving on campus, I discovered where the *hot* spots were on campus. I spent much of my time meeting other men in the bathrooms or cruisy areas on campus. And I was able to travel into Manhattan often to meet other gay men. In 1964, these were heady times for me. I was finally coming out and finding other men who were just like me.

Although this was still pre-Stonewall, Manhattan had plenty of bars and outlets for a young, horny gay man. And I took advantage of nearly every one of them. I connected with a lot of men during this time, but only on a sexual level. I never really got to know the person behind the genitals. I look back on my years of cruising and acting out, and I realize that I never gave myself the opportunity to connect with anyone on a non-sexual basis. That makes me sad.

I did make friends at school. I hung around with a crowd that was friendly and collegiate. On one level I wanted to be accepted as *normal*. However, I kept the two lives separate. My frequent forays into the "City" were made under the pretense of seeing friends. I never acknowledged anyone I had met in a men's room on campus if I was with my "straight" friends. Looking back, I'm amazed that I was able to pull this double life off without losing my sanity.

The summer after my freshman year, I worked at the Post Office in Queens at night. Every day before work I'd stop at the bus station men's room for a look around. One evening I met someone, went into one of the stalls with him, and within minutes was under arrest by vice police who were watching behind a wall. In that one moment, I felt totally devastated. I thought my life was over. I was now a criminal. At nineteen, I was caught with a man with my pants down. And no one in my family knew that I was gay. Not the best way to come out to your parents.

I was able to delay the inevitable for several months. The day of my arrest my parents and brothers had left on a two-week vacation. I couldn't see calling them for help. (I had stopped asking for help years ago.) I would "spoil their well deserved" vacation. So I called the father of a friend. I told him I had gotten into a fight and he came to bail me out. I found my own lawyer, went to court alone twice. On my third appearance, the judge asked my lawyer where my parents were. He responded that they were not aware of my arrest. Because I was underage at the time, the judge instructed me to have them with me at my next appearance.

I almost fainted. I couldn't talk to my parents about the simplest of life's problems. How could I tell them I was gay? I gave my parents' phone number to a court official and asked him to be the bearer of the bad news. All the way back to school on the train, I realized that when I walked into my dorm room the phone would ring and they would know. There was no way out.

The phone did ring, and my parents were not pleased. We arranged to meet that Saturday in the Bronx where I was running in a cross country track meet. I remember seeing my mother on an overcast November day with sunglasses covering her red eyes. There was more shock than anger; more disappointment than compassion; more why's, when's, and how's, than understanding.

At my next and final court appearance, my father was at my side in support. The judge gave me a suspended sentence and said I didn't belong in court and that he didn't want to see me there again. I knew that I didn't belong there, but I was yet to learn that I didn't belong in men's rooms, in the bushes, and in the other hunting grounds of anonymous sex either. That realization was still twenty years away.

The rest of my college years was much the same. I never did go back to that bus station john. But my arrest didn't keep me out of others. I just became a little more cautious, a little more *streetwise*. During my college years, I spent three summers traveling around Europe. The first time, at nineteen, I spent almost the entire three months traveling from country to country from one bed to another. I never connected with the person behind the genitals.

At college, I was well known. Editor of the school newspaper, resident assistant in the dorms, on the cross-country team. As a cover for my being gay, I had a girlfriend. At that point, I felt I needed all the trappings of the straight world to be accepted. Eventually, my girlfriend and I had sex, and she became pregnant. Like little adults, we discussed our options. I was willing to do whatever she wanted, including getting married. We decided upon an abortion—a difficult choice for both of us.

When I look back, I realize we almost put ourselves in the same position as my parents. The marriage would have been a disaster. I would have been guilty about being in the closet and angry with my girlfriend because I had to get married. I would have repeated the same mistake that my parents made and I would have been just as angry. Through the grace of God we were steered to the right decision.

My sexual acting out continued at graduate school in Ohio. But my acting out became much more compulsive. I spent hours going from men's room to men's room on campus, seeking brief encounters with men. And occasionally I would bring someone home. I found my life taking on a pronounced split. By day, I was a graduate student/teacher, respectable, intelligent, and urbane. By night, I was a driven sex addict. I hung out in the bathrooms; I drank at the bars. I couldn't get enough. How I managed to have an active "straight" social life and an even more active cruising life without having a breakdown—mental or physical—is a miracle.

Part of my graduate program required spending six months studying in Europe. I think that was the main reason I accepted the scholarship at the school. Before long I was in Europe again. And in Berlin. Having become a connoisseur of sexual acting out, I picked a city to study in that was notorious for its sexual and political openness. In Berlin, I discovered a new arena for sexual escapades—the big, beautiful outdoors. Soon I was traveling to the forest almost every other night to have sex with shadows next to trees. My studies suffered and so did I.

This was now the age of gay liberation. I felt I had a right to express my sexual desires. They were just as valid as any straight person's. I used my sexual orientation and the liberation of the times as excuses to act out. And when I got VD, I proudly accepted that as a badge of battle.

During my college years, I had occasional, short-term relationships with other men. They never lasted more than a few months though. And they usually ended because I got bored, or because the other person discovered my promiscuity, or because a relationship was getting too intimate for comfort.

Eventually, I finished my degree, came back to the U.S., and settled in New York City. I could think of no better place to live. (I hadn't discovered San Francisco yet.) I could satisfy my addiction on almost every corner. I found a job as a journalist on a good publication and soon went about establishing myself. I was twenty-four, gay, living in Mecca, discovering the bars and bathhouses. Often, I spent a long lunch hour at the baths, at the YMCA, or at various and notorious men's rooms in Midtown looking for action.

Action I may have gotten. But my self respect, esteem, and self worth suffered. I never felt people would like me—for me. I had gotten used to people liking me for my sexual prowess. And I had long ago become an addict to the sexual hunt, to men's genitals, and to using acting out as a way to "pleasure over"/plaster over my feelings. I had a perverted sense of values.

During this period in New York, I did meet a man. I fell in love with him. We established a household together. While he was the first man who loved me for my looks, for my smile, for my ability to love and enjoy life, his love came with too many conditions. He was jealous and possessive—traits that I had a difficult time handling. It wasn't too long before I was back in the bathrooms, back to my addiction. We fought a lot, which I hated because it reminded me of my parents. After nearly three years, I walked out of the relationship.

I moved into Manhattan, into my own apartment. And I tried to forget him with a continual parade of men I would pick up on the streets, in Central Park, or in the bars. My cruising took on dangerous overtones as I spent more and more of my time at night in unsafe areas. I was not happy. I wanted a relationship. Yet, I did not know how to have one or how to let someone get close to me. My acting out papered over the pain.

I was offered a job in Boston and took it. I was ready for a change. Even though I thought I could never leave New York, I figured a change in geography would lead to a change in my life. How wrong I was. The bars had different names and the people had a different accent. But that was the only difference. I moved into an apartment on Beacon Hill, just steps away from a prime cruising area. Nearly every night before I went to bed I would go out to the river, no matter what the weather was, for a midnight snack. Without my fix, I would toss and turn and have a hard time going to sleep.

After two years in Boston, I met my second lover. This time it was love at first sight for me. We dated. I swore off anonymous sex. We had a courtship. We moved in together. But when the honeymoon wore off, I was back in the Combat Zone (a seedy district in Boston) during my lunch hour acting out. My old patterns resurfaced. Whenever there was conflict, I ran for a fix. I would go to the Zone to make me feel good when I was depressed or to make me feel bad when my ego was inflated. I always found some excuse to go.

This relationship lasted five years. He became the critical deprecating parent and I became the unfaithful one. We had many arguments, yet I stayed and hoped for the best. In this relationship I was very much a love addict, taking whatever abuse was dished out and coming back for more in the name of love. It was not a relationship made in heaven for either of us. This time he took the walk.

Within weeks of our split-up, I was amazed at how happy and relieved I felt. I didn't go around depressed or pouting for months like after my first relationship. I did continue my acting out, however.

Three years ago I met my present lover. Although my addiction continued, I was able to confine it largely to other cities when I went on business trips. I was like the faithful husband at home. But once I got onto that plane, I couldn't wait to act out on my addiction. Many times I carried it to extremes, traveling great distances to get to a particular bar in another city or staying up nearly till dawn until I was finally satiated or exhausted from the hunt. How I was able to put in a full day's work after my marathon acting out sessions still amazes me.

During this time, the AIDS epidemic began to make headlines in the media. Although I was concerned, it did not stop me from continuing my sexual binges. My sexual practices were getting more bizarre and, in light of AIDS, unhealthy. Despite the epidemic, I was unable to stop. During this time I was in therapy and my therapist mentioned S.L.A.A. to me. He had given me the 40 questions pamphlet. I answered the questions and didn't like the frequency of my positive responses. I threw it away and chose to ignore the obvious.

On a trip to New Orleans in September, 1984 I vowed to stop acting out. For health reasons, I had come to realize it was not safe. But despite my firm resolve, I spent the week in some of my most outrageous acting out episodes. I was not in control of myself. I was addicted. I was not able to help myself, despite the risk to my health and my life. I felt scared. I was depressed. On the plane back, I knew that I needed help.

I told my therapist about my experiences and my inability to maintain my resolve. He again mentioned S.L.A.A. and gave me the number of a member whom I called that night. He told me about the meetings in the Boston area. I went to my first S.L.A.A. meeting a week later.

The last eight months of my life in S.L.A.A. have not been easy. It took me two months before I stopped acting out. I said a lot of goodbyes to slippery places. I experienced withdrawal. I was angry about coming to meetings. I spent much time comparing rather than identifying.

But then I began to get in touch with my emotions and feelings. Listening to others share their experiences brought up many feelings and memories. I could no longer avoid them through acting out. Now I was experiencing my emotions—the good and the bad. I found a tremendous amount of support in the Fellowship, from people who were going through the same pain and from those who had gone through the same feelings. I found a sponsor. I began to work the program. The first time I qualified was a cleansing experience for me. It helped me to understand that I was not alone. There were people who identified with my story and with my pain.

I now know that there are others out there who are making their imperfect way through life as I am. I have nothing to be ashamed of. I have everything to look forward to. I have one day at a time. I have myself. I have the opportunity to get to know people as I have never known them before and to enjoy the rewards of sobriety. I thank my higher Power every day for that opportunity.

I Couldn't Fool Myself
Any Longer

I was raised an only child in a small town in New Jersey. We were quite isolated from the community at large, associating primarily with relatives and a few other members of the small Jewish community in our town. Most of the friends that I chose were vetoed by my parents—either because they were not Jewish or because my friends' parents were not held in high esteem in the Jewish community. I was told that I would go to college and study business so that I would be a success and "make them proud." My parents, especially my mother, tended to be very overprotective of me, and feelings were not dealt with at all. If I was unhappy, my mother told me that she "loves me and if I am unhappy then she is unhappy," leaving me with a feeling of guilt for any negative feelings. If I showed anger, I was told by my mother that *she* "never got angry at her parents when they were alive, and if I didn't treat her better, I would feel guilt after she was gone." In spite of this general manipulation of my feelings, they occasionally erupted in violent screaming and yelling, followed by profuse apologies and kissing and making up. No painful issues were ever discussed.

Sex, of course, was denied entirely for years. My questions were put off or I was lied to. When I was about ten years old and finally old enough to hear about it from my friends, I summoned the courage to discuss it with my parents. My father sat there silently, as his attitude had always been that "your mother expresses things so much better than I do" and he let her do all of the talking. She explained in a few sentences the basic biological act of sex and then said: "If you are not married by the time you are twenty-five or thirty, then maybe you might want to go to a prostitute where you pay for sex—but they have disease and I would want to spray her for germs before I let you near her." That was my introduction to the topic of sex. Further questions brought only the simple answer that "we already discussed this, there is nothing more to say."

When I learned to masturbate on my own, it was something that I really thought I had discovered for the first time in the annals of human existence! I really had *no* idea what it was. So I asked my parents, who then ran to the family doctor in horror. The doctor told them to have me confess to them each time I masturbated. Each time I confessed, my mother would run screaming to my father: "He did it again, he did it again, what am I going to do, oh my god, oh my god!" After a month of this, the doctor decided that maybe if they would let me alone it would go away, and they no longer required me to report to them.

When I began to date, I was told that I was only allowed to date Jewish girls because they were "less experienced and don't require as much physical and sexual stuff as other girls." As a result, I dated girls who were so up-tight that they wouldn't even kiss for several dates, even if their parents weren't watching so carefully. Although certainly the times were different in the 1950's than they are now, I believe that my experiences were even more restricting and frustrating than those of most other kids. Even necking was not acceptable behavior for a "good Jewish boy." Once when my car had a battery problem, the mechanic asked if I did a lot of parking with girls with the motor off and the radio running. My mother took offense at this and chewed him out for daring to suggest that her son would do such a thing. I was eighteen at the time.

It was clear that anything to do with sex had to be hidden from my parents. In fact, they worried about me so much that almost everything that was fun, exciting, or different had to be hidden from them. This set a pattern which would be with me for years: fun and sex had to be hidden from my home—sex belonged to my private world—period.

I was about twenty-one years old before I had sex, with the girl who would become my first wife. We were engaged, so it was "O.K."—but of course we would never discuss it with anyone because we knew that it was really not O.K. Although I had not waited for sex until I was married, I had waited until I was engaged. I felt that I had made it "home free" (so to speak) and it was O.K. at last. All of the pent-up frustration was behind me.

With my sexual feelings no longer held back, I suddenly realized that I was attracted to *other* women also. I had one affair before I was married, but felt too guilty to break off the engagement, even though I wanted to. So I got married and decided to be a good husband and not have affairs. This lasted about one year. My marriage was not going well, primarily due to the fact that both of us were in school being supported by her parents, and because of a serious illness from which my wife was still recovering. Neither of us understood anything about how to deal with feelings; both of us had come from families where feelings were not dealt with openly.

My next affair was a real love affair. When I think back about it I realize that it was probably one of the most substantial relationships I have ever had. The affair came at a time that was obviously very stressful for me. I had finished my advanced degree program, I had my first professional job, and my wife was pregnant. Life was moving along, but our marriage had not really improved. My wife refused to go with me to a marriage counselor so I went to a psychiatrist myself. The psychiatrist did not seem to understand my situation at all—never helping me to get in touch with my feelings, or even to recognize how I had failed to deal with feelings all of my life. He pronounced me "well," but I was as confused and frustrated as ever. Now I was living the first of a long series of extra-marital affairs, and I was learning how to do it. I had a split life. My life at home with my wife was similar to the life that I had led as a child with my parents—full of quiet desperation and frustration. I hid my rage except for occasional blow-ups, and we pretended that nothing was wrong, even though we were both coming apart at the seams. Whatever fun and fulfilment I was getting, came from my affair.

I learned to hide my tracks very well, just changing the truth slightly. The project that I did during the afternoon was explained to my wife as a project that had to be done on Saturday. For every business trip that I really went on, I told her about another one that didn't exist. Every lecture I attended during the day became an evening symposium. I had real experiences to relate—I could talk about the meetings because they had really occurred—only they had occurred at different times. Most important, I learned to completely insulate one part of my life from another.

I realized that I was in love with the other woman, and this caused me, at first, a great deal of pain and frustration. But soon I learned to handle that better. I didn't have the courage to leave my wife, and I didn't have the courage to cut off the affair and deal with my marriage honestly. My feelings were compartmentalized and so was my life. I began to enjoy the ability to lead two lives—it was fun and exciting to balance it all, and I orchestrated my time like a new hobby. I always had several different projects or jobs or careers going at once, and this kind of juggling became very natural to me. Extending it now to my love life was fun. I would occasionally have fantasies about leaving both lover and wife and going off to start over, and sometimes I would have acute anxiety attacks, but most of the time I would congratulate myself on being so efficient as to keep it all running as smoothly as I did.

When we moved, I decided that I would have to cut off the affair. We had a new baby, I had a new job, and it was time to make a real attempt to make the marriage work. I didn't know if it would work or not, but I felt that I had to try. I would occasionally see my old girl friend, or have a one night stand now and then, but, more than I had in the past, I put my energy into the marriage. However, I started to notice that something was wrong. I became aware that every affair that I had had occurred just after I moved or accepted a new job. I realized that when I was insecure I looked for an affair to give me courage or calmness. I also realized that I was always involved in some kind of romantic game. There was always a friend, or a wife of a friend, or a colleague, or a secretary, or someone for whom I was on the make. I had an affair or a major flirtation going at almost all times. It had become a major part of my lifestyle— it was the spice of my life. It was my drug. Then I discovered other drugs.

During the late 60's and early 70's I worked as a volunteer counselor for a drop-in clinic. The experiences there were good for me in many ways, for the work and the people whom I hung out with all helped to bring me closer to my feelings. However, they also brought me closer to drugs. I was soon dealing grass and using it at incredible rates. This was a perfect "smoke screen" for my growing sex addiction as the dealing brought me in contact with many available women, and the constant use of grass helped me to hide from the feelings that were beginning to emerge through the counseling work. Dealing gave me an excuse to be out at all hours of the night. It was the perfect cover for my sex activities. This new pattern also contributed to a full split in my life. On one side, I had a home and family and a professional job. On the other side, I was constantly on the make, servicing two or three women at a time, and dealing and consuming large quantities of drugs. As an alternative to my old up-tight lifestyle of quiet desperation and frustration, it felt just fine. But I knew that I was out of control. I didn't have the words for it, but I knew that my sexual activities were becoming more than simply cheating on my wife. I was filling every available moment with sex and spending a lot of time developing relationships, with sex as the sole purpose. If one of my sex partners asked why I hadn't seen her, I would make up excuses about being busy at work. The real truth was that I hadn't even thought of her since I left her. The next time I would think of her would be when I had an evening to fill or when she called me. I would kid myself that all of these women were "relationships," yet if they didn't have sex with me, I would seldom see them, except to *try* to have sex with them. In retrospect, it is amazing how replaceable and interchangeable they all were— although at the time I really thought that we were close and shared our feelings.

Some relationships were with women who were clearly emotionally disturbed. A number of these women, I realize now, were sex and love addicts themselves, and we fed each other's addiction. Looking through old address books, I am amazed at the number of women's names I have listed. And more amazing is that I forgot most of them almost immediately. Yet these names, as I look at them, still call to mind the quality of sex we had or the amount of time I devoted to getting to know them for the purpose of sex; *that* was the category under which they were filed in my mind. I was not conscious of lying to them or manipulating them. I always *felt* as though I was honest and open. I began to realize, however, that I was saying the same thing to each of them. Although I was being "honest," I was developing my "rap." I had always been horrified at the thought that people develop a "line" or a "rap" to use with the opposite sex. These things came into consciousness at times, but I avoided dealing with them. At times I would try to count the women that I had slept with, but usually I lost count or couldn't remember their names, even if I remembered the events. I was running full speed, but I had very few meaningful or growthful relationships.

My first marriage fell apart. We both realized that we were not happy together. I still don't know to what extent my sex addiction caused the breakup of the marriage. I think that we were really unsuited to each other, and I believe that I stayed with the marriage longer than I should have because it became part of my presentation of myself. As a person with a bad marriage, I was protected from real involvement with others, and of course, the affairs prevented real involvement with my marriage. I was still isolated from people, but on the surface it looked like I had a lot relationships going.

Within a year I was remarried. This marriage has been generally good, and I love my wife very much, but the sex addiction was still there. For a while I abstained. I hadn't expected to continue with my old habits as I attributed that to a phase of my life that was now over: a bad marriage, and my involvement with drug dealing. However, within a few years I was back at it. The addiction was no different, although now it was harder to make excuses. I was simply trying once again to get as much sex as I could from anybody that I could. I couldn't imagine saying no if asked to have sex; I couldn't even imagine saying no to the opportunity to pursue the possibility of sex! When I had my first affair during the second marriage, I felt like someone who had lost his virginity—now that it had happened I might just as well enjoy it as much as I could.

It had never been my style to pick up women at bars or on the street so I had to make sure that I was in contact with a lot of people to assure that the opportunity would come up. I lived a frantic life with two jobs and many activities. I had women whom I would see on business trips: I was like a sailor who had a girl in every port, often planning my trips to see my girl friends. None of these relationships were serious love affairs—I loved my wife and didn't fall in love with any of these other women. I also generally didn't have sex very casually—they were all "friends with whom I expressed my relationship by means of sex." Sometimes women would confront me—they didn't mind that I was married, but they didn't like my seeing other women also. Some would fall in love with me. As I was getting older, more of these women were older and some of them were married themselves. I realized that I didn't like seeing married women because they were deceiving themselves and were not comfortable with the affair. Then I realized that I saw in them my *own* style—deceiving oneself—living for the moment without really thinking through what was wanted out of the relationship. I felt used—I was the drug for someone else's addiction, a pawn in *their* melodrama. I didn't like that. And I especially didn't like becoming aware of my own game.

I was introduced to Al-Anon programs because my wife and friends were in the program. I decided to go into the program also in order to stop my use of drugs. This caused me no trouble, but I knew that the program seemed too easy—I was not digging very deep into my feelings. I saw people who were really coming to terms with themselves in the program, but I wasn't. I wasn't using drugs any more, but nothing else was happening at a deeper level. I knew that the bottom line for me was sex.

Months before, I had heard that there was a fellowship which dealt with sex obsessions. That was not something I really wanted to deal with yet, but I knew that if I were ever to write a Fourth Step inventory, or really become honest in my dealings with people, I would have to let go of my sex obsession. But I wasn't ready to do it yet. I jumped back into the addiction full force for a while. I worked on developing affairs when I knew from the beginning that each relationship would be destructive for both of us. I was denying my addiction and denying the consequences of my actions. Once again I had a number of women with whom I could have sex. I realized that I felt the way I had felt years before when I was seeing many women and dealing drugs. It was a frantic life: keeping my sex addiction alive was like working another job! I had to make a certain amount of phone calls, spend a certain amount of time, money, and dinner dates in order to keep the relationships going. It was too much! I was tired—it wasn't worth it anymore. I cared about my marriage, and yet I truly couldn't imagine a life without the extra sex. Even more important than the sex was the thrill of the chase, the excitement of seeing whom I would be with the next weekend on a business trip, the thrill of making it all fit together without getting caught. But it was beginning to wear thin again, and I realized that I was once again counting how many women I had had, how many in the last month, etc. It was like taking inventory for a business! There was just getting to be too much extra baggage to carry. My marriage would not survive another year of this. I was getting to see myself too well in Al-Anon to kid myself that this could continue.

My wife had known of some of my affairs, but had only guessed at the extent of the problem. I denied anything that she didn't already know and swore that my extra-marital sex life was over each time I was caught. It was now or never—I could stop now or go on another round of sex addiction. I was in a real bind. The old line, "my difficult home life," didn't have the power it used to have—because I knew that my wife was working on her recovery in her Twelve-Step program. I was not able to kid myself anymore. It was time to give up the addiction that had been my first addiction and now was my last addiction. For me it meant also admitting that I wouldn't have a double life anymore—my life at home and at work would be my whole life. I wouldn't have any game going or any part of my life that was hidden from the people with whom I lived.

One night, after an argument with my wife, I called my sponsor in Al-Anon. My wife had just told me that I didn't know what honesty was, that I was not capable of honesty. I denied that, of course, as I denied most evidence of my addiction. But even though I denied it to her, I knew that I was not an honest person. I didn't generally lie; I was not a bad person, but if anyone had any idea of my sex addiction, I would deny it all. If it ever became known, I would be humiliated. I was not honest. I had a double life that was continuing into the present moment and, when confronted with it, I denied it. I had bottomed out on dishonesty. I was exhausted. I wanted to stop. I still couldn't imagine a life without my sex addiction, but I was burned out and ready to try a different sort of life. My sponsor suggested the meeting of Sex and Love Addicts Anonymous.

I went to my first meeting and immediately felt at home. This was it. Here was the program for my addiction. This is where I had to surrender, turn my will over, and let the program into my heart as I had never really done before.

It has only been about nine months since I have been sober in the S.L.A.A. program. Most of the time it is wonderful to be free of the compulsion to have sex. The opportunity to tell my story in meetings has made it possible for me to remember the various incidents and see them in perspective. The problem was not even the number of people that I had had sex with. The real problem was the fact that it was an addiction for me, and as such I had to stop the compulsive pattern that was making my life unmanageable. I had used sex to hide from anxiety, to fill time so that I wouldn't have to be alone, to avoid real commitment in relationships, and to keep my life moving at a hectic pace so that I could avoid dealing with my feelings and growing as a person. Since I have become sober in S.L.A.A. I have felt more contentment than I remember ever experiencing in my life. I am "off duty"—I don't have to keep the hectic life going anymore. I can focus my energy on my work and my family. I feel whole and centered for the first time.

It is not always easy. Most of the women that I have seen or could still be involved with are not compelling to me any more. They can be friends without any of the sexual part of our relationship, or we can simply drift apart. There are times, however, when I meet someone new and I realize that it could easily start all over again. But now I can see beyond today and beyond the first time that I might sleep with a woman. I can see the entire progression— the melodrama of finding time to meet, the discussion of why I am having an affair if I am married, the guilt over cheating and dishonesty, the eventual end of the relationship. Since I can see the entire progression now, I don't have to go on the trip any more.

There are some women to whom I have to explain my new life. Most old girl friends are understanding—many knew all along that I was a sex addict! Some are addicts themselves and could not understand my new feelings. Now, however, I can make amends as needed and not have to lie to anyone. I am not out of the woods yet, however. Sometimes I hear of other people having a slip in sobriety in S.L.A.A. or in other Twelve-Step programs, and I am tempted to note that as a justification for when and if I have a slip. I don't trust myself yet, but I notice that the compulsion is leaving me. I have more faith that my life will change because of the loss of the compulsion, than simply because of my will to remain sober.

The tools of the program have been essential to my recovery. My relationship to my higher Power was at first very much symbolized by the group. Even though I believe in and pray to a higher Power the most important part of the program for me is still the fact that I have made a commitment to the group. To ignore that commitment would require that I admit to them, and thus to myself, that I have been unwilling to work the program. My criterion for my actions used to be, "What can I get away with?" That is changing: now the criterion for my actions is, "What can I do that is going to help me in my spiritual recovery and in the maintenance of my serenity?"

When I am tempted to have sex with someone other than my wife, I look at the person carefully and say to myself, "Is this person and my relationship with her worth the loss of my recovery? Is it enough to warrant going back to what I once was?" The answer is easy—and the desire simply leaves me. I realize how much of attraction is based on compulsion. With the compulsion gone, I find that I am much more attracted to my wife, for in my marriage the love is what causes the sexual attraction. I used to *start* with the sexual attraction, and then try to find the thrill, but the thrill was really in the chase. The program helped me to see that the chase was making me crazy. Without an active sex addiction, I am also becoming more aware of my love addiction. I am often dependent and demanding toward my wife. The need for "strokes"—sexual or emotional—still drives me. But that addiction is also beginning to lift as I continue to work the program.

It was very difficult for me at first to admit that I had a problem and even more difficult to go to my first meeting. In going I realized that I would eventually have to do the Sixth Step and be "entirely ready to have God remove all these defects of character." Clearly, my sex addiction was a defect in character, but it was one that I could hide for years and I had done so. For me, coming to my first S.L.A.A. meeting was surrender. I had hit bottom, and I was going to recover. The path would lead to asking God to remove the defect in character that had caused my compulsive sexual behavior. So once I had begun there was no turning back—I couldn't fool myself any more.

Somehow I just never seem to get around to calling up the women that I occasionally fantasize about. Somehow I seem to keep going back to meetings, even when I say earlier in the day that I am too tired or too busy. Somehow, one day at a time, I am living the program—and no one could be more surprised than I am! It is starting to feel natural. It is becoming less of a struggle. And it is good to know that my friends in the program will be there for me as I continue to work on my emotional, physical and spiritual recovery in S.L.A.A.

. . . And in the Meantime, I Get to Have My Life

I've stopped trying to look back into my childhood to find reasons why I'm a sex and love addict. I keep drawing blanks. In fact, the more I look for reasons, the more I deflect myself from the essential task of determining my own addictive pattern and then abstaining from it. But I'll mention my childhood because I think it gives an important backdrop to the scenes in which I later found myself.

I was born the youngest of four children in an upper-middle class family during the post-World War II baby boom. My father was a scientist, my mother a college-educated housewife. No one drank, took prescription or non-prescription drugs, beat anyone, or sexually molested anyone in my family. We went on family picnics on Sundays and family camping trips in the summers. We were instilled with humanitarian values but were given virulent anti-religious messages. We were one of those families that seemed to "work."

But because I was the youngest, I always felt left out, like I didn't belong. To compensate, I put tremendous stock in my friendships with the other little girls in the neighborhood. I remember endless happy hours spent with my best girl friend playing eight-year-olds' games.

When I was nine years old, my father was transferred to Europe for a two-year stay. We rented our house and were packed off to a country where we knew no one, not even the language. Though I mastered the language within six months, the social customs of the country were very formal. To play with someone after school, one's parents had to exchange written invitations two weeks in advance. Needless to say, it wasn't at all like dropping by a friend's house to see if she could play.

I was terribly lonely during those two years, but because I knew we would be returning to our old neighborhood eventually I would comfort myself by dreaming about my reunion with my best friend. It was then that I discovered "relationship fantasies." They were a powerful anaesthetizer.

When we finally did return to the States, my anticipation about meeting my best friend again was almost unbearable. What I hadn't considered was that during my absence she would take another best friend from among the other neighborhood girls and would scarcely remember me! When I was met with a distant welcome from her, I was devastated. I was thrust into a depression that would not lift for another four years.

I mention this experience in detail because it not only describes my first love-addicted relationship, it encapsulates the essential need behind my addictive pattern: the need to feel that I belong; my need to feel special, my need to feel loved.

After three abysmal years in junior high school, I "reawakened" to another "best friendship" with another girl during tenth grade. We would spend hours on the phone talking about war and social injustice and our relationship. We prided ourselves that we didn't waste our time discussing such trivialities as clothes and boys. Once again I had specialness in my life. This girl was very beautiful and in fact was considered one of the more desirable girls on campus. But she didn't date; she spent all of her free time with me. This was bliss! Eventually she did fall for a boy and changed to suit his needs. I watched in agony and disbelief as she faded away from me.

I talked with my mother about my pain, and she—a life-adventurer from the start—responded with, "Life's joys are worth the pain." And so began a cycle of intensely joyous, intensely painful friendships with other girls. Love and pain were now inextricably linked. I accepted it as a fact of life. The songs on the radio bore me out.

I didn't date in high school. My emotional energy was bound up with my best friend(s), and boys seemed awkward creatures in those days. My main use for a boyfriend would have been to increase my acceptability among the girls; I was already having nagging doubts, barely audible, about my own sexual orientation.

When I graduated from high school, I tried a geographic cure. With a string of broken female friendships behind me, I decided what I needed was: (1) to get as far away from my past life as possible, and (2) to focus on boys instead of girls. (I believe this is something like an alcoholic deciding to switch drinks in an effort to control the intoxicating effects.) I went to a prestigious college 3,000 miles from home where I would be sure to find a boyfriend/husband who came from my class and cultural background. Needless to say, it didn't work out that way. I got to college in withdrawal from another friendship, discovered I had no skills or even natural instinct in attracting men, and so in my pain and loneliness I turned once again to women for emotional sustenance. Within four months, I was once again someone's best friend. Only this time we were all budding into sexual maturity and I realized in horror one day that I wanted to make love to my friend. Actually, she realized it in horror. I couldn't see any reason why we shouldn't give sexual expression to those intensely loving feelings. But if she thought it was horrible, well, O.K., it was horrible. Just so long as she still loved me. To make myself more acceptable to her, I went into therapy to "become straight." I didn't realize until years later the almost comical contradiction in that proposition. Anyway, in the course of therapy it became clear that I was gay, and so I had a reason that explained all those broken friendships: I was in love with them! The solution, I thought then, was to find women like myself. But where? I still had three years of college to complete where no one ever breathed the word "homosexual" outside of Abnormal Psychology class.

Those three years "in the closet" were hard and lonely times for me. Sexual and romantic fantasies played a major role. I did manage to have a few sexual escapades with both sexes during that time, mostly to prove to myself that I could get *someone* into bed; I had always believed myself to be singularly undesirable sexually. To compensate, I would make myself emotionally indispensable to one woman or another around me.

It would be yet another two years, after college graduation and coming out into a gay community, before I would get into a sexual relationship lasting longer than six weeks. During this period I had a few two and three-night encounters with other gay women "to get experience" while I pined hopelessly (still) after some other unrequited love (always a heterosexual woman).

My first "real" relationship with another lesbian came when I was 23. She was a sex educator, and believe me, I got an education! We had very little in common; I knew even then that I didn't particularly like her. I remember saying to my friends, "I can't get out of this relationship. She's too good in bed." This woman introduced me to the incredible adventure that lovemaking can become and I loved the hours spent in sexual bliss. But I also remember having that silent despair: this was the "wrong" woman for me and I was going to have to wait for Fate to free me. I could not free myself.

"Fate" freed me by giving me another woman. She and I truly believed we were the match of the century—after only thirty-six hours of knowing each other! This woman lived in another part of the country and at the end of the weekend we'd spent together, she promised me she would move to my city to live with me. She would do this in four months time when she graduated from school.

The next four months were living hell. I was in almost constant withdrawal and *had* to phone her every other night for two-hour conversations (my phone bills were astronomical!), in addition to exchanging letters and visiting with her monthly (I paid). I counted the days to when this woman would come and save my life; release me from the horrendous ache and loneliness inside. She never did. Two weeks before she was scheduled to arrive, she called to tell me she'd fallen in love with someone else. The next day my doctor told me I had a bleeding ulcer. Shortly thereafter I was fired from my job.

Again I was thrust into a depression, desperately hoping some woman would find me. I felt so unworthy that I never believed I could initiate anything with anyone. I knew I was good in bed (thanks to the sex-educator lover) but felt incredibly incompetent in all the lead-up-to preliminaries. At age twenty-five, with some twenty-five sexualized contacts behind me and having been in love (addictively) for sixteen years with some fifteen people, my life still felt characterized mainly by loneliness and periods of involuntary celibacy.

My first long-term relationship lasted a year and a half. There is little to be said about this, and yet so much. The woman was caring, but terribly controlling. I gave over my power to her, and yet I also learned to stand up for myself in that relationship. She taught me about feelings (mine were all repressed), about communication skills, about introspection and about spirituality. I was an eager student, but we had different sexual appetites and regularly fought over the frequency of sex. I always wanted more; I could never get enough. Eventually I did begin adventuring and she left at the first sign I showed of being interested in someone else. In my pain and rage I took on two other women as sexual partners, believing it my due after all those years. But all I wanted, really, was to be loved, and these women were simply feeble shields against the loneliness.

The relationship that brought me into the S.L.A.A. program looked like it was going to be "it." We were careful to become good friends before becoming sexual with each other; we had a strong spiritual link, and lots in common. Over the years I grew to love her very deeply. But we had tremendous power inequities. It was here that I learned I could "buy" a lover through money and rescuing. She was a newly sober alcoholic who needed both from me, and I so desperately craved being loved and needed that we exchanged these commodities for one another. We almost never had sex. I was in a lot of pain over this, but refrained from saying anything because I remembered those brutal fights I'd had over sex with my previous lover. Solitary masturbation, sometimes compulsive, played a large role in this relationship. Again I was hooked into a love relationship with no sexual satisfaction. And again I hoped for Fate to save me. My prayers were that my lover would sexually awaken one day; instead she left me abruptly.

By that time I'd been in Al-Anon for over a year and I dragged myself into a meeting looking like death warmed over. An acquaintance asked me how I was and I told her that my lover had left me and that I felt like I was in physical withdrawal. She told me about S.L.A.A. and I began attending meetings immediately.

I was very resistant to S.L.A.A. in the beginning. In Al-Anon I had struggled to integrate the Twelve Steps with my own radical Feminism, a difficult struggle but one made with the help and support of other lesbians in an all-lesbian Al-Anon group. In S.L.A.A. I was at that time the only lesbian, perhaps the only gay, and one of very few women. Over the previous six years of my life I'd had very little contact with men, and suddenly I found myself talking with them about my most vulnerable and most potentially explosive points. I felt these men to be anti-gay, anti-love, anti-sex, anti-fun. I would run to my lesbian support group and discuss my reservations about the program, but still kept coming to S.L.A.A. meetings, listening, listening.

Much of what these men talked about I initially mistook for blatant (hetero)sexism. "Of course *men* would sexually objectify women or try to make them into their mothers," I told myself. "But I'm a political, conscious lesbian. *I* don't do those things." Only I *did*, and in much the same manner as the men did.

While in the program for six weeks and out of the last relationship for eight weeks, I was still not convinced I was a sex and love addict. I went out for what I hope will be the last time. I met an incredibly attractive, fun-loving, warm, sexy, intelligent woman. We had an affair and I felt myself falling, falling too quickly and too deeply after only two weeks together. I wanted only to be with this woman. I wanted not to deal with the pain of my previous lover's abandonment, not to put energy into rebuilding my own life or into building a relationship with a higher Power, all of which were goals I had held for myself. It was during this exciting, ecstatic two-week affair that I realized I was powerless, truly powerless over the sex and love that this woman was offering me. Though I was emotionally bankrupt from my previous relationship, I was willing, and was beginning to give over anything in order to stay in that bliss. But my higher Power had other plans.

One early morning I awoke in a terror so black that the night sky couldn't compete. I tried to tell myself to just lie still, to wait until the woman lying next to me awoke. We would make love then and everything would be O.K. But my eight weeks in S.L.A.A. had sunk in, and I knew that love-making could *never* be more than the most temporary of antidotes for this level of terror. Something was very, very wrong. Right then I surrendered to my higher Power. I told the woman I would have to stop seeing her, and went into withdrawal for the second time in eight weeks. I wasn't sure I could survive it, but I *was* sure I couldn't survive another addictive relationship. If S.L.A.A. offered me nothing else, it offered me hope that I wouldn't drown in that black terror. And I was willing to chance it, even though this withdrawal was the worst yet. I swear there were days when I was literally writhing on the floor, believing that I would somehow die if I didn't call my most recent lover/addictive object.

That day was exactly six months ago today as I type this. I am still in early sobriety, still have terrific fits of despair and loneliness. But the difference between this despair and loneliness and those same feelings I had during my active addiction is that today I have hope alongside those feelings. Today I have hope that I can have a life as full and free as I've always wanted.

I finally have a way to explain why and how I have had such unsatisfactory relationships. Because I'm an addict, I have looked to lovers and sexual partners to fill a void in me that cannot be filled by another person. The void was in part a spiritual void: I only knew how to experience love in a sexual context, and since my hunger was for a spiritual kind of love, sexual and romantic love was never quite enough. But the void was also a void of self: unless I had a lover, I didn't know who I was. I didn't know how to structure my time, how to plan for the future, how to infuse meaning into my life. I always saw myself primarily as someone's lover (or unrequited lover); I didn't know who else to be. I grew to need relationships, real or imaginary, as much as I needed the air I breathed; for without identity and meaning, in effect, I had no life.

But not today. Today I have a program and supportive and caring people, men and women, who have helped me to see that I can be whole without a lover. Today, with the help of S.L.A.A., I can create a life born of my own needs by discovering my own Self. I have a sense of direction today, a sense of internal meaning. I have energy for my relationship with my higher Power (always a struggle for me, coming from such an anti-spiritual home); I have energy for my friendships, for my family relationships (sorely in need of repair), for my hobbies, for my work.

Today I *choose* not to be in a sexual relationship. I no longer have to wait for a woman to come along and claim me and then wait for Fate to release me from a relationship I did not choose and could not leave. Today I have the dignity of choice, and I no longer have to flail around in the darkness. With my higher Power's guidance I will know when to get sexually involved and with whom. I know that as long as I'm in this program I stand as good a chance as anyone to have a satisfying love relationship. And in the meantime, I get to have my life. Today I have a sense of personal power and freedom I would never have imagined possible.

But the core of my sobriety, my true freedom, comes from feeling myself connected to the loving power of the Universe. I no longer have to use sexualized love to fill my great spiritual void. Today, feeling myself to be a child of the Universe, I *know* I'm loved; I *know* I'm special; I *know* I belong. And that's what I've wanted all along.

Thank You, God, for What You've Given Me

I grew up in the 1940's and 50's, in a home that appeared to conform to the typical middle-class, Midwestern stereotype. Dad commuted each day to Chicago from our tidy suburb and Mom stayed home to raise me and my younger brother. School, church, and Boy Scouts filled most of the time.

Dad was distant and remained uninvolved while Mom moved in to fill all the empty spaces. I never saw much closeness between them, and not much closeness existed between either of them and others. Dad, in particular, was self-contained. Mom, though, kept busy with community work like PTA and the Women's Church Auxiliary.

Until I was seven or eight, I would help Mom with her afternoon baths, rubbing her dry with deep-pile towels and spreading talc over her body. We shared less obviously sexual intimacies as well—mind-melding to replace Dad as confidant and to assure that my every thought and deed met with her rather vague and always endless list of expectations.

During my pre-teen years, I found little to interest me in others boys' play. My pleasures were in less manly pursuits than sports. I read a lot and enjoyed writing stories and poems. When shared, these solitary activities were most appreciated by girls my age. With Mom as a guide, I learned to be sensitive, particularly to doing things that made her happy and proud.

At eleven or twelve, I began to be confused by changes in my body. At home, Dad either paid no notice or just teased me about my squeaky voice; Mom left a "How to Tell Your Son about Sex" pamphlet on my bed one night and the next morning suggested I talk with our doctor if I had any questions. At school, required gym classes and locker room showers exposed me to much curiosity from other boys my age who were a bit behind me in growing up. We all were fascinated by "how big/how hard it is." For the first time, among boys my age, I was the center of interest and a recognized leader in our sexual explorations and experimentation.

The day I first masturbated was a hot August afternoon just before I entered sixth grade. I'd just come home from camp where an older fellow had explained things to me. With the first climax came guilt and never-again resolve. Later again that afternoon, then again that night—twice—followed by an uttered, prayerful hope that, if I did this often enough, "it" would wear out quickly. For thirty-three years, once, twice, thrice and more daily masturbations continued.

In junior high and high school, I dated mightily—with each date carefully examined by Mom to assure fidelity and conformance to some set of unstated standards. It seemed okay, within limits, to date and a bit of "gentle" kissing was to be expected as I got older. Touching, though, was the start of trouble and an effective block was carefully built to prevent dangerous intimacies.

We never talked much about my boy friends. Here, Mom never seemed to be concerned, never suspected intimacies beyond those explored on "Leave It to Beaver." Hers was a woman's world and what she knew of men was limited to her own woman's experience.

Through all these teen years, regular heavy weekend dating with girls included after-good-night-kisses sex with boy friends. The early evening hours were warm, loving, caring closeness—times that promised much but times that left too much undone. Later, hidden and unspeaking, others boys and I "came off" in fireworks excitement.

With college, there was a move from home and a growing realization that the way I'd organized things during high school really didn't fly quite right in this new world. Drinking began with a start-of-freshman-year fraternity party, joined with terror that my darker side would be revealed to my new friends. For the first time, I heard negative comments about masturbation and rumors of fellows who were excluded because they were "strange." The second semester ended with a suicide attempt and my first contacts with psychiatrists. Later that summer I travelled alone to the East Coast. In Boston, I spent my first night in a thrifty hotel and slipped into male-sex unexpectedly in the "for everyone shower" down the hall from my room. The next day I fled to spend the remainder of the trip sequestered with friends in New Jersey.

The next three college years were spent in my fraternity room and the psychiatrist's office. Isolated, I drank, masturbated, and did only enough school work to avoid being sent home. On two occasions, encouraged by fraternity brothers, I dated, and these relationships moved through pinning to engagements. Both ended on nights of necking when blouses came unbuttoned and bras unsnapped.

In my senior year, someone jokingly pointed out a gay bar and, after asking what "gay" was, I determined to return later that evening. It was New Year's Eve and I arrived before eight. By 8:15, I was on my way to a man's apartment. He had been drinking heavily and was angry that his lover hadn't shown up. In bed, my eagerness belied my inexperience. In the midst of sex-making, his lover walked in, drunk, and now enraged at the naked infidelity. I dressed quickly and left—back to the bar and a second friend who introduced me to a turkish bath just around the corner. Quick sex followed, along with a curt goodbye, and the first of many, many walks to the "room just down the hall."

I did not finish my senior year, in a sense graduating instead in my own way. I said goodbye to the psychiatrist and moved into the netherworld of my new answer, the unliberated early 1960's of Chicago's gay community.

Several months of unconfined "freedom" was broken only by hepatitis hospital-time and recovery. Then, to put some structure into my life, I sought out a lover. For the next four years, our relationship was organized to include as many others as possible. We bar-hopped and entertained constantly with one goal—new, untested sex partners to keep excitement at a fever pitch.

To escape, from time to time I would move into skid row cage hotels for a few days or weeks. Here, I could drink and have sex without ever having to talk.

When I was twenty-six, my lover attempted suicide. I felt responsible and slipped towards depression as the relationship dissolved. His psychiatrist felt I needed to be hospitalized to provide a safe spot in which I could sort things out. Released several weeks later, I was out of work and returned home for a year of searching.

This year was one in which gay sex was very limited, liquor was replaced with prescription drugs, and therapy resumed on a twice a week basis. I also moved back into a more acceptable world, primarily through church, and began to make friends whose interests were different and broader than those I had pursued for several years.

At church, I came to know, very tentatively and cautiously, the woman who became my wife. We became friends first, then lovers, then husband and wife in a marriage that has lasted since 1968. We talked before we were married and discussed openly many things with our priest. Aware somewhat of the past problems, we moved into the marriage with hope that things would be different. In a sense, our hopes were fulfilled.

Our relationship was close, as my many relationships with girls and women had been. We were and are good friends. At the same time, we worked together as I finally completed school and began to build a successful business career. To some extent, my dreadful fear of sexual intimacy with women was masked.

On the underside, I continued solitary sex, drank, and pleasured myself with almost daily release in public washrooms, gay movie houses and adult bookstores. These "moments" were somehow separated, somehow not really a part of me, somehow "blacked out" through liquor and dissociation.

With things going so well, this period was one in which I chose not to share insights with a psychiatrist. After ten years, though, work pressure added to the stress. My business now provided considerable time for travel, time spent to expand drink, drug and sex adventures. At home, my anonymous sex time was before work, at lunch, and after office hours. Later in the evening, with my wife asleep in the next room, I drank, drugged, and sexed alone in the den. By New Year's, 1978, I was again trying to sort things out with a psychiatrist, tried suicide again and, after hospitalization, began to look for a new job.

In a real sense, recovery began in 1978. My new psychiatrist and I talked a lot about sex as addictive behavior and, God's gift, this doctor recognized drug abuse and refused medications as a part of the therapy process. With alcohol not then a big part of the picture, we failed to consider this and focused on ways I'd used sex to relieve stress.

I quickly moved into an involving new job and enjoyed initial business success once again. Sex activity reduced greatly, but from its high base even a substantial reducation left a major problem. Unnoticed, my use of alcohol increased over the next five years.

On a daily basis, with business opportunities to drink, my drinking moved to heavy use and maintenance levels. My sex acting-out became binges, usually all-night adventures following evening dinner business meetings fueled by drink.

Finally in 1982, the toll was taken. The job was moving to termination. While secure at home, my wife was distant. We struggled as we faced financial collapse. A co-worker and friend, the man who was firing me, casually mentioned my drinking. With everything else so wrong, this was one problem I did not need, and I chatted with my physician who also headed an alcoholism treatment center. Within hours, I was at my first Twelve Step program meeting.

In moving into alcoholism recovery, I felt at gut-level some understanding of addiction and the struggle I had been having with sex for so many years. All the insights already learned were like the many pieces of a jig-saw puzzle. With the Twelve Step program, I had a firm table on which to put these pieces together. Even in the first few confused days of sobriety, I understood similarities in these addictions—compulsive, obsessive behaviors determinedly leading me to self-destruction.

Sex and Love Addicts Anonymous was not available to me during my first year of recovery. I was still living in Chicago and Twelve Step programs there were pretty much confined to alcohol and drugs. However, my first A.A. meeting and most of those that have followed have been made up of gays, providing me the opportunity to move into the community on a non-anonymous and non-sexual basis. For the first time, I found the loving, caring friendships and intimacies I thought could only be developed sexually. I also met others who had stories of sexual addiction and recovery to share as a result of the Twelve Step programs.

After about a year, I switched therapists, turning now to an alcoholism counselor. Together we began to deal more completely with sexual identity questions. I surrendered to God's will for me and became open to alternatives. The anonymous sex was briefly replaced with one or two short-term special friendships. I joined a second gay married men's support group. Through this all, my wife stayed involved and informed. We were determined to work this out together.

In November, after more than a year of recovery and unemployment, I had my first full-time job offer. This required immediate relocation and temporary separation from my wife. The new job was in San Francisco.

I arrived in San Francisco on Friday, November 11, 1983, spent the weekend South of Market, started work on Monday, and met with a gay therapist on Tuesday. He suggested Sex and Love Addicts Anonymous at this first meeting and the next night I was at my first S.L.A.A. meeting. With two brief slips, God's loving grace and this fellowship have now given me several months of life without sex outside a committed relationship—no anonymous sex, no spot relationships to fill in the time, and infrequent solitary sex.

My wife joined me for the Christmas holidays and moved to join me in San Francisco late in January. We have been moving towards new intimacies and honesty in our relationship. We are working together to build anew a love we hope will be much different, confident that we now have the tools to make possible what had seemed impossible.

This is all very new, and much remains unsettled. The past many months have been filled with God's gifts and, in learning that prayer for knowledge of His will and the willingness and strength to carry this out one day at a time will be answered, life has become bright and promising.

Thank you, God, for what you've given me
—for what you've taken away
—and what you've left behind.

Free at Last!

There didn't seem to be any reason for continuing to live. I could see no alternative. As I drove North, thoughts of those close to me entered my head as I made my peace with the idea of killing myself in a matter of hours. The torture of continuing to live obsessed by sexual thoughts and actions was finally unacceptable. My guilt was overwhelming; I felt totally crushed by it, my spirit lost in a suffocating darkness. Life meant nothing but agony and unrelenting, insufferable pain. The thought of suicide actually gave me a sense of relief, a feeling of freedom and end to the misery. I felt both agitated and calm as I searched for a gun shop.

A few hours later, I stood before the counter staring at the cold, hard metal of the deadly thing I intended to use on myself. As I looked at the gun, I knew I couldn't do it. I had to face the fact that I wasn't capable of taking my own life. It was a moment of truth. I was going to have to find another solution. At that point I didn't know what that would be, but that moment was to stand out as a turning point, the beginning of my recovery. On the heels of this encounter with death, I began a two week sexual binge, totally lost in frantic obsession. I bought prostitutes, watched strippers, masturbated compulsively, lost the alcohol sobriety I'd gained in Alcoholics Anonymous, and endangered my very life in this last despairing binge before I was finally convinced of my powerlessness over my addiction to sex.

As a child I was fearful of my father's criticism and his unpredictable angry outbursts, and sought refuge in my mother's protective warmth. Only with her did I feel safe expressing feelings, but even then I thought it best not to express any negative feelings. Over time, without realizing it, I sacrificed my own individuality in my efforts to maintain this sense of emotional security derived from dependence on others. I thought that in order to be loved I must do whatever others would like me to do. I was therefore determined to be the super kid; I would do no wrong. But occasionally my frustration at not being able to earn my father's approval would be unleashed in explosive temper tantrums.

When I left home and tried to function on my own, I discovered how handicapped I was by this deep emotional dependence. I had never learned a sense of independent thought or behavior. All my responses to life were gauged in terms of what my parents would expect of me. While this is undoubtedly true of many people, I'm not sure it lasts well into most people's thirties. I was a prisoner either to my father's rage or my mother's protection. I had no concept of myself as anything more than an extension of them and what they would permit me to be. It was against this backdrop that I entered the real world to experience life!

Needless to say, my orientation to the world as a self-effacing, scared little boy was not adequate to meet the realities that began to confront me. I had developed no experience with setting limits for my own behavior and no sense of how to make decisions that were healthy for me. I began to do what felt good, which very quickly proceeded to take me in inappropriate directions—to take me in, period. When life confronted me with pain, I responded by running away. I had learned that I could use one relationship to protect me from another, and I was to repeat that pattern in a multitude of variations for the next fifteen to twenty years. Eventually I even sought escape for its own sake, without regard to external painful experiences, and simply got lost in a maze of escapist activities and the resultant load of crushing guilt.

My earliest memories of avoiding the realities of life were of listening to the romantic escape music of the 1950's while dreaming of this or that girl in school who would save my life. I remember that even before the escape of the music there was the thrill of having a girlfriend in the sixth grade, and the transforming magic of losing myself in the fantasy of loving. All at once the turmoil in life seemed to stop and the fantasy was enough to temporarily obliterate pain. It worked! I hadn't discovered masturbation at this point. I only remember the joy of my discovery that beyond my personal misery there was an oasis, a promise of relief.

My early dating was not very significant except that I always had a crush on someone. At seventh and eighth grade parties, we played the usual kissing games. During one game, instead of being kissed by one girl, I was slapped, when I had done nothing inappropriate! In retrospect, it was my first indication that I had entered an area that was full of exciting promise and yet, at the same time, had its share of risk and even guilt. That slap at my innocence changed my perception of the task at hand. I was going to have to be more careful, but I was no less intent on harvesting the promise of obliteration inherent in the pursuit of girls. At about this time I discovered masturbation, adding a new dimension to the experience of sex. What had been the beginning of love addiction now become complete with the discovery of the obliterating magic of sexual fantasy coupled with masturbation.

From the beginning, I had a vague sense of guilt about masturbating. It seemed someone was always saying that masturbation would give you warts or make you go blind. Just sensing my way around this new territory, it was easy to be led to believe that it was wrong. People even said you might become insane; little did I know then what truth there was in that! Early on in my masturbation experiences, my mother surprised me by announcing that it was alright to masturbate, but that I shouldn't use my underwear to clean up with because it caused stains. Totally humiliated, I wanted to run as far as I could; I felt my deepest privacy had been invaded.

I can remember the excitement of early petting and how the desire for sexual gratification became the primary objective in my encounters with early girlfriends. Of course, this was not unusual for an adolescent, but it never really changed. I was never able to see women for anything more than their potential to give me sexual gratification. Again, this is not unlike many other men, but with me it felt all-consuming and unusually important.

At this point in my life, my parents felt I hadn't matured sufficiently to go directly to college, so they made arrangements for me to go to prep school for a couple of years. Away from home for the first time, I can remember masturbating a lot and always having a pretty girlfriend at home to write to. She had to be pretty so that I could own the beauty and lose myself in it, and at the same time build up my diminished ego. This was also to be a recurring theme in my sex and love addiction. Beauty was an especially alluring paradise, a place to hide from the ugliness I felt inside. My development to this point looked fairly "normal," from the outside, as I had not begun the sexual acting out that characterized the next fifteen to twenty years.

My first recollection of acting out behavior happened on a camping trip that I took with my family. Camping excited me when it dawned upon me that people must be taking their clothes off inside their tents. There was also a primitive aura to the experience which seemed to bring out the sexual urge inside me. One night I left our tent, went to an area where the toilets were, completely undressed and stretched out on the ground in front of the women's room and masturbated. It's almost as if that experience came out of nowhere. It shocks me now as I write it. I didn't get caught.

Soon after this experience, I entered college and eventually began roaming the streets fantasizing about the women in laundromats late at night. Then I started feeling the breasts of women as they passed me at night on the street. I'd run away and never got caught. I also began peeking in the windows of the houses surrounding the college. Without attempting an analysis, suffice it to say that I had developed rather suddenly a desperate need for sexual oblivion. Prep school had been a benevolent extension of my mother's protective atmosphere, but at college I was really on my own for the first time and felt psychologically abandoned. I was not aware at this time that sexual acting out was serving to transform my experience of a painful reality. It's only in retrospect that I can see the pattern. I began to see myself as a pervert, further diminishing an already internalized picture of myself as a person of little or no worth.

I withdrew from college while "in love" with a new girlfriend and without informing my parents of my decision in advance. My angry father insisted that I return to some college by the next fall. My parents thought it was a good idea for me to see a psychiatrist. If they had only known half the story!

I went to work at a local hospital where I met Mrs. D, a nurse ten years older than I was, who began to pursue me sexually. Here I was, a twenty-year-old virgin obsessed with sex, with an attractive married woman sneaking around the ward looking for places to get me alone! I couldn't have prayed for anything better! We began a weekly escapade that elevated my miserable existence to a place I thought was reserved for very few. The power of my sexual experiences with Mrs. D was overwhelming! In a matter of hours she made me feel like a man. She initiated and satisfied sexual desires I never knew were possible and literally transformed my vision of the world!

We continued our clandestine meetings in the back of my car throughout the summer as I lived in ecstasy from week to week. These days were significant because I learned on a deep level that sex could give me a sense of myself I had never had before. I sensed I had the power to overcome all the pain of my past—it even seemed to just melt away. Initially, the positive rewards were so great that I can't recall feeling guilty about what I was doing. Sure, Mrs. D was married, but that consideration seemed minor in light of the benefits I was receiving. The drug "sex" had distorted my values and any concern I had with morality. Besides, I had never developed a strong independent sense of my own values.

By the end of that summer I had been accepted by another college, so I left this incredible woman and managed to get a new girlfriend right away. Petting was all I could manage with this new girl, who eventually decided to return to her regular boyfriend. I was devastated. Perhaps I had been riding on my sexual high from the previous summer, thinking I could have any girl I wanted. She rejected me, and that struck a painful chord. I began my voyeurism again and almost got caught. I was called to the dean's office to explain my reason for hanging around the women's dorm. Since my sister also went to that college, I said I was looking for her. This brush with humiliation wasn't pleasant, and before long I was feeling suicidal and a long way from the memories of the previous summer. Life seemed empty without the intrigue and release of sex. With no girlfriend, I was in enforced withdrawal, wholly involuntary, smack up against the ugliness I felt about myself.

That year a grandmother whom I was very close to and who had soothed many of my earlier pains died suddenly, and her death resulted in my trying to behave in a moral fashion. In the spring of that year, when I was home on vacation, I met Mrs. D and refused her overtures to pick up where we had left off. In retrospect, I can see a major conflict that was to repeat itself throughout my addiction. I desperately needed the escape that sex gave me, if only temporarily, but coupled with it was a sense of ever increasing guilt over my behavior. I was powerless to stop despite the guilt and pain that my behavior caused me. *The pain from my past that I felt compelled to escape was compounded with each new inappropriate behavior.* I would embark on self-imposed periods of "monasticism," only to eventually return to some form of sexual oblivion.

By the end of that year I left college again and went on active duty with the Navy. Depressed and lonely, I wrote to Mrs. D begging for the sex I had refused two months earlier. She never answered.

While in the Navy, I spent a lot of time drinking, going to porno movies, and masturbating, but I was unable to avoid the more dangerous voyeurism. As luck would have it, I met another married woman whose husband was fighting in Vietnam. Married women felt "safe" on some level. I mean, I didn't want to take responsibility for using a single girl *just* for sex, and thought that having sex in a situation such as that was wrong. As a fledgling sex and love addict, I had a strange sense of morality!

Married women, I surmised, just wanted the sex. There was no confusion about emotional involvement. It didn't matter that the woman's husband was fighting in Vietnam. I needed what she could give me regardless of the circumstances. On some level, though, my guilt was always being stockpiled.

When I got out of the Navy, I came to Boston. I knew no one and soon began to find prostitutes to get what I desperately needed. These were my first experiences with prostitutes, and the guilt and growing sense of myself as a pervert resulted in my frantically going to the yellow pages to find a psychiatrist. Lonely and confused, I went to see him expecting that he would listen to me and make me all better. It didn't work that way. He referred me to an associate whom I saw for the next year or so. During this period, I met the woman who was to become my first wife. It is significant that soon after meeting her I told the psychiatrist that I would be alright for awhile. A new woman had entered my life and that always meant that I would feel whole again. In retrospect, it was probably the excitement of having a new sexual partner that was the key factor in my sudden "health." I didn't know anything about love; I needed sex and if that meant marriage, then so be it! Inevitably, as I have come to learn but didn't know then, all relationships go through phases where the sexual intensity is diminished. But to an active sex and love addict, this is unacceptable. I was in no way prepared to work on the marriage once the difficulties began. My focus was genital; my illness saw to that, and I needed my fix. I began to feel trapped by the closeness, bored by the sex, and desperate to smother these feelings. Panic swept over me as I contemplated ways to sexualize the overwhelmingly threatening feelings that I was having. A strange mix of morality and sexual need resulted in some bizarre decisions regarding my sexual behavior. I ruled out affairs with other women (at least initially) because that was wrong. But going to the strip joints in Boston's Combat Zone, peering in windows, compulsive masturbation, and eventually exhibitionism were not "cheating" on my wife!

I was trapped. While I had entered the marriage with hopes and dreams for our future, in reality I was an immature, sick man, hooked on sex in order to survive. I would spend spring and summer nights exhibiting myself, masturbating, drinking, peering in windows, and gradually getting sicker. The psychiatrist I was seeing gave me valium and a lawyer's number in case I was caught. Nothing stopped me. One night I went out, drank, and drove West in the middle of the night, fleeing frantically from the mounting confusion and desperation in my life. On this particular morning, I arrived in Hartford, Connecticut, fantasizing about taking off all my clothes and running nude through a girls' school cafeteria. I was never able to do it, but I wanted to so much. It felt like the only way I could blot out the pain inside. I called home in tears and agreed to meet my wife in the psychiatrist's office. This became a pattern. I would try to summon up the will to live a sane, "normal" way of life and eventually would explode in an orgy of self-destruction, only to return to my misery exhausted, penitent, and ready for another period of good behavior.

My most disturbed behavior, in addition to the exhibitionism, was a return to grabbing women on the streets. For a few years during my marriage, this was the staple of my addiction. I look back on it with a great deal of guilt, but it is lessened to a great extent today because I am able to see that I was ill and not bad. What I would do is follow women and as I passed them I would feel their asses and then run like hell. It's not an attractive picture of myself, and not one that's easy to share with you. In retrospect, I think I needed sexual excitement desperately, but wasn't able to get it on a level that would obliterate. The adrenalin surge that filled me as I followed a woman and felt her temporarily catapulted me beyond any pain. There was immediate guilt, but another ass would take care of that, and so on and on. Once started, I was powerless to stop. Only exhaustion or the light of daybreak could intervene. My inclination as I write now is to try to analyze this behavior in the light of a period of sexual sobriety and years of therapy, but I'm not sure that is useful. What *is* useful is the knowledge that through S.L.A.A. I haven't found it necessary to act out in any form, even if I want to.

My story over the next few years essentially repeats the patterns I have already mentioned. I left my wife after an affair, and in a desperate quest for new sex. I went back to school after graduating from college and met a student whom I got pregnant. We had the child and within two years I had left them, only to find someone else whom I eventually left as well. It was during the period of these serial relationships that my sexual acting out and increasing alcohol and drug dependency resulted in my making a serious attempt to take my life. Fortunately, I blundered the attempt and was hospitalized, which led me to begin a five year period of sobriety in Alcoholics Anonymous. However, despite my sobriety in A.A., I continued to harbor a relatively quiet, but nonetheless potentially fatal, addiction to sex and love.

My serial relationships certainly indicate an addiction to love and romance as well as sex. In my early sobriety in A.A., I began to have some sense that my sexual activities might possibly be curbed with a Twelve Step approach, but I was nowhere near ready to go that road. Ironically, this was during the time period when S.L.A.A. was being founded. But, alone in my misery and certainly not ready to let go of the destructive patterns, I continued using sex and love to ease my journey through life. While the guilt over my need for sex was often unbearable, the negative consequences of my activities had not reached the point where I was ready to do anything to stop.

Over the next couple of years, I became heavily involved with religion and felt strong enough to greatly reduce my sexual obsessions. This represented a relatively happy period for me and was my first indication that when I didn't act out I felt better about myself. But since I was without the support of other recovering addicts, this period gradually faded away and I was back in the soup again. This time, however, I was actually beginning to get a little more healthy, and managed, after leaving the last woman, to live alone for six months. I began to take care of myself and to feel a sense of dignity for the first time in my life. In living alone, my view of myself improved, but not acting out was the most important factor. At the end of six months, I had a one night stand with a woman, and shortly thereafter I met the woman whom I have stayed with now for four years (a record) and whom, because I am now sober in S.L.A.A., I plan to marry. Her suffering and my own resulted in my coming to S.L.A.A., getting sober, and growing sufficiently to be able to make a commitment based on love. It's that final chapter that I want to share with you now.

Our early relationship had all the earmarks of love addiction. We swept one another off our feet. Within a year we started living together and within a few months I had returned to the local red light district after two or three years of being away. I had the same trapped feeling I had experienced in my first marriage. All I knew how to do was react, and the "Combat Zone" area was my safe harbor. I called the psychiatrist I had when I was hospitalized after my suicide attempt and began more therapy. This new woman was special, and I didn't want to keep repeating the patterns of the past. You reach a point where, even though you feel powerless to stop acting out, you know it's all leading downhill and you've just *got* to stop!

Throughout the years since I had left my son, I had continued regular visits to see him, yet this brought continual reminders of the failure of my past, not to mention the pain of leaving him each time we got together. Many of my visits with him had been followed by trips to the Combat Zone. I was feeling trapped in a new relationship, guilty and sad about my son, and stressed-out by a new and demanding job, all while I was still unaccustomed to experiencing feelings and knowing how to handle them. I simply couldn't hold up, and acting out was all I knew. Compulsive masturbation, porno magazines, walking the beaches, watching the strippers, and not going to A.A. meetings was my way of handling the stress. Why I never returned to exhibitionism or grabbing women I don't know. Maybe I was getting better! Two days before my fifth anniversary of sobriety in A.A., I drank in the Combat Zone, and when the night was over, I was several hundred miles away, in Philadelphia, calling home in the early hours of the morning, crying in a phone booth. It was also my womanfriend's birthday and she flew to Philadelphia to rescue her sad, defeated lover. Some birthday present.

I had never been very active in A.A. and so spent the next year going to meetings almost on a daily basis. This helped, but I knew I wasn't dealing with the underlying problem. I continued to go to the Combat Zone off and on; I didn't drink there, but my guilt was intensifying. My womanfriend and I stayed together but I moved out of the house, which gave me the space I needed at that time. My job as a counselor in an alcoholism program really began to get to me. Here I was only months away from my last drink, and active in another addiction, trying to help other people get sober. The contradictions were too much even for this sex and love addict.

One night at an A.A. meeting the speaker, a woman, made references throughout her story to being obsessed with men. Later, after the meeting, I saw her talking with a man in A.A. whom I had heard make references in his story to sexual behavior that had troubled him. Without hesitation, I intruded upon their conversation and learned that the man was a founder of S.L.A.A. and that there were meetings in the Boston area. I was ecstatic! To think that a fellowship existed, built on the principles of A.A., which dealt with sexual and romantic obsession!—just what I felt I needed.

I attended my first S.L.A.A. meeting the next night, and after hearing a few speakers, I announced to the group that I was finally home! The reality of what was ahead of me had not yet sunk in. I was simply overjoyed that I had found a place where I could talk freely and without judgment about the hidden parts of myself. As was my tendency, I ascribed some magical power to the group, half expecting that my attendance at meetings would lift my obsession. I began a period of withdrawal from acting out, which for me meant no masturbation, no visits to the Combat Zone, no porno magazines, no following women on the streets either to grab or just watch their asses, no exhibitionism, no subtle touching in crowded public areas, no prostitutes, no cruising the beaches incessantly searching for naked women, and no serial relationships for "legitimate" sex. I lasted just short of six weeks before drinking again and returning to the Combat Zone to watch the strippers and compulsively masturbate. Within a week, I had stopped drinking, but I continued going to the Combat Zone periodically over the next ten months, leading up to Memorial Day, 1981.

I had not returned to S.L.A.A. since leaving it in the summer of 1980. Well-meaning friends who knew of my sexual history felt S.L.A.A. wasn't the solution. I was advised that I needed to learn how to engage in these activities without guilt! Privately I knew better, but just wasn't ready to stop watching those strippers. My life was fast becoming emotionally unmanageable. I would make secret trips to the Combat Zone, get home in the early morning hours after masturbating in the car on the way home, and go into work, visit my womanfriend, or pick up my son as if nothing had happened. I played the responsible, mature adult and the emotional burden was awesome.

I spent the first couple of days of Memorial Day weekend with my womanfriend and soon realized that she would be working on Monday and I would have the day to myself. Not only that, but good hot summer weather was expected. The freedom of the hot weather, the eternal promise of spring and the chance to cruise the beaches surged within me as I made secret plans to indulge the next day. No obligations to anyone, a day to escape into sex!—nothing could be better. Almost twenty years of acting out and more recent exposure to S.L.A.A. aside, the promise of each acting out possibility was enough to wipe out the pain of the past, the pain of the present, and any future pain that could possibly exist. What began that day was three weeks of total sexual and alcoholic binging. I need to recount those three weeks since they represent the end of my active addiction, one day at a time, and the beginning of my S.L.A.A. sobriety.

Memorial Day was hot and perfect for the beach. I began early to cruise the dunes. The cruising always had a pathetic flavor to it and this time was no exception. In essence it symbolized the entire nature of my sex addiction. While cruising, I would frantically search for the naked women. The dunes were impossible to walk through. Since it was early in the season, I had to be careful not to get burned. The dune grass would stick into my burning feet as I ran from hilltop to hilltop, hoping to glimpse the magic I craved. On this morning I wore sneakers and the sand poured into them and gradually began to force its way under my toenails, and yet I trudged on in search. Blisters and lost toenails were the aftermath, but they meant nothing in the desperate drive of my sickness. Inevitably, I spent the entire day looking, only to leave and masturbate in the car. Now what would I do? The pain was creeping back and I needed another fix. That meant the Combat Zone.

For the next three weeks I drank, watched the strippers, went with prostitutes, compulsively masturbated, went to work, went out again, saw my therapist, saw my womanfriend and son, and kept on running, but I couldn't get away. The feverish pitch reached the point at which I began my story, where I felt once again like I had to end it all. It was all too familiar. The patterns were tiresome. Again, I couldn't take my life. I had a few more days of constant sex and drinking, ending finally at four a.m. with a prostitute in my car at the Prudential Center in Boston. I zipped up my fly, said goodbye to the hooker, and drove home, only to get up three hours later to pick up my son for the day. I struggled through that day, waking up the next day to begin my sobriety in S.L.A.A.

I really had no choice but to get sober. Nothing was allowing me to escape any longer. I needed stronger and stronger doses of sex to get high. I had developed tolerance and was left each time looking at myself in miserable shape. I was either going to eventually kill myself or go crazy. I knew that S.L.A.A. could help me but that I was going to have to do the work of getting sober for myself. Again I entered withdrawal, abstaining from the litany of behaviors that had been everything, and led me nowhere. I was still involved with the same woman and continued to make love to her since this was, and was going to continue to be, a committed relationship. She was now aware of most of my history and had a great deal of trouble accepting it, but was willing to embark on sobriety with me.

The withdrawal period, lasting for me almost three months, was quite difficult. Since it was summertime, the temptations were many, and as a result I spent much of the time in the house. I couldn't safely go to the beaches or even just wander around the city. I found I had to have definite destinations in mind or I was set up for trouble. It was always hard for me to ask for help from other people, but I found it absolutely necessary to let go of my false pride and pick up the phone when I felt things slipping away. I began asking for help from a higher Power in the morning to help me stay away from a drink and an addictive act for that day. Each day was an experiment in growing up, which continues into the present. I found that once I stopped acting out I began to experience the feelings that I had been running from for so long. I learned things about myself that weren't pleasant and also had some realizations that were gratifying. Most of all I learned that I don't have to act out even if I want to.

I have a sense of personal dignity and personal power that I never felt before. I don't have to apologize for my existence any longer. I have an illness and am not a morally bankrupt pervert. I still have the desire to act out on occasion and probably will continue to feel this way from time to time, but that only serves to remind me that I must put energy into my recovery and do whatever is necessary to stay sober. Withdrawal also helped me to see how the addiction feeds itself. When I was active, I needed more and more sex to begin to alleviate the pain. But once I stopped acting out, I found I didn't experience an overwhelming horniness that threatened to take me to the Combat Zone. When the pain comes now, I don't automatically resort to a sexual thought or solution. I have time to process the feelings and to realize they can't overwhelm me, by going to either my higher Power or a member of the S.L.A.A. Fellowship for help.

I have also had the experience of allowing myself to be swept up by uncomfortable feelings into some preliminary sexualizing that has threatened to reactivate the addiction. This can happen when I cease to be open with those close to me about what I'm currently experiencing, and begin thinking that there is a sexual solution to the problems in my life. What I have learned, however, is that by sharing this with someone I can defuse the urges and block the negative downward spiral that makes the active addiction seem like the only way out. Once the negative thinking is allowed a beachhead, my addictive nature is all too quick to respond. I mention this in order not to paint sobriety unrealisticaly. The rewards of sobriety are immense, however. Life is more beautiful than ever before, and the promise of a future with some peace of mind is real. And yet sobriety for me, after twenty years of acting out, can be a daily struggle. After all, I'm a kid at thirty-seven, finally learning to grow up! But also like a kid I'm experiencing life in a new way. The challenges are exciting. The learning is painful, but not nearly as painful as all that guilt and acting out.

The Twelve Steps of this program offer a way of life we all deserve. My life has shown me how powerless I am in the face of this addiction. I have come to believe that a Power greater than myself can restore me to sanity. On a daily basis I make the best attempt I can to turn my life and will over to that Power. I have made peace with my past and amends to those I have hurt, and the process goes on. I love my God and the Fellowship of S.L.A.A. that has made it all possible. My prayer is that I have communicated to you the pain that went before, and the way I have been given to overcome it. Today I don't have to lie in the gutters of the Combat Zone. I can breathe fresh air, walk with dignity in my world, and thank God for my sobriety! Free at last!

What I Did for Love

I had been living with S. for two years, and was struggling with trying to decide if I should stay or leave. Actually, I was obsessed with that question and stuck in a rut of non-decision making. I was accustomed to settling for less from the men I dated, and the image of actually moving out and being without him filled me with fear and anxiety. As God would have it, I was blessed with an Al-Anon sponsor who was in several other Twelve Step programs. Tired of being asked to make "The Decision" for me, she suggested that I attend a meeting of Sex and Love Addicts Anonymous.

That was in July 1983, and having learned in Al-Anon to take suggestions, I went along. It seemed awful—a room full of people (mostly men) with all sorts of "perverted" histories, giving details of their sexual acting-out behavior. Every few moments, when I listened more open-mindedly, remembering to identify and not compare, I heard things that I could identify with as the "me I used to be." But none of that seemed relevant to the struggle I felt in a caring, committed relationship.

Of course, this "caring" relationship had begun—several years earlier—like so many of my others. I had lost a job and was filled with self-pity, self-hate, insecurity, and loneliness. Trained to be a master's level professional, I was making ends meet by waitressing because I did not have the confidence to pursue a job in my field. I met S. in a bar and was immediately attracted to him although he was too drunk to say anything that made much sense. Two weeks later I met him again and that night we went to bed together. His wife had left him not too long before, and his mother had just died. He needed to fly to California the next day, and in the middle of our first night together he awoke with alcoholic tremors and needed to be taken to an emergency room. It was a perfect set-up for me, pushing all my "rescue" buttons. Naturally, I told him that I had enough of my own troubles and couldn't get involved in his. But from the time he returned from California we spent every evening together. S. lived across the street from me, and I would go out on a date—to show him I wasn't getting involved—and call him as soon as I got home. Every rational fiber in my being told me that this was a mistake—but I was hooked. A month later, S. went into detox and got sober. Two months after that we moved in together.

I had developed a pattern of "falling madly in love"—and leaving as soon as the going got rough. I was determined to make this relationship work. That meant I would stick it out through his alcohol slips, his near suicide, his criticism of my friends, and his emotional unavailability. There were good moments together and some actually intimate sharing, but neither of us was healthy or mature enough to survive the disagreements, to work through our differences and to engage in a true partnership.

After three years, in October of 1983, I decided that I couldn't "play house" anymore. Since S. was neither able to communicate effectively nor to make a commitment to the relationship, with the help of my recovery in Al-Anon and my higher Power, I left him.

Initially, using the Al-Anon program and the supportive help of my sponsor, I approached the move with a positive outlook. It was clearly God-given to me. I had found an affordable apartment that was cute, if not luxurious, and I gave myself permission to spend money on making my new place feel like my home. One of the struggles I had had with S. was about redecorating the apartment we shared. He would not allow me to try to make it feel like "our home," and so it was freeing to be able to establish a home for myself. I thought that practicing the Al-Anon program and having God in my life would get me through the separation and help me to continue to grow. But I didn't know that I had an untreated addiction and that it would not take long for it to become overpowering.

Shortly after I moved, I began to feel that I had made a mistake and became overcome with feelings of guilt, despair and longing to return to S. My sponsor again suggested I try S.L.A.A. and I began to attend meetings on a fairly regular basis.

I still felt out of place in the program. I was grieving the loss of a three year monogamous relationship and most S.L.A.A. members at that time still seemed to be focusing on giving up their "sexual fix," whether it was multiple affairs, "red light district" activity, or compulsive masturbation. They suggested I not go back to my lover, but I thought that maybe if we kept in contact we could work towards an eventual reconciliation.

At this time I was seeing S. just about every Sunday. As was traditional for our Sundays together, I cooked a chicken dinner, we relaxed together, watched TV, and made love. S. seemed to be content with that, but I needed to talk about our separation, how I felt, what I hoped for—and he refused to. After a month of these visits, it felt more painful for me to be with him on this superficial level of relating than to be without him. He also began drinking again and after not hearing from him for two weeks, I responded to his "rescue" call and re-entered the enabling behavior that Al-Anon had taught me to leave behind.

So, I finally surrendered a little piece of my self-will and committed to my sponsor that I would not call him. I was angry. I was obsessed with wanting to talk to him, see him, sleep with him. It was torture not to act out on that obsession. I still thought this was because I loved him so much and remained reluctant to label myself an addict.

In December, I began the journey toward the "bottom" that would make recovery possible for me. At an A.A. dance, just before the holidays, I met a man who set off sparks of sexual energy. I had enough S.L.A.A. and had done enough reading to know that I should not accept a date with this person. I wrote in my journal that night that if he did call I would only meet him for coffee; I would not begin any serious relationship, and I would not go to bed with him. But as soon as I saw him again I knew I was in trouble, I could not resist the sexual arousal I felt in his presence. We had coffee, went for a walk, and several hours later, on his living room floor, he forcefully had sex with me. It wasn't that my body didn't want him, but when I closed my eyes, I saw the face of S. and began crying and begging him to stop. He didn't care about my feelings, but I was already too overcome by the addiction to be able to resist his plea for forgiveness. So began a three month downward spiral during which I completely lost myself to this man. I allowed him to rule me—to have access to my home, my car, my time, my body—all at his convenience. I was hurting myself in many ways and my life became extremely unmanageable. We had sex for two months without using any birth control as I had taken myself off the pill to help me resist the temptation of sleeping with S. I suffered with the anxiety of possible pregnancy and experienced several psychosomatic symptoms.

When my sponsor questioned my behavior and my involvement with this man, I defended it and justified it. At that time I felt that J., who was sober in A.A. and active in that fellowship, had the recovery that I had so badly wanted S. to have. J. and I shared discussions of the Twelve Steps, got down on our knees together at night, and went to meetings. J. also had friends in the program and was very sociable, whereas S. had been so isolated. We enjoyed dancing and other activities together. J. was very enthusiastic in his praise for me and could even be adoring. He said he loved me, and I had never heard that from S. He was supportive during a rough time in my life when my mother had open-heart surgery in 1984.

I used all these things to justify my involvement with J.—and to deny my need for S.L.A.A. I was not able to see the obsessive nature of this relationship and how it was affecting my emotional and physical health, my work, and my sense of self. However, this relationship—the relationship that I had thought was proving that I did not need S.L.A.A.—became the one that clearly showed me the progression of my illness.

There had been some warning signals during the first two months of my involvement with J. that he could become moody, aggressive, and unpredictable. But in true addict style I avoided the discomfort of acknowledging those traits. In February, however, just around Valentine's day, the man I had described to myself and others as caring, honest, loving, and communicative became overtaken by another personality.

J. became uncommunicative and unavailable. Weeks went by without any word from him, and if I called his house he would be enraged. He became verbally abusive, telling me I was "unimportant to him," that I was a "sick person," and so on. If I tried to discuss my feelings of confusion about his sudden change, he'd tell me to take my own inventory, not his, and that he wasn't responsible for my feelings. He twisted the wisdom of the Al-Anon program to manipulate me and confuse me even more.

In the midst of an increasing sense of powerlessness and unmanageability, I had moments of insight which were recorded in my journal—that I was trapped in an addiction, that I was hurting myself, that I needed to stop—but I couldn't. I remained at the mercy of this man's power over me—responding to midnight phone calls to pick him up, allowing him to keep the key to my apartment, loaning him money, and beginning to believe the insulting things he was regularly saying about me. I clung to the memories of those first months and waited for reality to change.

Finally, the pain became too great. J. made a decision that he wanted to stop seeing me and then made it seem like it was my decision. Several days later the "mind games" worsened. He had called in a moment of vulnerability and asked to stay with me because he was overwhelmed and afraid he would drink. He talked from his heart, he was loving and affectionate. I made him dinner, listened, and tried to be comforting. A half hour later he was heading out the door refusing to say where he was going or when he'd be back. When he saw how hurt I was, he responded even more nastily. A few moments after closing the door behind him, he came back in, threw off his coat, and wondered if I could go out and get us some ice cream. I did. I was frozen with bewilderment and fear. I didn't want him there, but I couldn't ask him to leave. I didn't want him to touch me, but I couldn't say no. I thought I was going insane.

It was the next day, when a therapist labeled the behavior I had described to her as sadistic, that I became able to break away from this man, enter recovery in S.L.A.A., and begin to have hope that I could put my addictive patterns behind me.

Amidst the pain of withdrawal—the sleepless nights, the nightmares, the endless crying, the raw feelings of aloneness and abandonment—I reached desperately for the help of the program and my higher Power. I began to gain clarity about my addictive past, the feelings that had been suppressed beneath the obsessive/compulsive behaviors, and my emerging sense of self.

I was raised in a relatively "normal" family. There was no substance abuse, no physical abuse, no sexual abuse. Yet the feelings I grew up with are very similar to those of the people I have heard in S.L.A.A. who grew up in a much more obviously troubled environment. My mother was a strong-willed, hot-tempered woman who found it easy to criticize but difficult to offer praise or reassurance. As I entered adolescence, I was already experiencing strong feelings of self-doubt, self-hate and insecurity. I had seen my mother disown my older sister when her lifestyle didn't meet my mother's expectations, and I could not trust that her love for me would not be withdrawn just as easily. I felt unlistened to, judged, and unaccepted. Those deeply embedded feelings became the foundation of my addictive patterns, and my relationships with people, men in particular, grew out of an endless inner sense of neediness.

I became prey to a man's attentiveness without being able to exercise much, if any, choice about whether I liked or wanted to be with that particular man. I needed to have continuous approval and affirmation from everyone. Because of a lack of a strong identity, I readily identified with people of many divergent backgrounds and interests, and assumed theirs as my own. I couldn't tolerate being alone with myself, and I was driven to promiscuous sexuality in part to soothe the pain of loneliness and self-loathing. I was driven by an unconscious need, based on the patterns established in my childhood, to choose men who would never be able to give me what I felt I wanted—just as my mother would never be able to do—and would ultimately reinforce the parental message that I was unlovable and unworthy. I became a sex and love addict—searching obsessively for the man who would make my life happier, and being driven further and further away from finding a sense of serenity and contentment.

This knowledge about myself became available to me as I continued in my recovery—going to meetings, reading the literature, learning to live in the Twelve Steps, seeking guidance from a higher Power, and reaching out to my sponsor and others in the fellowship.

The clarity I gained during withdrawal uncovered memories and feelings that had been repressed by obsessive/compulsive behavior. Recovery allowed me to grieve the loss of my relationship with S. which I had avoided doing by acting-out. Recovery allowed me to own the truths about myself that I had previously resisted, and by doing so, to begin to loosen the chains of the addiction.

When I chaired my first meeting, after six weeks of sobriety, I read some passages from a journal I had kept in 1977. Among the entries was this one: "Why do relationships always have to be so screwed up for me? Why do I let them be?"

With the exception of three relationships (among many in a period of fifteen years), I had been driven into obsessive "love affairs" or compulsive sexual promiscuity ever since I was fifteen years old. As a child I had entertained obsessive fantasies or crushes, but had not acted on any of them. When I was fifteen, and working in a summer camp away from home, I was introduced to a twenty-five year old alcoholic, and so began the whirlwind of relationships that would make my life unmanageable.

As I entered young adulthood, the disease progressed and I found it literally impossible to spend time alone without becoming severely depressed. I was unable to maintain a relationship with my high school boyfriend because I couldn't stay faithful during our periods of geographical separation.

During my junior year of college, I found it virtually impossible to say no to any man who showed an interest in me. I have never been an active pursuer, but I was always a ready recipient. I had a bunch of one-night stands, an affair with a married man, an involvement with two men who were roommates. If the relationship lasted any length of time, I was hopelessly "madly in love" and obsessed with fantasies of a lifetime together.

My feelings for one man were easily transferred onto the next and I had little, if any, space between lovers. The summer after my junior year of college is a good example of how unsettling this could become. I had left my most recent lover for summer vacation and went to work at a camp in New Hampshire. There I became infatuated with an employee, and when he was fired, I quit. The two of us took off with dreams of hitching across the country. I had my parents recover my belongings from the camp as I'd left with only a knapsack of clothes. My friend and I made it as far as Reading, Mass. He left to go to New York to get some money and didn't return. I called another male friend, living in Boston, to rescue me. Although I insisted on renting my own room, during the next six weeks I only spent one night there. At the end of August, my lover from college picked me up at this man's home. I spent two weeks with him and returned to my parents' house just one week before school started again in order to get my belongings together. Not only was the addiction hurting me, it was affecting the people I cared about as well.

Most of the men I became involved with were older, with different interests and values, and many were alcoholic or otherwise "troubled." I was unable to keep what little self-identity I had; once I became involved with someone my life was shaped by his needs, interests and demands. A psychology professor from whom I sought counseling in college once made me wear a sign that declared "Don't Tread on Me," but I remained incapable of shaping my own life.

During graduate school, while living on my own in Boston, the disease progressed further. I was in a state of increased neediness due to the death of my latest boyfriend from cancer. Tim had actually been an emotionally healthy man, and we were good friends. He died at age twenty-three, and I had taken care of him since the illness was diagnosed nine months earlier. After this loss, I became obsessively involved with a sensitive, caring, introspective man, who would have been a great partner except for one thing—he was gay. Realizing his ultimate unavailability did not stop my longing for him, but since I couldn't "have" him, I sedated my anxiety, sadness and emptiness with a lot of casual sex. Again, it was during withdrawal in S.L.A.A. that my memory of those years became clear. Riding past the building I had lived in at that time, three weeks into sobriety, I suddenly remembered going to bed with—the guy I met in the laundromat, the guy who worked in the liquor store, the guy who lived upstairs, and his roommate, and the man I met when my car broke down. I continued in these sexual liaisons until I could hook my next obsessive lover.

The next three and a half years brought a series of obsessive relationships with what I considered inappropriate men. I lived for two years with a black man from Barbados who was uneducated, illiterate, but charming. I wore my hair in an "afro," let him choose my clothes for me, and learned how to cook West Indian food. Following that relationship, I became engaged to a man whose last name I still cannot recall. He was emotionally unstable and became abusive. I left him under police protection. I then had a series of intense, but brief, relationships, always feeling that I "loved" each man I was with. I lost a job during this time, and realize now it was because my energy was so consumed by three ongoing obsessions that I did not have any energy left for work.

By now, in my late twenties, the addiction was affecting every area of my life. It especially devastated my emotional well-being and self-image. Although I have always had many friends, I felt isolated and unworthy unless I felt I was wanted and needed by a man. I was so absorbed in the pursuit of "love" that the rest of my life seemed meaningless and unfulfilling. I had vague longings of wanting to pursue certain activities or interests, but these were quickly diverted and made subservient to my many obsessive entanglements. I was aware that I wanted my life to be different, but I was helplessly enslaved in an increasingly destructive, insidious addiction.

When I finally came to S.L.A.A. out of a sense of my own vulnerability, I had everything to gain and nothing to lose. The pain of withdrawal would eventually have an ending; the pain caused by my addictive behavior could have gone on endlessly. Through accepting my powerlessness over sex and love addiction, surrendering my will and my life over to the care of my higher Power, and humbly accepting God's guidance, I regained control of my life. I began to feel dignity and respect for myself. The loneliness subsided and I began to enjoy being alone. When I shared the company of friends, I was with them in body and mind. I was no longer plagued by an unceasing sense of longing. I started to pursue interests and activities that I desired for myself. I returned to my religion to study and to worship. I became increasingly involved in the Fellowship, doing service at the group and intergroup level. I began to have the ability to exercise choice. My life felt complete and purposeful.

When my recovery and my sobriety became the prominent focus of my life, when I began living "one day at a time" and putting "first things first," the possibility of a true partnership was given to me by God.

From the very beginning I approached this relationship with caution and discipline. I had known R. for twelve years. We had been good friends, had had a romantic involvement which I had chosen to end a long time before, and had remained friends. We had not visited together for seven years, and maintained contact mostly through letters.

Just as I was beginning withdrawal, R. unexpectedly asked if he could come to visit. My initial response was to jump at the chance for yet another escape from the work of recovery. However, I knew I couldn't afford to allow that to happen. I chose instead to "get current" with my friend—to tell him that I had recently learned I had an addiction and that I needed to treat it. I told him that he had always been a great "rescuer" for me, and I didn't want to put him in that position again. I was able to ask him if he would be willing to postpone the visit until I felt more healthy, more stable in my withdrawal. He was willing to do this, and we scheduled a visit for several months later.

I talked about his upcoming visit with my sponsor and at S.L.A.A. meetings. I borrowed a cot so that R. could sleep comfortably in the living room. I committed myself to call S.L.A.A. members during his week-long stay.

The visit went very well. We were very comfortable with each other and I was able to share freely the story of my addiction and the program of recovery in S.L.A.A. R. had never been someone who "sparked" immediate sexual energy in me, so that was not a problem. I was aware that I felt some discomfort about having a man in my home, but *that* was an affirmation of my recovery. I was not going to "lose myself" at any cost as I'd done in the past.

As a result of this visit, R. and I decided we wanted to start to explore the potentials for a lasting relationship. We would have to do much of our getting to know each other via the telephone, and planned to call each other once a week until our next visit, several months away. To eliminate any possibilities of slipping into a dependency pattern regarding the telephone calls, I did not allow myself to call him except when it was "my turn," and I did not call if I was feeling lonely or needy.

It is difficult to describe the process of the next six months as it has been a new experience for me, with a new perception of relationships and of myself within a relationship. There has not been any obsession, and my life has continued with the same vitality and enthusiasm for those activities I had defined as important to me during withdrawal. The first time I felt myself "missing" R., I wondered if that was an O.K. feeling to have. I needed to learn the difference between missing someone and having an obsessive longing. I have not run away from any of my feelings and have been able to "keep current" about them with my partner. Together we have addressed all sorts of issues that affect the possibility of our future commitment. This has not been easy; I have often wished I could blind myself to reality and encase myself in the romantic fantasies that sustained my addictive relationships in the past. However, this is no longer an alternative for me.

I have tried to stay aware of God's will for this relationship and to avoid any tendency (which I certainly have had) to willfully "force situations." R. has respected my need to approach the relationship at a pace that feels comfortable and sober. I have exercised choices based on my commitment to recovery, rather than on desires and instincts.

Physical intimacy has followed emotional intimacy, and was approached slowly. Our first kiss resulted in fifteen minutes of laughter. The first time we slept next to each other, I had a nightmare and returned to sleeping in my own bed. The first time we made love, I cried. I do not take it for granted that we will be sexually involved each time we see each other. It depends a great deal on each of our emotional and spiritual states of being.

In a wonderful book, *The Road Less Travelled*, M. Scott Peck defines love as "the will to extend one's self for the purpose of nurturing one's own or another's spiritual growth." He states that love is "effortful," and that "true love is not a feeling by which we are overwhelmed; it is a committed, thoughtful decision." At this time, R. and I have hopes that our exploration of a partnership will result in marriage. This is not a certainty for me, although I would hope for it to happen. However, whether we marry or not, I have been blessed with the opportunity to experience a relationship free of the driving forces of addiction. And I have surely learned something about my capacities to truly love.

I Had Everything
(Except a Life)

I see my story is in the stories of many others. As one of the later contributors, I've had the opportunity to consult the book manuscript for quite a while, and in reading the earlier stories came to feel that my identification and empathy with every writer meant that I might not have anything of value to share.

In thinking about this point, however, I realized that perhaps this is the very thing I could share: the process of my identification and the conclusion that was forced upon me (by the facts) that I belong in this fellowship.

During my first S.L.A.A. meetings I was repelled by the stories I heard: accounts of voyeurism, exhibitionism, run-ins with the police, stories of dealings with prostitutes, compulsive masturbation, and other gory, repulsive tales. I wondered what I was doing at such meetings.

I had no experience with any of the above. My addiction, as I originally saw it, was comparatively innocent—and certainly "socially acceptable." I was simply a Great Lover. In all modesty, I did not claim this title for myself. It had been bestowed upon me by my peer group. This group consisted of colleagues, friends, and fans in the West Coast entertainment world. After all, getting into bed with as many beautiful women as possible seemed to be the ideal most valued in the society I knew.

Advertisements, films, TV, magazines constantly promote the idea of attractiveness, beauty and sexual charm as the objective of our otherwise dull lives. It seemed ironic that because I excelled so well in these highly touted virtues, my life became such a mess, and finally unraveled.

I will pass up the litany of my deprived childhood; I had screwed-up parents who offered neither role models nor affection so necessary to healthy growth. My desperate need for love/approval, and my denial of this need, led to thirty years of frenetic behavior in a number of areas. In some of these areas, like sports and my business career, the frenzy paid off with developed skills and economic prosperity.

To the observer, my life was the American Dream come true: beautiful wife, two handsome children, large home, pool and tennis court, cars, travel, etc.

Behind this staged setting was a driven, scared boy who didn't believe he had any intrinsic value, whose goodies might be taken away at any moment, and whose only workable tool to handle this papier-mâché world was a series of ongoing love affairs and intriguing escapades around the world.

I wanted the stability of a home and the family I never had, but I was simply incapable of investing the energy and manifesting the patience required for the construction of that life. I wanted it all and I wanted it now—and I was willing to accept the mere appearance that I had it all. Of course, I had nothing but a stage-setting; tragically, I developed the skills to lie and deceive (mostly myself) that the sham was working.

Within my peer group, the sham was life itself. There seemed to be an unending amount of laughter, parties and fun, but when the parties stopped and the laughter subsided, the quiet was—literally—unbearable. For in those moments, my "H.P." (though I didn't so identify it then) would have me look at what was really going on: the marriage was a lie, both my kids were into dope and police problems, my deceptions were multiplying, and my energy was running out.

That magical energy which enabled me to live three and four lives (living one or two was amateur stuff) was being short-circuited. For years I had learned to live with the low hum of floating anxiety. Psychiatry, workshop weekends, and incessant reading of self-help books would allay the pain, but then off I'd go again on another "love affair" with an aspiring model or young actress.

Against this background of helter-skelter was my brush with the Twelve Step program, via Al-Anon. Although my initial reaction to the higher Power was a cynical turnoff, my H.P. did establish a beachhead and, during the years of my "progression" in this sex-love addiction disease, H.P. was crucial to the initiation of my recovery.

For it wasn't too long (conventional time-divisions are lost to me) before the floating anxieties became anchored. I began experiencing full-blown panics, the kind that would make me grip the table to make sure I didn't float off into space—or burst into a doctor's office begging for a whiff of oxygen to keep me alive. The mounting sexual activity and growing deceit had finally broken me. Divorced after twenty-six years, business now on the skids, facing the fear of becoming that "dirty old man" I had so long derided, I had reached the point which is the prelude for change for most addicts: I was at my bottom.

Withdrawal, for me, was a grace. My frenzied sexual and intrigue activities were lifted; all that energy was as deceptive as the other shams in my life. I can look at pretty girls (or pretty flowers or buildings), but I am no longer "on the make"; my hungry little boy does not have to move into fantasies.

The journey for that transformation is, I believe, outlined in this book, in the stories of fellow-addicts, and especially, for me, in the fellowship of the S.L.A.A. meetings. It was in the meetings, which were initially so repugnant to me because of the stories of abject neediness and bizarre acting-out which were shared there, that I finally heard *myself,* saw myself, and eventually cultivated some compassion for myself.

For though I disdained those in the thrall of compulsive masturbation (an act labeled ugly and evil in my childhood memory), I ultimately came to see that all of my love conquests, my romantic achievements, my incessant braggadocio were also forms of masturbation. Among the scores of bodies and costumes and names, there was no emotional contact, no exchange, no communication; there was only a neurotic (and therefore never-to-be-satisfied) neediness momentarily allayed by romance, intrigue and orgasm.

The form manifested by the neediness is incidental to the substance—the motive behind the actions—and part of my sickness was to judge the form, once again placating my need to be superior and thereby deny the constantly pressing pain of not being anything or anyone.

I am still seeking to develop and nurture that love-needy boy, but with the aid of this fellowship and the Twelve Steps, I no longer misuse my energy or the people around me in my natural and deserved quest for love—a love I am now beginning to understand for the first time. It is the quest for the authentic experience of this value which I share with my fellow S.L.A.A. members.

An Unmerited Gift

There are two images before me as I write: one is a snapshot of myself at the age of three—and the other is a mental image of the face of B., who shot himself to death just a few days ago, while in the grip of this disease. If I look closely at the picture of the little girl I can see that she appears, from the way she looks downward, her hands clutched together in front of her face, from her untidy curls and her inward gaze, dispirited and "somewhere else." And what about B.? B. was, to many people in the outside world, a success, and had been sober in A.A. for several years, but sex and love addiction was the disease that killed him. I didn't know him very well; we talked frequently on the phone for the brief period that he came back to S.L.A.A.—he'd "visited" a few times a year ago. The anguish and paranoia he was suffering from were terrifying to witness, and it was disheartening to see that it was likely that whatever hope I had to offer him was not a match for the progression of his disease. B. was trapped by his sex and love addiction into thinking that if only he were reunited with his lover, his world would be alright. When she rejected him, he shot himself in such a way that he would be propelled out a window on the top floor of a ten-story building. This disease does progress as do alcoholism, compulsive eating and debting—I know, I suffer from all of them.

As a child I was trapped by a punishing father (who had the money disease) and a mother who ate compulsively. I am the daughter of two love addicts. I love my mother and I loved my father. He died a year ago of cancer. It was running away from the pain of his death into the arms of yet another inappropriate lover that propelled me into the arms of S.L.A.A. over eight months ago.

All my life I sought the love I felt I merited. Surely Daddy was about to become that wonderful, kind, patient, generous father he could sometimes be. It's just today that he's in a bad mood/spanks me with a ruler/shuts me into his bedroom to give me a lecture for an hour and a half, explaining that I must learn a lesson, that it hurts him more than it hurts me . . . And what do I learn there? I learn to daydream. I dreamed myself out of that claustrophobic room, away from his voice that told me over and over, no matter what he actually said, that his love was conditional, and once again, I had been unworthy of it. And where was my mother? Surely she would defend me. But she sided with her addiction, her love dependency, of course. Hadn't he saved her from an unprotected life, marrying her soon after her mother died? When my father died, I asked my mother how she'd felt when she lost her mother (she was only in her early twenties, I'm in my early forties). She said she couldn't remember . . . that she had my father . . . and her voice drifted off. That was the answer to my question.

Three years before I was born my father wrote this poem called "Not to Be in Love." It opens

> Not to be in love
> Is to conduct an endless search
> O'er every newly met with face,
> A search for some instinctively familiar grace
> To make a soul whose selfmost rhythm
> Is blendable with mine;

He writes of looking for "that lost chord (. . .) /To match the glorious memories of that breathtaking daybreak sky/That taught me heart for that same beauty's sake/To search until I die." He says he wants to find someone so that "we two may ever move as one." "[S]ome empty nook within the heart or mind or soul seeks filling; because some haunting pain needs stilling, because a life of one, another one for life keeps calling, Nor can ever be denied." It all means nothing, if in the end, he's not in love, if he hasn't found someone to still the pain.

Whatever my father said when he scolded me endlessly behind closed doors, he taught me unwittingly that somewhere, somehow, there was another person who could be everything to me as my mother was to him, and I set out early to do what he did: to still a haunting pain. Mine was that I didn't feel I had his, and perhaps my mother's, unconditional love.

I'm looking at the snapshot of me again. Standing behind me is Elf, my first playmate after my sister. Looking at Elf's blond hair, Irish face, thin bones and boyish look, I see the features of many love addictions. All the women I was addicted to looked a little like Elf. And Elf looked like Marie, my sister. Marie was little, frail, passive and admired me. From Elf I went to Josephine, and to Julie, a girl I knew in Campfire Girls, who was my lover at the age of twelve, until her mother sent her off to a Catholic girls' school.

Shocked and dismayed, I noticed that the girls had begun to be interested in boys. I determined not to be left behind. I got a boyfriend. I went to "boy-girl" parties. I played spin the bottle. I had no idea how to be equal with someone. I either dominated or was dominated. If a person was abusive or emotionally cold (like my father) that meant he or she truly loved me. If I found someone weak or willing to look up to me (like my mother or sister) they would love me forever (and if they resisted I could force them to). Still, I managed a few equal friendships and stayed on good behavior with them and through high school, particularly repressing my feelings for women, and centering my life around my boyfriends. My love addiction was particularly kicked off by triangles: dad and mom and I being the original one. I guess I thought I could catch affection in the crossfire. I picked boyfriends I had little in common with, in order to avoid intimacy. When a relationship bored me, I would inevitably break it off. Less frequently, they broke off with me.

This happened with Michael, and when we got back together again, he left me, to go back to the third in the triangle—a girl he'd been seeing in the interim. My reaction to the breakup was to hide in a novel, then rip it to bits, cry in my sister's arms that I was falling into a black hole, wait until she was asleep and tip-toe downstairs to take a handful of aspirin. Fortunately, 20 aspirin only make your ears ring. I immediately got a new boyfriend.

"Escaping" my small town, I thought I would enjoy independence at college. But when my part-time job ended, I immediately moved in with a man 14 years my senior and I picked him because I knew my parents would not like him. He called me "Pet" and became my new father. He fit the image to a "T." We ran away together. He physically abused me. I verbally abused him in order to incite him. I felt right at home. I wrote my parents that we'd got married, and I spent the next six years with this man, trying to earn his affection. I supported him and his business; nothing else occurred to me. I was a mistake and he, Philip, was the punishment. After five years of this, I met some feminists who gave me support to leave Philip. (We were living at that point in a group marriage with another couple.)

We'd met Sarah and John in a sex ad for swingers. John, in contrast to Philip, was a sensitive man. I think the final year of that arrangement was held together because of his kindness. But he was married and only available to me part-time, and so I left the group of them and proceeded to sleep with a dozen men over the next summer. I met one man hitchhiking and another was a neighbor. I don't recall being really interested in any of them. The sex wasn't very good. I was becoming interested in women, and finally slept with one in a menage a trois (another triangle) but I found it too exciting, too frightening, and so I stopped.

Peter was a good friend I'd known for years through an avocation. One Sunday night he visited and stayed the night. Philip had been sexually disloyal, but Peter was monogamous with me. We had a good relationship for a few years, enjoying similar hobbies, interests, and friends; but when Peter went to Europe for a vacation alone, I sought out a relationship with a woman I hardly knew, becoming instantly drawn to Jean. She had a boyfriend; I worked with him. She and I became best friends. At this time I had been in severe stress: a teacher of several years' duration had died. I had had cancer (but fully recovered). These traumas had given me an excuse to "drink, eat and be merry." I couldn't go for more than a day without seeing Jean. In the last years of my six-year relationship with Peter, I spent more time with her than with him. Eventually I realized—she had rejected me sexually—that she was heterosexual and that I would have to come to terms with my feelings alone. I thought the pain of withdrawal I constantly felt around her was part of being a lesbian. I decided I must come out, but avoided leaving Peter for yet another year, seducing a fifteen-year-old student in the interim as a kind of cross-over lover. He was slim and beardless, and so fit the bill.

I left Peter and developed a crush on Aurora, the one lesbian friend I had, and immediately began an anxiety state that was probably a breakdown. I took care of it by sleeping with Aurora. I felt that it restored my self-esteem about being a lover of women, and I began to be optimistic about being a lesbian. I was fired from my job during this time; I could hardly think with all the anxiety I was feeling, and took another male lover just weeks out of a marriage. I got drunk frequently. When this relationship (which had previously been a good friendship) failed to work, I began dating women.

To screw up my courage, I got drunk, finally meeting a woman who looked like Elf. Laura was a love addict, and a sex addict, too. I suppose I'm taking her inventory, but I believe the addiction was mutual. After six months of obsessive love-making, she moved in with me, even as she continued to see other women on the side, which infuriated me. She was not articulate, had a limited education, and put me on a pedestal. I felt lonely and foolish, but I could not leave her. Laura and I smoked marijuana daily and lived as one person, never doing anything alone. With great regularity she would go off with other women. Once, distraught, I tried to break off with her, walking five miles to a friend's house, where I cried on her bed for five hours. I then walked home again and made up with Laura.

In the fourth year of our relationship I went into A.A. I was addicted to the woman who introduced me to the program. Martha and I had been flirtatious friends for years, a friendship fueled by an interest in literature, but more by intrigue and mutual addiction. During the next four years I was able to put down alcohol, drugs, cigarettes, compulsive eating, caffeine, and debting. But my love and sex addiction flourished: in the next three years "sober" I suffered through nine obsessive relationships—as many as I'd had in my entire life previously (sober or drunk). I spent many an hour in an A.A. meeting trying, without knowing it, to get support for my love and sex addiction, only to be told it was a symptom of getting sober. But this was getting worse.

When my father died, I ran to the first woman I met to get relief. (I was also in withdrawal from Martha, with whom I'd attempted a sexual relationship. Out of mutual fear, we'd abandoned our one attempt in several years of incredible attraction, and I'd remained sexually abstinent for three months on my own—a painful time.) With Alice I was bored the first few dates, but soon I was hooked and "in love." We experimented with sado-masochism, inventing sexual games in which I was the masochist. The more exotic our love-making, the more I liked it—anything to distract me from mourning my father. When she was unfaithful with an acquaintance, I left her, vowing never to speak to her again. In three weeks, we were holding hands.

During this time I cried daily and felt so much tension that I had begun to bleed vaginally. I was due for treatment (similar to an abortion) and asked Alice to accompany me. (Hair of the dog, you might say.) Afterwards, I invited her over to comfort me. I knew I was truly insane. The very next day someone told me about S.L.A.A., and the following week I went to my first meeting, getting 6-8 phone numbers, and a temporary sponsor. I braced myself for the withdrawal I knew would come, and set a bottom line, knowing I would be seeing my "drug" the next day. After a few weeks I found a permanent sponsor and set a bottom line which included no masturbation, no dating for a year, and no attendance at lesbian social events or making new lesbian friends. I also made no attempt to see either Alice or Martha, and I avoided places and meetings where I might run into them. I made one exception for a particularly important meeting, and, terrified, ran into Alice there about twice a month for half a year. It was to become a barometer of my recovery, for gradually it became not so painful to see her, though I avoided ever saying hello.

A quiet, physically-exhausted, depressed state set in, after an initial period of hyperactivity. I was resting from a lifetime of acting out. During this period I wrote and read, re-examining my life and my relationships. Not one failed to undergo my scrutiny. Many of them fell by the wayside. I spent weekends in bed, reading. I went to all four area S.L.A.A. meetings every week, called my sponsor daily, and had incredibly vivid dreams. I found myself peaceful and joyful on a beach. A man was in my bedroom about to murder me. My father stumbled off a building and was killed. I made love with someone I didn't know. I slept for twelve hours a night. Then I slept for three. I cried and cried for my father, mourning him as if he had just died. Gradually I felt my addiction loosen its grip. Alice went away for a time, and Martha moved away. I joined a special, focussed Twelve Step group for the first six months of sobriety. I took a profound Fifth Step and let go of some secrets I'd never disclosed in A.A. The relief was wonderful.

At three months I ran into Martha on the street, believing her to be thousands of miles away. I cried and called my sponsor from a pay phone. It was a little test. I spent the rest of the day in bed.

I began working at my art again; I felt my brain returning. In the spring, feeling tense, I took up jogging, and worked up to three miles a day, when my neck gave me trouble and I began going to a chiropractor for three months. I took formal instruction in Transcendental Meditation at seven months, and now, at eight, I find I am again questioning my sexuality. I again feel attracted to men. I have no idea whether this is to stay safe, to avoid women—the real focus of my attention—or if my "coming out" was really an aspect of sex and love addiction, and I am really heterosexual. It is frightening to see how much of my identity has been masked by this disease. I have the comfort of knowing, whatever my sexuality may turn out to be—lesbian or "straight"—that I will know with a clear mind and spirit what it is this time.

At eight months, I feel enough recovery and energy to discover myself obsessing with people in the program and one or two out of it. These obsessions are mild and I do not act on them. My sponsor assures me that the disease is not going to let go of me in eight months, and that these "mild cases" will instruct me further to identify the pattern my disease takes.

Today, when I look at the snapshot of me, of that little blond girl with her dusty hands clasped in front of her, I feel great hope. Compulsion for *somebody* in my life to fix the pain has been lifted. And the pain underneath has been bearable. It is a healing pain that I endure because of the gift I have received from God—the first partnership I have ever formed. And the second is with myself, with the child in me who was the victim of this disease. I am learning to love her unconditionally, just as I loved B., who this disease made its terrible target. Why him and not me? S.L.A.A. sobriety is an unmerited gift. I cannot explain why it has been given to me, but I can be grateful.

Trouble in Paradise

My name is Fred and I am a sex and love addict. I have been this way since I started escaping into rock music at the age of eight. My parents abused me, both physically and emotionally, and I looked for anything to avoid feeling the constant pain. We rarely hugged or kissed in my family, and we never talked about our feelings. Love, security and affection, I first heard about in rock and roll music. I took what they said in the songs literally, and when they promised eternal peace, love and security, I was ready to believe. I knew that if I could just wait until puberty, the dull aching emptiness I felt inside would be exchanged for these treasures, with romantic excitement and a feeling of belonging thrown in. All I would have to do is find the right person.

When my mother became very sick, and my older brother who had always been close became interested in other things, I became withdrawn and depressed. My escape into music and fantasy was not enough. I needed something stronger for the pain. I found it at thirteen when my friend showed me how to masturbate. I was hooked for sixteen years.

Not completely satisfied with daily masturbation, I started looking for someone in whom I could completely lose myself, satiating my most infantile needs and desires. I wanted to reach out to girls my age, but I was absolutely terrified of rejection. I wanted them to "read me," understanding my needs and taking the initiative to reach out to me. So I kept to myself, continued to masturbate like crazy, and waited to stumble into the relationship that would save my life. I frequently traveled on Greyhound buses, and I had a fantasy that I would find "her" sitting alone in the back of the bus. I would find the courage to sit next to her. Without a word, she would start kissing me. My life would finally be saved.

Because of my compulsive masturbation and romantic escapism, I stopped growing emotionally. I hated myself. I discovered drinking and pot, which helped me to escape even further. Because I was so afraid of the opposite sex, I became obsessed that I might be gay. I started going steady with girls and learned how to make out. When my brother and his friends became romantically active, I watched their pursuits like a sports fan. They seemed to get a kick out of my hanging around their wild parties, and once they gave me the job of babysitting a girl who had passed out drinking. I saw my chance and felt up her breasts.

When I later discovered that I could have girlfriends, I stopped worrying so much about being gay. I spent hours on the phone, which I usually took into bed at night. I received the shock of my life at fifteen when my fourteen year old girlfriend left me for a seventeen year old. I couldn't believe she had done it. I wrote her several letters, and when she didn't respond, I went into the garage and started the car. I left a suicide note, hoping I would hurt her very deeply. Before the fumes overcame me, I ran into the house and called the suicide prevention hotline. I tore up the note and never told anyone.

I continued to escape into masturbation, fantasy, music, and drugs. I was getting high alone until the fear and depression were too much. I started drinking heavily with friends, hoping that the deep, dark secrets I kept inside would not destroy me when they finally came out. I felt more alienated than ever at home. There was nobody I could talk to. Girls at school were noticing me a lot, but I couldn't respond to them. The best I could do was to go home and masturbate while fantasizing about them.

Suddenly, when I was sixteen, my bus fantasy came true. I was working long hours in a pizza shop when my friend asked me to double date with a girl who had seen me in the store. Terrified, I refused. Several weeks later, she came to the door after I closed up the shop. She was very pretty, and I could tell she had been drinking. She told me her name was Marie, sat on the counter, and invited me to kiss her. I was hooked for two years.

My relationship with Marie was more than I had hoped for. We had sex almost anywhere, all the time, narrowly escaping detection by our parents more than once. I felt like I was alive for the first time. Finally, I could do all the things I had been afraid to, like going to parties, dances and football games. We spent every spare minute together. My whole life seemed to come together. I was in love; I had a reason to live. All the songs made perfect sense to me. I had a mystical feeling when we were together. I felt powerful, important and whole. I had arrived, finally. I couldn't imagine life getting any better than this.

I never experienced Marie as a person. I didn't know what she liked and didn't like. I never knew how she felt or what she thought. I didn't know if we had any common interests. The truth was that I didn't care. As long as she wouldn't leave me and we kept having sex, nothing else mattered.

When I left for college, Marie and I started to drift apart. She came to see me once, and we spent the weekend taking drugs and having sex. She seemed like a stranger to me in my new environment. I told her I didn't want to see her any more.

When Marie left my life, all my fears, doubts and insecurities returned. I started doing poorly in school. Then several of my friends told me they were gay. When I went with them to a few parties, I thought I had found the answer to my lifelong problems. I started going to gay bars and having sex with new and old friends. I read gay books and magazines. I went to gay rallies and picnics. I tried having sex with strangers. I tried to get into a few dependent relationships. Several months later, I found myself alone and depressed. I tried therapy. I tried to outwit the therapist, hoping he would be good enough to guess what was wrong with me. I couldn't stand the thought of working to find out what was wrong with me. Before long, I quit. I was so depressed that I only ate, slept and masturbated. I stopped seeing my friends. Again I felt suicidal.

After a few months, I felt better. My fantasy life returned and I started seeing friends again. My roommate had a friend named Alice who sounded interesting on the phone. When I met her at a party, it only took us a few hours to wind up in bed together. I was both attracted and repulsed by her. For more than a year, we met briefly for sex, but wouldn't speak for months at a time. I felt like I hated her, but I couldn't resist the sex. We fought a lot. As the sex became more frequent, we spent more time together. I told my roommate Sam that I was afraid I might wake up some morning married to Alice. He said I was being ridiculous. She was still having sex with other people, and I hoped she would fall for somebody else, forgetting about me—the *only* way I could hope to be clear of this mess. She didn't. A friend told me she was really falling for me. I didn't know what to do. I wanted to break off the relationship but I was unable to do it.

I also became aware that I was unable to control my masturbation. I needed it to go to sleep at night, to get up in the morning, to relax, to stimulate me, to cheer me up, and to calm me down. I masturbated when I was bored. I masturbated when I faced any unpleasant feeling. I told myself I needed it when I wasn't having sex with anyone. I looked for stimulating books and magazines to read. I was masturbating so often that I was afraid I would damage my sex organ.

The issue with Alice was causing me so much confusion that, for the first time, I turned to God for help. I knelt down and prayed for guidance. My sexual desire took over, and I was "guided" right to her door. She had been strung out for several days on drugs, and she looked like a ghost. I was repulsed, but I couldn't get away. Why I continued to spend time and have sex with someone I disliked defied my imagination. I finally decided it was "God's will," and resigned myself to whatever might happen.

When an opportunity came up to vacation where Alice was staying, I felt torn. I was afraid I wouldn't be able to stand her presence and my vacation would be spoiled. I decided to go anyway. Three hours after the vacation started, I was back on cloud nine. We had non-stop sex for two weeks, never leaving each other's sight. When it came time to go home, I couldn't. I turned to God for help. Being a spiritual infant, I didn't know that when I prayed for guidance, I heard only the deafening roar of my own selfish will and sexual desire. I was hopelessly addicted to Alice.

Alice and I decided to live together. We knew that our friends would never support us in this, so we abruptly uprooted our lives and moved to a small town, actually named Paradise, which was several hundred miles away. When we were turned down for housing because we were unmarried, I was crushed. I suggested that we sit down to pray about it. The answer I got was frightening. True to the fear I had expressed to Sam, I decided not just to get married, but to do it that very afternoon! I was hooked for eight years.

Soon after our married life began (later that afternoon), things started to come unraveled. When I experienced sexual and emotional abuse, I clung more desperately. I knew something was drastically wrong, but I thought everything would fall back into place if we could only get back onto that cloud. When Alice became upset or abusive, I tried to coax her into bed. We moved a lot trying to find the right circumstances for our love to survive. I lost contact with reality in my quest to make the relationship work.

When Alice became pregnant a year later, I was panic stricken. I was still a child myself, and the thought of being a parent was unimaginable. We fought bitterly. It felt like we were on a sinking ship together, and only one of us could survive. When I was going to survive, she desperately clung to me and I hated her. When she was going to survive, I desperately clung to her. My life was out of control, and the only thing I could think of was how to keep the marriage together.

When Samantha was born, the fights continued. I felt neglected and abused. Alice became severely depressed and would not seek help. The day she threatened to beat the baby, I thought I would lose my mind. I called adoption agencies. I threatened to move out. Then I decided the solution was for me to take on Alice's responsibilities myself. I walked on eggshells. I took the baby everywhere I went. Our marriage continued like a see-saw for seven more years. When I finally got counseling, things seemed to improve. We had several years when our lives seemed relatively stable. While I experienced frequent sexual abuse, I thought the problem was not getting enough sex. I continued to masturbate as I had throughout my life. Now I blamed it on the fact that we didn't have sex very often.

During our eighth year of marriage, a financial crisis brought us to marriage counseling. The counselors advised us to spend more time alone together, communicating with each other. We decided to take a vacation together which would finally duplicate that original experience which brought us together. We just had to get back on that pink cloud!

I decided that I was too defensive, and would spend the time trying to open myself up to Alice. I was unaware of how drug dependent she was by then, and of her decision to leave her supply of drugs at home. When the fights started, I was crushed. I was able to pretend that things could be better for a few days until it was just too much. I came home alone and made plans to separate from Alice. I felt a sense of relief unlike anything I had ever experienced in my life.

I joined a Twelve Step fellowship to help me recover from the effects of Alice's drug addiction. I took to the program like a hungry babe. I heard people talk of experiences I had kept inside for years. My relief turned to exhilaration as I filled my spare time with meetings. I found a new relationship with my higher Power. I found a sponsor and began to recover from years of destructive living. In the Twelve Steps I found a way of living which I had only dreamed of before. Unknowingly, I had also entered the early stages of withdrawal. The worst was yet to come.

One evening my sponsor and I were talking about love and affection when he told me there was a high powered sexual energy which some people mistake for love. I was stunned. "Where on earth did you ever hear that?" I demanded. He patiently explained to me that he was a sober sex and love addict, and explained about the S.L.A.A. fellowship. I wanted to know more. When he gave me a pamphlet to read, I couldn't identify with the stories of chronic promiscuity. After all, I had been lonely, fearful, and miserable for most of my life. Once I got a hold of someone, I held on for good. And besides, I never cheated on my wife (if you didn't count masturbation).

I was still haunted by the idea of this Fellowship, and made plans to attend a meeting. I listened as people talked about their addiction. When it came my turn, I said my name and passed. The elation I had found in my other fellowship was nowhere to be found. After the meeting, my sponsor asked me how I felt. "I think I've got it," I said sullenly. It was like discovering that I had VD.

I went home and sat down to figure out what to do next. Even though nobody had mentioned masturbation, I knew it was part of my "bottom line." Years of masturbation flashed before me that night. I remembered hiding behind closed doors, afraid of being interrupted by my mother or my wife, hiding semen-soaked kleenex, towels, or underwear in the waste basket or the dirty clothes hamper. I remembered the haunting realizations that I was out of control. I called my sponsor and told him that I was going to go through twenty-four hours without masturbating. The first thing I noticed when I went to bed was that I didn't have to check the cracks in the curtains to make sure the neighbors in the next building wouldn't see me masturbating. Then I moved the kleenex box and the dirty clothes hamper away from my bed. Little did I know that I had entered into full withdrawal from sex and love addiction.

As the days passed, I expected to start climbing the walls with a sex drive gone cuckoo. What I did not expect was for my emotions to go on a wild see-saw. Normal everyday experiences became unbearably intense. Some days I barely got through my job, often only by locking the office door. Other days I couldn't get out of bed. I was on the verge of committing myself to a mental hospital when I asked my sponsor to meet me at work. As we drove around in his car, he told me he had experienced the same feelings in withdrawal. He had been ready to commit himself when someone in the program told him he was going *sane*. He assured me the feelings would not last forever. In fact, he told me, I might expect them to subside temporarily within a few weeks. Those were the longest three weeks of my life. Going to meetings, asking my higher Power for help constantly, and phoning people for support were the only way I made it.

I experienced periodic bouts of withdrawal for a year. Each time it was less intense. I started learning to experience feelings I had only obliterated with my addiction. I started to discover who Fred was. Life began to take on a perspective it never had before. My relationships with friends and family improved. The part of me which was stunted began slowly to grow again. I started the long task of growing up.

In sobriety I have learned things that I completely missed, growing up as a sex and love addict, things like the difference between loneliness and being alone. I had to find appropriate and healthy ways to depend on the people in my life. I had to meet my responsibilities to myself and others without being a martyr or "people-pleaser." I needed to trust people and to be myself in many situations. I needed to know what were my physical and emotional limits. I needed to know what sets off my addiction.

For the first nine months of sobriety, I had to avoid movies and all music that wasn't religious or classical. I was overly sensitive to any sexual or emotional stimulus, and I found that I was set off easily. I found I needed to stay current with other S.L.A.A. members about brushes with the disease. I completely avoided women and gay men, including those in the Fellowship. Sometimes I became paranoid in meetings, thinking that certain people were trying to set off my disease. I didn't realize that many people were as sick as I was, and that they had no more intentions of bothering me than I did them.

After a year of sobriety, I found that I could talk to women and gay men without losing my sobriety. I could listen to music that I liked, ignoring the sick messages. I still needed to monitor the movies closely, and had to walk out more than once. I found, much to my surprise, that I could be around people without being swallowed up by them or ending up in destructive relationships—being sentenced to prison from a day to life.

Today I am going on two years of sober living. I have found self respect and dignity which allow me to make choices in my life. I can pray for God's guidance in my life, and *know* when I'm deluding myself. I still need lots of help in the form of therapy and support from the program. I keep a list of S.L.A.A. telephone numbers wherever I go. I have had to make long distance phone calls, change plans, and go to other lengths to protect my sobriety.

For me to stay sober today, I cannot have sex in any form. While I do not intend to become a monk, I do intend to save certain parts of myself for the most intimate *and* appropriate relationship I can have. Today I am too busy growing up to give much thought to when that relationship might be, if it even happens during my lifetime. I owe my life to God and to S.L.A.A.

The Objects of My Affections

In 1938, my parents came to America from Czechoslovakia, in flight from Hitler. My brother was born in Prague, and was only a few months old at the time of the immigration. My family settled in Cleveland where my father was able to get an American medical license and began to practice medicine. I was born in Cleveland in 1943. When I was two, we moved to Minneapolis where my father achieved some notoriety in medical research. For years I told myself this story about the early years of my life—that the period in Minneapolis was idyllic, that we were all together, just one big happy family. Then it felt like suddenly the bottom dropped out with my parents' bitter divorce. My father sued for custody on the basis that my mother was an unfit parent. He charged that she was having a lesbian affair. My mother eventually won custody, although her own mother (my grandmother) had testified *against* her at the trial. My mother, brother and I then moved to New Jersey. I date the beginning of my life's internal chaos to that move.

My brother teased me incessantly about being fat. I *was* chubby (not really obese) and made an easy target since I was five years younger than him. We moved very frequently and I went to a different school for each elementary grade. I spent summer vacations with my father. A year and a half after the divorce, he married a divorcee whose daughter from her first marriage was slightly older than me. Every summer we played together happily and enjoyed each other's company. But, at the end of the summers, my brother and I always had to go back. My mother began working in the field of speech therapy with children. When I was seven, she married my stepfather, an active alcoholic. The contrast between the two households I lived in felt like going from fire to ice. My mother's second marriage was terribly volatile, complete with verbal abuse, unpredictable upheavals and sudden mood swings. For years I bitterly resented the fact that my mother had "sold her children up the river" for an alcoholic, and I hated my stepfather. In total contrast, during the summers, in my father's second marriage, I almost never saw arguments. Only once do I remember ever seeing my stepmother angry at my father; she yelled at him and ran out of the house. In neither household did I have the sense of clearly defined limits or organized discipline set by my parents for either my brother or me.

My happiest times, though, were during summer vacations when my father and I played piano duets together. The keyboard was the place where I received a parent's undivided attention, and so I came to love music, and found refuge in it for many years.

On the basis of good grades and a high score on an IQ test, I was skipped from fourth to fifth grade; from then on I believed I could rely on being smart (and not having to work very hard) for academic success. In 1953 when I was ten years old, my half-sister Deborah was born. I was terribly jealous of her. I was deeply envious of "regular" families, where no one was divorced, mothers stayed home, and fathers worked. I had absolutely no sense of fitting in or belonging; I blamed everything on my parents' divorce and subsequent remarriages.

Toward the end of the sixth grade, we moved to the house we lived in until I left for college. This meant another new school. A boy named Robert was attracted to me. One day he held my hand and kissed me. I was completely unaccustomed to what had happened—it felt as foreign as someone speaking Chinese to me. I didn't know what it meant. After a short time, his interest in me waned; my interest in him, however, waxed. In short, for the next three years I followed him around like a puppy dog. For those years I was part of his group of friends: smart, precocious (and probably obnoxious) Jewish kids. We had frequent parties and played "post office."

I became terribly disillusioned toward the end of the ninth grade when I discovered that people were gossiping about me just as much as I gossiped about them. I made a conscious decision to use humor to win friends, since I had learned I could amuse people. Also, at this time I found a new hero through the movie, "The Spirit of St. Louis," which I saw eighteen times! I immersed myself totally in the study of Lindbergh, aviation and airplanes. I believe now that Lindbergh's main appeal to me was this: he depended on no other person but himself, the Lone Eagle. Emotionally, I had adopted that stance to the world—I spoke to no one about my inner life.

By this time my mother and stepfather lived in separate locations; my stepfather had a house of his own in Connecticut. Occasionally on weekends we were all together there, but you never knew if he was going to be charming or verbally abusive to my mother. I tried to stay out of their way. My mother did try to explain the situation to us: he was the villain, the wolf, and she was the helpless victim, the lamb.

I did not date in high school. I made friends with Ellie, an older college student who was working in the college bookstore. She and her friends were amused by me, a precocious high school kid who read a lot and hung out in the bookstore. The night of the junior prom Ellie, Jake (a friend of hers) and I went to the beach for a picnic. On a romantic beach walk, Jake kissed me. Once again, I thought someone was speaking Chinese to me—I didn't know what it meant. After that, Jake and I went out occasionally and necked; that was the physical extent of our involvement. For me, the emotional extent was much greater. I was certain this was true love, and any day I knew Jake would leave his wife and kids for me. I knew also that his attention had made me feel alive and vital, and without it I felt barren and sad. Gradually, he spent less and less time with me.

One summer while visiting my father, my stepsister arranged a date for me with a friend of hers from high school. I was so nervous I completely forgot his name; I found it by going to another room and rifling through the yearbook until I came to his picture. This form of nervousness (totally forgetting a man's name) plagued me often for many years afterward; even if I had gone out with someone, I had to work at remembering his name.

When I was a senior in high school, my mother rented a few rooms to college students. I was very attracted to them, but no relationship ever developed. I remember, though, walking around in my bathrobe; it was the first time I was really trying to attract male attention.

I went to a small college whose curriculum centered on the classics. My freshman year I was one of "The Three Musketeers" as we called ourselves—Susan, James, and myself. We were great pals and had a lot of fun together, just being silly. Toward the end of the year, James and I became more romantic about each other and Susan faded into the background. That summer I went on my first diet and managed to lose about twenty pounds. I went back to school, outfitted with some new clothes and anxious to pick up where I left off with James. He was equally glad to see me. My memories of the first two weeks of school that year are like the greeting card pictures—nothing existed but the two of us, flying kites together in golden fall colors—bliss.

Suddenly it all shattered. Because James had been involved in a homosexual relationship at school the previous year, his home town psychiatrist recommended that he take a year off. (Remember, this was 1961.) I was devastated by James's departure and quickly gained back all the weight I had lost. I became very anxious before classes and would masturbate frantically while attempting to study.

My roommate that year was a beautiful blond girl who took vitamins, ate health foods, and drank Tiger's Milk. Her boyfriend was equally handsome and the two of them made a striking couple. I saw her rarely since she spent every night in his room. She tried to answer my questions about sex, but finally my curiosity got the better of me.

James had left behind a circle of friends at school, and in his absence we stayed together. On the periphery was Frank. One Friday night before Thanksgiving, we had a party at which the liquor flowed freely. I decided simply not to go back to my dorm. I used to blame it all on the fateful blackberry brandy—it would be years before I realized how true that perception was.

Frank, with whom I spent the night, was neither prepared nor gentle nor concerned. Even more shocking was the discovery the following morning that he didn't even know my name. I was consumed with shame and guilt, but no longer curious. I was "late" by Christmas and alerted my mother. Although my parents had been divorced for sixteen years, and there *were* other doctors in the world, there was only one person she could think of with whom to discuss this situation: my father. I listened to the conversation on the extension phone, and remember to this day how mortified I felt. Mercifully, it was a false alarm. When I went back to school in January, my mother's advice was simple: "Don't get pregnant."

That spring I became involved with Vaughn, who drank a good deal. Basically I didn't like him as much as I liked James, but I drank along with him, and we had a good time.

My third year at college was quite different from the first two: James had returned to campus, and Vaughn had dropped out and was living in a nearby town. I tried to maintain relationships with both. With Vaughn, I felt like I was "playing house" in his apartment; we'd go grocery shopping, etc. Back on campus, James was attentive, but never as attentive as I wanted. I spent weekends off-campus with Vaughn, and spent weekdays trying to explain to James where I'd been. There was little time for books and studying. I remember vividly standing in the shower one day, feeling certain that no amount of water and soap could ever get me clean.

Vaughn wanted to marry me, but I wanted James. When Vaughn was drunk, he became verbally abusive to me, just like my stepfather behaved toward my mother. It all felt strangely familiar, as though I had become my mother. I still could not break off the relationship with Vaughn.

I decided to let distance do the trick. The opportunity appeared to go to Israel with a student group for the summer and work on a kibbutz. I remember clearly asking my father for the money for a round-trip ticket, knowing deep in my heart however, that it was going to be a one-way trip for me and I was not coming back. I told no one of that decision.

Further motivation came when my college informed me that it would prefer if I attended elsewhere in the future; in other words, I flunked out. I was terribly ashamed of my academic collapse, and so the trip to Israel came at an opportune time.

I became involved with the first man who paid any attention to me. At the end of the summer, when the American students went back to America, I moved in with Julian. In no way was this relationship based on communication; he spoke French, Moroccan Arabic and Hebrew (no English); I had completed one year of college French. We were married in December 1964. Four months later I was ready for a divorce and a return trip to America. Julian was stunned, since he thought we were the perfect couple. There were many transatlantic phone calls as I made arrangements to come back. The divorce papers were practically in hand when there was one final transatlantic phone call. I heard the operator in Israel call the operator in Connecticut, and then heard the

Connecticut operator ring the house. I heard my stepfather answer the phone, and all he said was: "Mrs. Jameson has cancelled the call." The mere sound of his voice was enough to remind me of how much I hated him—I thought, things may be bad here in Israel, but they're worse back in America. I cancelled the divorce and stayed in Israel.

In 1965 my daughter, Carla, was born. Pregnancy was the first time in my life I felt "normal"; it was a happy time for me. I became the English teacher in the kibbutz school, and was the liaison when other student groups came to visit. One year a girl who came with one of those student groups seemed able to look right through me and the "picture-perfect" impression I was attempting to give—American girl meets Israeli and lives happily ever after. In 1966, I became pregnant again, but I was quite ill with this pregnancy.

1967 was a year filled with major events: In April, I lost the baby in the seventh month of pregnancy. In May, Julian and I decided to come to America to stay, where my father said he would help us get established. In June, we were trying to leave when the Six Day War erupted. (My family, of course, thought it was 1939 all over again, and tried unsuccessfully to get us out of there before the war started.) In July, we (Julian, Carla and I) came back to America although, deep in my heart, I knew that the marriage would never survive outside of the kibbutz's protected environment. At first we lived with my father and stepmother. In August, I was hospitalized for surgery. In September, I discovered I was pregnant and had an abortion. (It was illegal at the time and had to be done secretly, with no possible trace to my father, a local physician.) In October, Julian, Carla and I moved to Miami Beach.

I went through all of these things and talked to no one about my feelings. I just knew I was going crazy. I was having recurrent dreams of going back to college, looking for James. I watched soap operas and cried for hours; I was terribly depressed. I made plans to get away and visit my mother in New Jersey for Christmas (she had finally divorced my stepfather). My secret plans were to find my first love, James, just like in my dreams and pick up where we had left off.

Carla and I did go north for Christmas. Before I could set eyes on James, my mother arranged a date for me with a group of her friends, including a college professor named Simon. It was love at first sight; he would be my ticket out of the marriage. I simply never went back to that apartment in Miami Beach. Still believing we were the perfect couple, Julian came to see us, but there was no way I was going back.

For some legal reason, I had to establish further residency in Florida. So for six weeks, Carla and I stayed with friends of my mother in Gainesville, Florida, until the divorce would become final. Gradually, it became clear that the long-distance affair with Simon was dissolving and he and I were not going to live happily ever after.

As the date to go to court in Miami and finalize the divorce came closer and closer, I began to have insomnia and listened to all-night radio. I started calling the late-night disc jockey, and that's how Doug entered my life. It was love at first sight, or at least, to bed quickly. I could not be alone, but most of all, I could not face going through the divorce alone. Conveniently, Doug lost his job at the radio station, left Gainesville with me, and came to Miami. After the divorce, the three of us took off for Cape Canaveral where Doug thought some friends might be able to give him a job.

Doug was much more sexually experienced than I was, i.e., "good in bed." I thought it peculiar that sex was so enthralling, even though I didn't like him very much as a person. The situation deteriorated; I began having fantasies of walking into the ocean and never coming back.

Finally, I got a job as an employment counselor at an employment agency. I made lots of flirty phone calls, but placed no one in a job. In June 1968, Doug moved out. My father came and rescued Carla and me. He moved us down to Miami where I went back to school to finish my degree. I am deeply grateful to my father for picking up the entire costs for that year.

Ironically, the subject I majored in was an interdepartmental potpourri called "Human Relations." My first professor had just returned from a week at Esalen Institute and was trying out new Gestalt techniques on us. One day a local therapist came to class and led a few exercises; I began crying and could not stop. Shortly thereafter, I entered therapy with her. I felt that my inner life was totally insane, except for that one hour a week with the therapist where I felt some type of honesty. It was the first time in my life I told anyone what was really going on with me; I was twenty-four years old.

Shortly after my arrival back in Miami, some family friends asked me to talk about kibbutz life at a meeting. I knew, too, it was a set-up, since a recently widowed university professor (with a young daughter just Carla's age) was going to be there. He and I became "an item." Visions of sugar-plums danced in my head; I had the scenario all planned—wife of university professor, mother to two young children, etc. Ron was twenty-five years my senior, but "love conquers all." I had a few disquieting moments when I realized his three-year-old daughter was not yet toilet-trained, and that Ron was totally passive about her.

The four of us (Ron, his daughter, Carla and I) flew north to spend Thanksgiving with my mother in New Jersey. I used to think my mother hexed my relationships because somehow, under the stress of that visit, the whole house of cards Ron and I had built together quickly fell apart. Ron and his daughter flew home Friday, two days earlier than scheduled: I rejoiced and planned never to see him again, ever.

At four a.m. on Saturday, my father called from Miami. There had been an accident on the way home from the airport and, at that moment, Ron was undergoing neurosurgery. The child had only minor injuries. I did not return immediately to be at Ron's bedside, since I had decided to escape from the relationship. Ron was in a coma for a week and hospitalized for months; he lost his mobility on his left side. His personality never returned to what it was before the accident, although he was able to maintain his teaching career. Over the years, while he became an advocate for the physically handicapped, I became racked with guilt at the mere thought of him.

Suddenly I discovered I had been in school for six months and had no friends, since I was totally absorbed with Ron. I made friends with a flashy, very rich guy who, like me, was older than the other students. I designed elaborate seduction plots which never materialized; he just wasn't interested. That spring my mother came to visit for a few days; my friend acted more animated with *her* than he was with me. I seethed with rage and jealousy. Eventually, mother went home. I wrote reams of poetry about these encounters and near-misses of the heart.

I began dating Chris, my milkman. Like me, he had not dated as a teenager, and had had his first sexual experience at age twenty-two. He was much less experienced sexually than I was, but he was in the "personal rescue" business; his hobby was handwriting analysis, and I was convinced he knew more about me than I knew about myself. I needed someone to turn to, although (once again) I never felt that I liked him very much.

After graduation from college in Miami, I found an administrative job in a social service agency and was able, at last, to support myself and Carla. After six months of dating Chris, I became pregnant. I thought that the abortion would be the convenient way to end the relationship, but afterward I found I needed Chris more than ever, and he *was* there to take care of me. We began going to encounter groups together, trying to "fix" things. After a year we became engaged, and a year later (1971) we were married. At last I was going to become the American Housewife, which I had not been during my first marriage on the kibbutz. My dream was that Chris would continue working so that I could quit and stay home. It ended up with me working and putting him through college. I attributed our unhappiness to the fact that he was going to school and we had so little time together. We tried lots of things to liven up our sex life—pot, pornography—we even went for a series of modified Masters and Johnson counseling sessions.

After five years, I knew in my heart it was over. The only reason I stayed longer was my belief that I could not sleep alone. I stayed for another two years, gathering resentments to power my lift-off from that relationship.

During Labor Day Weekend, 1977, we separated. In my mind he was the villain and I had been the victim. The second divorce was even more devastating to me than the first; now I *knew* I was a failure in love and had two divorce papers to prove it. Professionally, by this time, I had become the director of a social service program, but I had too many troubles of my own to be able to talk to anyone else with problems. For the next six months, my boss transferred me to straight administrative paper busywork.

My life of serial promiscuity began about three months after the second divorce. I would meet someone, and it was always total love at first sight. If a man called me three times, I already had the wedding planned in my head. Gradually disillusionment set in, followed by my complete rejection of the person. In order to meet people, I went to singles' groups and dating services.

In 1979, I began to prepare for a career change. I hated my job, but had always loved music and was very active in local choruses, etc. To get my degree in music education (a two-year process), I began a schedule of working part-time and going to music school full-time. It was a "mid-life career change" and sounded great; secretly, I was terrified. I faced a tremendous salary reduction; I had no idea if I could even pass my classes (since I believed I was twice as old as all the other students and half as talented), and I felt total panic at the thought of actually teaching children in the classroom.

When I began music school, I was seeing three different men, one of whom was married. I thought, "At last I'm dating" (as opposed to being totally wrapped up emotionally in one person). In October 1979, I discovered I was pregnant and I was not sure who the father was. I was in total despair. I believe now that the Hand of God touched my life at that point. I had to have a sonogram test; the results revealed not only the precise length of the pregnancy, but also that this was a placenta previa and would not go full term. The exact date enabled me to identify the father, and he was emotionally supportive to me, at least beforehand. I hated the idea of another abortion, but arranged for one anyway. Mercifully, the night before, I began to miscarry.

This was one of the lowest points of my life emotionally. Of course, I told no one at school. However, the experience did propel me into group therapy, for which I am grateful.

I continued my life of music school and working. The pattern with men became frighteningly repetitive—very brief encounters. I noticed that if I had anything at all to drink on these "dates," it was a certainty that we landed in bed. So I decided that the way to control this was, simply, not to drink. However, even this resolve did not keep me from the behavior I regretted so deeply afterward.

Right before I was to start student-teaching, I made a play for a friend, a fellow student. He wasn't interested, but that evening he gave me the book by Ken Keyes, *Handbook to Higher Consciousness.* I could see that my relationships with men were what Keyes called an addiction. But now what?

I got a job teaching (elementary school music) almost immediately after graduaton. I wanted to quit every day during the first six weeks. I died a million deaths in the classroom. It felt like "feeding time" at the piranha cage—children can smell insecurity and I was much too frightened to admit I had no idea what I was doing. Nonetheless, I knew in a peculiar and deep way that the elementary school classroom was The Last Stop for me. I couldn't get married and solve my problems; I'd done that and that hadn't worked. I couldn't relocate and solve my problems; I'd done that and that hadn't worked either. I couldn't change jobs and solve my problem, since I had *just* done that, and that didn't seem to be working either. It began to dawn on me that maybe, just possibly, *the problem was me.*

Throughout all this time I was going to therapy. Finally, in the summer of 1982, the issue of being sexually compulsive arose. At first I was furious that my therapist would use such a term with me. I finally decided, though, that since I was compulsive, I might as well just go with it, and stop trying to control it and fight it. The next person to enter my life (August 1982) was Charles. Within three weeks we were living together. It was perfect—we engaged in a joint "rescue mission." I was going to "cure" him, and he was going to "cure" me.

But something unexpected happened. A year later (summer 1983) when I reached the highest weight in my own "recorded history," I joined Overeaters Anonymous. (I had tried everything else—Weight Watchers, etc.) I lost the extra thirty-five pounds very quickly that summer and fall, but my problems really started when I got to goal weight. For years I had thought that everything would be great when I was thin. At goal weight, though, the only change was that now I was packaged in a thin body, while remaining the same person inside. I had innumerable food "slips." It took me thirteen months to get thirty days of back-to-back Westminster abstinence. During one of these periods of slip after slip, I began to attend open A.A. meetings. I was certainly NOT (I thought) an alcoholic—I never drank that much. I just needed to hear from people for whom a slip was more dangerous than just having one "M&M"—or so I thought at the time.

One night as I was driving to the meeting, I happened to ask myself, "How had alcohol affected my life?" I almost drove off the road in shock when I remembered that a point had come in my "dating" when I realized I could not control my behavior if I drank, and that I had resolved not to drink if I went out with someone on a date.

That night a young girl in the program said, "It doesn't make any difference how old you are, or how much you drank, but if you don't like the results in your life, you have a problem . . ." After much agonizing, I joined A.A. the next day. For a long time, though, since I had drunk so little (just two glasses of wine or even one strong drink) I thought I had a "mild case" of alcoholism, not like those *other* people who REALLY drank—and certainly, not like my stepfather.

Through an incredible (and miraculous, I now believe) chain of events, Pat Carnes's book, *The Sexual Addiction,* fell into my hands in August 1984. One of the first stories is about an elementary music teacher who leads a double life. At last I had seen *my* story. I experienced the kind of surrender I'd heard people talk about at A.A. meetings, but had never really felt with regard to alcohol or to food—the shattering pain, and the relief at having a diagnosis. The next day I called all over Miami, looking for a Twelve Step group dealing with sexual addiction. Nothing. Finally, I called the hospital in Minnesota where Pat Carnes had done his work. The secretary sent me the address of S.L.A.A.

My recovery has involved severing my relationship with Charles. I believe that this was one of the *first* decisions *I* have ever really made. Today Charles' name is on my gratitude list, as are all The Men, and my two former husbands. If they hadn't been in my life, I wouldn't be where I am today. Thankfully, I know, too, that my experience with Charles is the last relationship like *that* I ever have to have.

Withdrawal is serious business. I read the withdrawal chapter in this book frequently. I was able to get to an actual S.L.A.A. meeting in Boston recently, and I found a sponsor who had helped me to define what my sobriety in this program means. I am trying to start an S.L.A.A. chapter here in Miami, and I believe it will happen at the right time which, apparently, is not yet.* I am learning who I am, which I never knew. I always relied on a man to tell me, and then I would try to be like a chameleon to fit him, or try to get him to fit me.

In the book, *Twenty Four Hours A Day,* the entry for March 12 says: "Your alcoholic self is not your real self. Your sane, sober, respectable self is your real self." What a gift!

During the years my life revolved around men, my daughter was not the focus of my life. I am grateful that I have a program to help me make amends to her. I am beginning to value this period of sexual sobriety as a time to get to know myself, and I make continual discoveries.

I know now that everything I ever wanted from a man is contained within Step Three. I have the seeds of a relationship with the higher Power, and the miracles are too numerous to tell. I used to think that strange coincidences happened in my life every few years or so. Now I find the Hand of God touching my life every day.

I have told my story in some detail because of this quotation from page 124 of the A.A. Big Book:

---

*Ed. note: There are now S.L.A.A. meetings in the Miami, Fla., area.

Showing others who suffer how we were given help is the very thing which makes life seem so worthwhile to us now. Cling to the thought that, in God's hands, the dark past is the greatest possession you have—the key to life and happiness for others. With it, you can avert death and misery for them.

In the choruses I used to sing with, we often sang Masses, which included the phrase, "Salva me, fons pietatis." For me it has come true, for I have been saved from a life of despair and hopelessness by the Fountain of Mercy.

The Flame
That Didn't Blow Out

My parents were, I now realize, very young, reluctant, babyboom, "GI bill" parents. When I was a boy, they seemed very unhappy. My spunky mother—rarely "sweet"—was at times hostile, at other times withdrawn and depressed. My father's drinking and working clouded what I hoped were the good intentions of a sad man. The atmosphere at home was usually tense and argumentative, and I felt unsafe except when my grandfather visited. Then my parents acted like T.V. parents.

My grandfather often took me for rides, which I loved. When I was in kindergarten, he died, and I felt cold, scared and alone. I knew then that if I were going to grow up and be normal, I would have to make it happen myself. At the same time I felt protective of my parents and my younger brother, responsible somehow as if I were the adult/parent.

Because home was so volatile I got very good at predicting what was going to happen next. I had a kind of radar which "knew" when a miscommunication was just another step on the way to an inevitable argument. I became a people watcher, paying more attention to eyes and actions than to words. I learned to see what was happening between people.

About this time I noticed that when I started to tell responsible adults what was really happening in my life and at home, their faces would become grave and concerned. These looks made me aware that I would have to make up or add "normal" experiences in my childhood that I could talk about, then and later as an adult. So I consciously climbed trees, played Little League, joined a church choir, and became a Cub Scout and later a Boy Scout in order to be "normal"—and later hopped freights, dived off highway bridges, and was a daredevil to distinguish myself.

By the fourth grade, kids called me "The Professor" because I knew so much about sex. I was really obsessed. I had gone to the library and learned how to find information. In seventh grade we had "lights out" parties, and although they weren't very "hot," they were the hottest thing going on. Occasionally I'd have nonorgasmic sex with other Boy Scouts. But mostly that was just experimental stuff which I pretended to dislike more than I really did. I really found it exciting and fun, which concerned me some at the time.

The summer of eighth grade, my father was newly sober and we moved away. In the new town I started off on the wrong foot and was never really accepted. Sexually and socially the kids were much slower than they had been in the previous town.

There was a kid there whom I'm sure was homosexual. He and I would sleep out and have sex together occasionally. That was a very strong connection for me. For the first time, shared sexual excitement was a "time out" from the social isolation at school and the arguments between my now united parents and me.

The summer I was fifteen, I went to a church conference. My roommate had a beard, and when he talked (the first afternoon) about smoking pot and having sex, I said, "I do that, too." He looked at me and flat knew it wasn't true.

But that evening as I was walking by a group of people, one of the college girls reached out, pinched my cheek and said, "Ooooh, when you grow up you're going to be something special." Bold as brass, I put my arm around her and replied, "Anne, I'm grown up now." And we walked off together toward the orchard. After an hour or so of preliminary kissing and hugging, she asked me where my room was. What happened next was very special. There was no struggle to remove her clothes. This wasn't flirting. She knew what she was doing, and pretended that I did too. Making love that evening was just wonderful—humorous, warm, and my young idea of heaven.

At one point my roommate returned, took one look at us in bed, apologized and left. Later, when we finally got up, he invited us to smoke a joint with him—which we did. What a great combination, I thought: sex and drugs all in one night!

During that six-day conference I had sex with two other girls. I bought an ounce of grass and came home feeling a foot off the ground.

The first night home I went to see an attractive girl who was a "buddy" of mine. I was animatedly telling her about my new sexual discoveries when I realized that I should shut up and kiss her. We became secret lovers that night.

So in that seven-day period my world really changed, although I was still socially an outcast. I became like the "bad girl" in town. Girls were made fun of if they were seen with me in public. It bothered me that they would pretend not to know me at school, but at least I had the intense sexual pleasure that was by now so important. And I sure kept a lot of secrets!

For the next three years, home was like a battlefield; school was torture, and sex, drugs and alcohol (in that order) provided the only relief I got. For the last year and a half I was in town, I rented a room I called "my apartment" (my parents never found out about this) and it was here that I invited girls.

After I graduated from high school in 1967, I went off to college. Within six weeks of being on campus one girl told me she was pregnant, and before Thanksgiving another girl was pregnant. I knew with my background I was too unstable to parent any children. But abortions were illegal and cost about $750. I had to scramble to come up with $1500. And scramble I did.

I figured out that the quickest way to make money was to deal drugs. By Christmas I had paid for the abortions, quit school, was flying around the country, and loved it. I discovered "big city women" in New York.

I now had money, and cocaine, and was still learning to figure out who women's fantasy lovers were and to "become" those guys. The dope dealing was scary; the money and women were exciting. But I couldn't tell anyone who I REALLY was, and was confused behind the facade. Sex was a way of "stopping the clock," a place to go when the rest of the world was too much.

What I learned during this period of my life was that although I was very versatile and confident sexually, I wasn't so good emotionally. I didn't know how to express my feelings. What I did was sexualize my feelings. I would be up in the mountains, say, and see a sunset which moved me, and I wouldn't know what to do with the emotions. So when I got back into town, I'd express those feelings sexually.

When I turned twenty later that year, I had the insight that I shouldn't drink, take drugs, or have sex with women I didn't love. I also realized that my spoken English had deteriorated, I was using "druggie jargon" and I hated it. So I decided to clean up my act. I got a job building houses during the week, and on weekends I climbed mountains. I only occasionally drank and drugged, did become physically healthy again, and still saw some women. During the spring I also again dropped into and out of college very quickly.

I moved to northern New England and ran a coffee house/rock-n-roll palace. There were lots of women coming in and out and I got a lot of sex. It looked like I was just another kind of "macho exploiter" because I had sex with so many different women. But inside *I* was always the grateful one. I acted more cavalier than I actually felt. I was really often very desperate.

People would frequently ask me, "Gee, how come you can connect so often?" I didn't tell them it was the most important thing in my life. When I didn't get sex, I had (what I later learned were) anxiety attacks. But sex didn't seem so important to other people and the fact that I was so preoccupied with it embarrassed me—a lot.

In September 1970 I took a job at a private school in the Southeast, working with emotionally disturbed high school kids. Within four days, the art teacher (Lee) and I had fallen head over heels, madly in love. I'd never allowed that to happen before, but her secret fantasy man was a lot like who I thought I was then. I thought she was the "perfect woman" and (I hoped) she thought I was the "perfect man." It started like a fairy tale with the addition of passionate, all-night sex. I used to say to her, "I can't wait to see how this movie (our life) ends."

We stayed at the school for a while, then moved to the Boston area. And before long there was trouble. We didn't know how to argue. *I* didn't know how to argue with people I loved, although I could argue with strangers, even have physical fights with them. But with people I cared for I could only be "nice" — or elsewhere.

Most of the time I would be "monogamous," but about every six weeks or so I would have sex with some other woman. It was always a "limited engagement" with no repeat visits. And it was always because of "special circumstances." I never thought that individually Lee and I were perfect, but I thought that together we were a perfect fit, the "Love of the Century."

Just before our second Christmas she went away for five days to visit her family. I was used to having sex so often that I immediately met another woman with whom I spent the night. The problem was that I couldn't get over this new affair. It wasn't really perfect with Lee. Part of living with her didn't work, and this new woman filled that part.

I was driving a cab, superintending a building, and doing an occasional dope deal, and I started paying the rent for this other woman too. Lee was devoting herself to her painting full time. And I was supporting both her and this other woman so that she too could devote more time to HER art and to us. So I was a twenty-two year old patron of the arts! I had a problem because I couldn't work twelve and fourteen hours a day and visit this other woman too. I somehow managed it for two to three months and almost came unglued!

I was terrified that Lee would learn about my new girlfriend, but I couldn't stop seeing her. My only hope was to leave town. Perhaps in rural New England I could learn to live with just Lee. Besides, wasn't it city living that caused me to drink and drug so much?

Away from the bright lights, I drank more, tried NOT to play around, argued with my business partner, and watched my investment evaporate. So I started yet another new job and became a supervisor on a construction site. Then things with Lee started to deteriorate. She felt she was too dependent on me, and I felt I should support us both. When I hurt my back and couldn't work or support us very well, the relationship just fell apart. The movie had started like a fairy tale and ended like a nightmare—she never wanted to see me again. How could anything that started so well end so bitterly?

Again I had the insight that I should stay away from alcohol, drugs and women—for at least six months, I thought. Well, I drank, of course, and was celibate seven days—until Lynn appeared. I was really pleasantly surprised that one century could hold "two loves, so big and so wonderful."

There was something different though. With Lee, I always thought she was the one who was under my influence, "under my ether." With Lynn, I would often wonder just WHO was "under the ether." I was willing to do whatever it took to keep her enthralled. And I could only relax when she was "really under." One thing for certain—it was going to take a lot of money. I moved back to the Boston area.

Although I'd been jealous with Lee, she didn't really give me any reason to be. Lynn was another story. She called my hand all the time—she threatened by deed and by word. She did nothing to assuage my fears. I was constantly worried about her screwing someone else (which she never actually did until the end). So although this was the second "love of the century," it was often rocky. Because I had hurt my back and needed to make money, I turned to selling. I found that I was a natural salesman. But I only seemed to be able to keep two out of three parts of my life in balance at one time. If Lynn was happy and I had money, I wouldn't have a social life. If my job would be going great guns and I had a social life, Lynn would want to leave. Or some other combination. I felt like the little Dutch boy plugging the dyke!

And there was another very real problem. My drinking, which had been going on since my early teens, was terrible. I finally got to A.A. and right away I could tell there would be conflict between A.A. and Lynn. She was intensely jealous of all the time I spent at A.A. If I weren't home by 11 p.m. she'd pretend to be asleep and I'd have to wake her up quietly so I could get my "sex fix." And then she'd be pissed off and say, "Why don't you go see your A.A. friends?"

It took me six or seven months in A.A. to learn about asking for help in the Third Step sense of "turn my life and my will over to the care of a higher Power." When I learned to do this, the higher Power handled whatever I turned over much better than I ever had. But it never occurred to me that I could turn over my sex life—or indeed, that I couldn't manage it!

At the end of my first two years in A.A., Lynn broke our deal. She stayed out all night with another man, wasn't contrite, and thought she'd probably see him again. Of course, I'd been sleeping with other women, but "only once," or only in "extraordinary circumstances," knowing that if I got caught Lynn would sleep around and rake me over the coals. I thought she was the best thing that ever happened in my life and that if she weren't there I would just die—really die.

When she broke our deal, I thought about it for a week before I moved out. I wasn't rational, and I thought about suicide. An A.A. friend said to me, "If you're thinking suicide, move out." And so I did—moved out one day at a time. Within thirty-six hours, however, Lynn and I had dinner together and then went "back home to the big bed." Although I'd looked forward to seeing her for dinner and..., being with her was terrible. In other words, the fantasy was terrific and the reality was terrible. And it had been for a long time. I just never admitted it!

My therapist later told me that the hardest thing he had to do then was to get me in touch with how terrible I actually felt, and how angry I was with her as I kept telling myself that she was the best part of my life!

I continued to get really excited about going to see her, and the experience continued to feel terrible. So I'd leave and begin to feel good again. I started cashing in rain checks with other women whom I would see at meetings, do business with, or know in some casual way. I dated around, and began to bracket my visits to Lynn with other women—both before and after. And I still paid her bills although I was living elsewhere.

One day I ran into Rich. I had known him from A.A. but had judged him pretty harshly. I thought he had shown bad taste and judgment by moving on an A.A. newcomer while his wife was pregnant. I hadn't really seen him to talk to for about a year. So when I ran into him I wanted to try to catch up on what he'd been doing. His baby was about eleven months old by then. He was living with his wife, and everything was great. I said that things were fine with me: I had moved out from Lynn, I was dating a lot of other women, and my new job was interesting. He told me he was talking with other people about sexual stuff— thinking of sex as an addiction—and that there were S.L.A.A. meetings every other Tuesday.

So the next Tuesday I went to his apartment for a meeting. Rich was the only other person present and he talked for about an hour and a half. Then I talked for an hour and a half. He suggested handling the sex problem "one day at a time." I responded with, "Forget that! I handled alcohol that way, haven't had a drink in two years, and I'm not going to live without sex one day at a time too!" He was married and that seemed easier to me. But I couldn't imagine being single, having all these women around, and not having sex!

However, I went home, did a lot of thinking, and then did a really intense First, Second and Third Step with sex. Over the next few days I realized I had never turned over my sex life to a higher Power. And I realized that I really could do that—that it was possible to adapt the one-day-at-a-time concept to my sexual and romantic life. Not one day at a time *to stay away from sex forever,* but to turn it over to the care of a higher Power. I was still afraid that my higher Power would forget about my sexual needs, and that I would fall apart and die. And *that* wasn't a casual problem to me!

I started to do a Third Step on a daily basis. In the morning I would ask for help and get centered, and get a sense for my higher Power's will for that day. Now, God never spoke to me saying, "Avoid blondes with long legs," or anything like that. What I did find during those meditations was a calmness. And using the calmness as my indicator, I tried to learn what circumstances, people or attitudes would cause it to disappear. At the same time I tried to notice what I could add and still stay calm and centered. I started going to the meetings regularly. I don't even remember if there were more people than Rich and me at those early meetings.

It was clear to me that I didn't have to stay away from sex forever in those early days, and that I could ask daily for knowledge of the higher Power's will for me. One night after what I crassly thought of as a "filler" date, it came to me that it might be best not to sleep with women in A.A. whom I hadn't already slept with or whom I couldn't imagine loving.

The first time I didn't move on an A.A. woman because she was someone "whom I couldn't imagine loving," I got home earlier than I would have and received a phone call from an A.A. friend of mine, a man. I realized that I didn't know very many men.

I was still going out with all the other categories of women during those weeks. But always after some actual experience or encounter, I would learn to limit categories of contact in the future. One week I included "women in Massachusetts whom I couldn't imagine loving." Another week I included "women out-of-state who might be nice but I couldn't imagine loving." And I found that as soon as I would let go of another category—that is, would not move on a woman in a bookstore or somewhere—I'd end up getting a phone call, going to a Red Sox game, or out to listen to a comic. It was fun. And I was able to keep the calm feeling I was learning to value.

I did notice that I would lose the calmness as my impulse to move on some woman would turn to action. *And* I noticed that I could ask for help and get centered again—and the calmness would return.

Today I can compare that calm, centered feeling to a candle burning steadily. That small flame guided me on my path. When it burned steadily, I was usually on good spiritual ground. When it flickered or went out, I was headed for trouble. The process of stopping what no longer worked, and learning new ways to add things which did work, was pretty smooth. And believe me, I didn't let go of anything that still worked!

Although at sixteen going to bed with someone produced euphoria for four or five days, by the summer of 1977 the same behavior satisfied my anxiety only temporarily. I had to go out and immediately meet someone else. That scared me because I thought I was abusing something, and I was afraid I would become impotent.

After I'd been going to meetings for six weeks or so, and daily asking for the help, cooperation and guidance of my higher Power, I would notice that maintaining a sexual relationship with a particular woman was an awful lot of work, and wasn't really satisfying. Another category would pop up—like "don't screw around with women on the road during the week"—and I would give it up. So sequentially—category by category—I was beginning to stop behaviors which felt bad and which weren't working any more.

Getting in touch with the feeling of calmness inside myself—which I called "being centered"—felt spiritual to me. So when I behaved in ways which interfered with that feeling, or left me feeling bad, I was able to stop the behavior which was producing that feeling. That led me into a pattern of action which was subsequently labelled "sequential withdrawal." I didn't drop everything at once. I did experiment. And I didn't beat myself by demanding that I do everything at once.

I followed the flame of my candle. I can't stress enough the importance of that. I acted and then watched the flame. If it stayed clear, and I felt O.K., I continued the behavior. If the flame flickered or went out, if I got crazy or felt bad, I stopped the behavior. And I continued to get centered every morning, and throughout the day.

I also extended this awareness to how I did business. When I would notice I was selling in a seductive manner, it made me feel bad. And I stopped sexualizing selling.

I was also beginning to see more A.A. people socially, and I was particularly enjoying having dinner with male friends. While I had been so busy with sex, I seemed unable to be a friend. And that was changing now.

On Columbus Day weekend in 1977, I went to see a woman I'd met fifteen months earlier at an A.A. convention. At that time we'd gone to bed, ending a nine-month period of celibacy for her in a blaze of passion. I had decided not to see her again because I was living with Lynn. Since Lynn was no longer in my life, I thought perhaps it was alright to go and see this woman. We went to a motel and had a marvelous time together. The volcanic sexual charge between us was so powerful I just felt insane. I arranged to see her again, but called it off. The sex was so powerful it could blow my candle flame out, perhaps forever. Previously I would have done anything to have sex that dynamic. Now I was more worried about my new inner calm.

At this point I was ready to do whatever my higher Power had in mind for me—ready to surrender to my higher Power—including "no sex with anyone else (for forever if necessary)." I did masturbate sometimes, but only when it felt right. Sometimes it did, and sometimes it didn't. Even when it did feel right, I didn't HAVE to do it—although I had no big prohibitions against it. I didn't need sex as much as I thought I did. I was surprised that, instead of anxiety at the prospect of a sexless night, I experienced calm. My candle seemed to flicker less, became more bright, and I felt good and clear.

On a late October afternoon I went to visit an A.A. friend. She'd asked me to drop by because a non-A.A. friend of hers (Julie) was coming over and she wanted me to meet her. I got centered in the morning, had a Russian Bath, went to the park for a while, listened to the birds sing, and finally, after realizing how pleased I was with my life, I went to Susan's house. There were several A.A. people I knew there. And there sat Julie: attractive, intelligent, powerful, interesting, and clearly not a man's woman. She was obviously living her life, involved with her work, interests and friends.

Well, four of us went for a ride. When I learned that Julie had a car, I suggested that she drive. Although there were people in the back seat, Julie and I were really talking just to each other. It was a warm, friendly, interesting hour's ride. What I didn't do was act like someone different than who I was. I was able to keep that good, centered feeling. I didn't have to become somebody else to keep her interested—she was already interested in finding out who I was. I didn't have to be a secret fantasy man. I just stayed in the place I had learned about in my meditations and with people in A.A. She left at the end of the ride, and I asked Susan if I could have her phone number. I called Julie on Tuesday and asked her if she'd like to go out on Friday night, and she said yes.

I thought our first date would be like one of those 1930's movies where we would have cocktails and dance cheek to cheek. But it wasn't like the 1930's movie. We felt awkward. Then I suggested we go to a coffee house I knew of and talk. And that's what we did. Time didn't stand still while we were talking. It felt enjoyable, and pleasant. Life was going along—a nice life, not a script or a movie.

My impulses were still all toward the movies, however, and that night as we came out of the coffee house it started to rain. I started to hail a cab so she wouldn't get wet, and she just laughed out loud. She didn't know anybody who took cabs so frivolously. She'd grown up on a farm and knew we wouldn't melt in the rain. And I realized again that this was the OLD impulse and it didn't feel right. So we just walked in the rain.

What I was discovering was that I had to learn how to *be* with somebody. I didn't know how, or what to do. All my habits and impulses were geared toward living a movie. I had to "let go," to become fifteen again, to learn new behaviors. I found that I was very awkward when I wasn't playing some movie role—nervous and shy. Instead of making me feel scared, it felt good. I felt "clean."

As we were walking, I put my beret on Julie's head and kissed her. It felt at the time like the natural, friendly thing to do next—and it felt awkward. We didn't know what to do, so we walked a block before we said anything. We held hands, and I noticed that I hadn't felt like this in a long time. When we finally got to my car, I asked her if she would like to come to my house for some home-made strawberry shortcake. She wasn't sure initially but then trusted me enough to risk coming.

We went to my small, furnished apartment, ate strawberry shortcake, and talked. We talked about traveling, teaching, and about old friends. We talked about the present, and I talked too much. Mostly we just had a very relaxed, pleasant time together.

When I realized where the evening might end up, I became really nervous. I excused myself and went into the bathroom, asked for help and got centered.

And the candle stayed lit. It felt like what was happening was right—not like many other experiences I had had. So I went back and asked her if she would like to see the rest of my place. I stayed myself; I didn't play a role in a movie.

The sex between us that night felt good even though we didn't know each other very well. In the morning I made cheese omelets. Later in the day when we stopped at her place, I felt very awkward with her roommates. But we went out for dinner that night, and talked a lot more. I noticed again that I didn't HAVE to tell her everything about me immediately. It felt right to say—or not say—whatever I wanted. No compulsion.

We started to date on weekends because both of us had demanding jobs during the week. Slowly we got to know one another. Sex was always rooted in what the relationship was as we proceeded. It was dependent upon the relationship, in RELATION to it, not to a picture that she or I had.

By Christmas time when she went to visit her family, I realized that this was the first Christmas since I was fifteen that I was going to spend not having sex on Christmas! Even so, Christmas was rather dramatic. I had caught lice from one of Julie's students; I had a cold which turned into the flu; I was nauseated, threw up and had chills. On December 26, I got a speeding ticket and went back to my apartment feeling just awful. And the phone rang. It was Lynn, saying in a seductive, sweet voice, "How are you?"

Instead of saying, "I'm fine," I said, "Well, let's see. I feel sick, I got a speeding ticket, just threw up and now you're on the phone. What do you want?" She started talking about her nephew whom I had been really close to and how much he missed me. Finally, she suggested she come right over and fix me up. I went through, in great detail, why I didn't want her to do that, hung up, and just lay in bed and realized I wasn't going to see her. Although I felt sick, I didn't feel crazy, and I knew *she* wasn't going to fix anything.

In February, Julie and I took a vacation together in the Caribbean. It was like being on separate vacations. We had very different ideas about what we wanted to do. I wanted to drive around, see people, try to speak Spanish, and be active. Julie wanted to sit in the shade and read. So we did different things during the day, and then we'd have dinner together at night. Although it felt fine, I was surprised that it did.

Since I met Julie, I had never entered the bedroom with "expectations." I was able to wait until I felt clear and centered. Sometimes I would be all jazzed up after a week of selling and traveling. And I would know that I wasn't centered enough to make love.

In the spring—on a business trip—I met a model at a trade show who looked like a Playboy bunny. I made plans to see her that night. But at the last minute I called her up and broke the date. Instead, after returning home, I went to see a woman I knew who ran a French restaurant. She wasn't there, and I ended up at the S.L.A.A. meeting instead. I told the people there I'd gotten distracted and started to go out with this woman, but didn't, and I guessed I was "safe."

But the next night I found myself back in that French restaurant dressed in a good suit. I got there late, and thought perhaps it would be more discreet if I waited for her elsewhere, which I did. After a lot of excited talking, hugging and kissing, I realized I didn't want her to know where I lived because I was going to keep her as my secret! And she was embarrassed about taking me to her house and didn't want to go to a motel, although she was willing to come to my apartment.

We finally made a date for the following Monday night, dinner at her place. She was going to make a great dinner and we would then—we knew where that was going. The next day, after talking to her until 4 a.m., I was mostly exhausted and felt terrible. So I went and talked to Rich, and realized that I shouldn't see her again. I sent her a telegram saying, "Lament Monday Meeting Impossible."

Julie came back to town that night and we went out to dinner. Of course, I had told her about S.L.A.A., and that I didn't seem to have a problem as long as I asked for help and went to meetings. I'd said I was no longer acting in ways which felt inappropriate, even though I still had the impulses sometimes. Anyway, we talked, telling each other about our week. And I told her in great detail about the model and the woman at the French restaurant and what I'd been doing. She listened to most of it, but before I got to the end, the telegram part, she left the restaurant. I finished my meal, did a massive Third Step, asked for help, and hoped I was doing to right thing. I really wanted her to know who I was, and that I did have trouble with this stuff, and that this was how it went sometimes. I didn't want to sugar-coat my message. So I had held the fact that I didn't actually sleep with the woman until the end. I was trying to let her know what my world was like when it was wrong.

When I finally left the restaurant and went outside, she was waiting for me in the car. I got in and we talked. I finished the story, making it clear that there was nothing she needed to do, and that it was my difficulty.

We continued to see each other. After we'd known each other nine or ten months, I noticed that we had more affection for each other. More was expressed sexually, and I thought sex this good had to be crazy and I must be in danger. I talked about my concern at S.L.A.A. meetings and other people didn't think it was so crazy. Here I was, growing sane, and feeling so different I assumed it MUST be crazy.

Shortly after this I started to realize that if I weren't very careful I was going to marry Julie. I had an idea that our relationship was going in that direction. I found myself, not fantasizing, but thinking what it might be like "if." Then I would think about my background, and the fact that I certainly didn't know of many good marriages, and keep silent.

I took her on a business trip with me in the fall for five days. She was able to see how hard I worked, how early I got up, how relentlessly I talked to customers, how isolated and lonely it all was. At the end of the trip, we rented a cabin in Maine. It felt wonderful to be there with her for several days. I liked the feeling so much that all the way back I talked about how I wanted to be a bachelor for the rest of my life. The day after we returned she took off for New York to visit a friend. And for a week I didn't hear from her.

I picked her up the day she returned. We didn't talk about love or marriage then. Only slowly did we begin to talk, at first hypothetically: "If you married . . ." or "What would your needs be if you married . . . ," etc. I still had major reservatons about marriage. And I didn't talk with Julie about it much—although I did talk about it at S.L.A.A. meetings or with Rich.

That Christmas we went to the mountains and spent ten days staying at various New England country inns. I promptly got sick and spent much of the time in bed. We talked a lot—great conversations about the possibility of marriage. I wasn't proposing exactly but I did talk about what we might need, about what our views of marriage were.

One of the most important issues was children. After my childhood and life, I thought there was about a 5% chance I could ever trust myself to have children. Julie thought there was about a 5% chance she would NOT want to have children. We each had a 5% negotiating position and were both very clear about how we felt, although we knew that change could occur. We trusted each other, though, and I said that she had a better case to argue than I did. I was still afraid she might marry me, then pull the rug out from under me and I would fold.

But six months later we were married by her minister father in a ceremony we designed. We held the ceremony in a Quaker meeting house: no sides to the wedding parties, and no giving away of the bride. It was a very moving wedding. My father cried (a first!) as did many others. We spent our wedding night at the Ritz, a hotel I had saved for a special night.

In July, Julie hurt her back and was to be out of work for a month. Ten days later I lost my job. I had the insight then that I should go to school and stop selling, but I didn't understand how to do it. We did go to the country for a couple of days and I remembered that I did have some other options—like carpentry. But I got another sales job and kept selling.

In November my car burned up, and I changed jobs again. The day after our first anniversary I lost another job—a real shock. But the message and pattern seemed clear: I was doing the wrong things for a living. When I asked for help, the direction seemed clear. So Julie and I talked it over and I went back to school. I stopped being the major bread winner, and Julie continued her work. We scaled down our standard of living, and at age thirty I became a student again. I had to start from the beginning as a freshman. I enrolled in an independent study program with a two-week residency every six months. And it worked very well for me.

Anyway, I went back to school, hoping the baby question would just go away. Of course, it didn't. Julie brought it up again. I would say, "We just can't do it. We have no money. It's crazy, with my background. We're all drunks, lunatics." And I'd hear her say, "We have to. There's no way we can't. I'll die if we don't." And we would find ourselves in black/white, "either/or" positions—with no "and/also" negotiating room.

We went into couples' counselling to learn how to talk to each other without ending up in absolutist positions. It took about a year for my position to shift. And then, in a two week period, I moved from "never" wanting kids to thinking about "how it might work." I realized that Julie would be broken in some important way if we didn't have children. That year—for Christmas—the only thing I had wanted was an erector set. Not for myself really, but for a child. I got it—a great big, old-fashioned kind. And one day toward the end of that time I said, "Yes, let's have a child. But not today—after I graduate." I was still stalling for time!

I knew by then that Julie and I had learned how to declare ourselves in affection and in anger. I had learned finally how to take issue—to argue—with people who were close to me. I was able to trust myself to be angry and clean at the same time. So the resolve to have a family meant more than just children. It was also a landmark in my ability to make a relationship work by not being "nice" to cover up issues, and by not selling myself short.

Much of the work had been done in continuing therapy, both with Julie and on my own. Some of the work had been carried out with an old A.A. acquaintance with whom I had become close. So now I had a relationship with Julie which was loving, full of trust, and workable—and I was also able to develop an important friendship with Tom.

As I look over this story and think about it, the thing which is more important to me than anything else is how I learned about the candle flame that didn't blow out. From my experience I was able to make sense of what felt right by experimenting and paying attention to what worked and what kept me centered. Bit by bit I was able to stop behaviors which made me crazy. I didn't stop everything all at once—only slowly, with the help of my higher Power, over time.

Early on, I was even afraid to talk about what was happening because it didn't fit the prevailing S.L.A.A. experiences which were being reported by others. I was afraid that from the outside, to someone else, it just looked like the same old pattern—sleeping with Julie on the first date, for example. From the *inside,* however, it was a qualitatively *different* experience. I was afraid to talk about it for a while because I didn't want to risk judgment by the few people around S.L.A.A. at that point.

In S.L.A.A., I learned to follow the candle flame, to let it glow clearly— and to pay attention when it didn't. As a result my life no longer feels like a movie. It feels like MY LIFE. I am living my life now. I used to say to Lee, "I can't wait to see how this movie ends." And then when we split up I remember saying, "This IS how the movie ends, I guess." Well, the movie did end, and my life began. I'm not trying to be the secret fantasy of anyone else. I don't mold my behavior to play a part which someone else writes. I can be who I really am, and where I really am now.

Much of the last five years has been spent developing the competencies I might have had if I had not made my life into a movie. As I said, I began and finished school (unlike previous jobs). I now have a job I like. And, even as I write this, my wife and I are expecting a baby any day. Life is good, different from anything I ever fantasized, and it is my life. I am living it, gratefully.

The Reconciliation of Love and Abuse

As a child, abuse meant love to me, and throughout my twenty-six years of adulthood, I have twisted myself and those around me physically, mentally, emotionally, and spiritually to perpetuate this belief. Looking back from the perspective of a newcomer in S.L.A.A. who has used the Twelve Steps to recover from alcoholism, cigarette and marijuana smoking, and compulsive overeating, it seems to me that self-abuse became my major coping mechanism for dealing with life.

Although certain American values were fostered in my parents' house—such as hard work, success, punctuality, obedience, political involvement, and maintaining a good appearance—there was no attempt to practice a spiritual approach to life. When the pressures of too many children, not enough money, or general neediness overwhelmed my parents, they had no higher Power to help make things easier for them, to cast their burdens upon, or to turn to for light and love. Instead, my parents made "higher powers" of each other, with the result that the four walls of our small house often resounded with anger derived from unmet expectations, creating intolerable tension for everyone. My father would deprive himself of rest, relaxation and help in his efforts to get ahead, and in resentment and frustration he would lash out at the family. This could stimulate my mother to emotionally manipulate us through suicide threats. Afterward, she would be very loving, both physically and emotionally. She also physically released her frustrations on her children, and I learned to fight with my siblings as a protection. I never suffered any broken bones, but no part of my body was safe and I was often hit about the face and head. I wanted desperately to love and be loved by my parents, and I decided that I must deserve abuse since they had to be right, and something had to be wrong with me that I would expect any better. At this point, I bitterly and secretly vowed *never* to be vulnerable again and to keep all power over my feelings to myself.

I discovered masturbation at around five years of age. Between then and age twelve, I often enjoyed myself privately in this way, but it became hard when I had to share a double bed with my sister. A desire to have sex with my sister occurred to me, but I did not act it out since sex was a powerful taboo in our house. I was ashamed of my curiosity about my genitals, the sexual act, pregnancy, and the difference between boys and girls. Even underwear was "dirty."

During pre-adolescence, I began to imagine what sex was like. I was a voracious reader and began to search for descriptions of love and sex in written matter ranging from *True Confessions* to medical books. I wondered how I would know when I was in love. It never occurred to me to look to my parents for a model since I had vowed never to be like them.

I began to have crushes on both male and female adults and, having no one to confide in (not even my peers), my imagination ran wild. I felt that I was capable of homosexuality, sado-masochistic love, prostitution, white slavery, and all the most sensationalistic forms of sex and "love."

I was allowed to begin dating at sixteen and, because I had learned flirting and manipulating techniques from my mother, I had many boyfriends. I wanted to be taken places so I used my sexuality by teasing men enough to obtain favors, but not going all the way. I began to go to bars and at twenty-one, in an alcoholic blackout, I came to, sitting in the bushes in my own vomit, my virginity gone. I guarded my body fairly well for two more years out of fear of pregnancy (there was no readily available birth control then) and at twenty-three met and married a fellow alcoholic/sex and love addict.

For sixteen years, a downward progression into alcoholism and sex and love addiction co-existed for us. Charles loved what I had—a female body—and I loved what he had—money, savvy, assertiveness, and a weakness through which he could be manipulated. Early in our marriage, after a country club dance where we had been drinking, I quarrelled with him and tried to slap him. He hit me and, when I saw stars, I felt a sense of power. I was again involved in the abusive type of love I knew from childhood. I thought I had license now to drink more, fight more and make up more.

I was raped in my own bed by a burglar after one year of marriage. Soon afterward I found that my skin crawled when I was touched, and I got the shudders. I tried psychoanalysis to cure my resulting frigidity but it did not work. However, increasing my use of alcohol and drugs numbed me enough to have sex. After five years, my husband told me he found our sex life boring, and in my desperation to cling to him I went to the other extreme and became very active sexually—talking trash, wearing revealing clothing, using pornography, going to strip joints and gay bars, seeking out swinging friends, getting into drunken adulterous episodes. Charles next wanted us to swap with other couples, but I was afraid he'd find a better sex partner and leave me so I would not consent. Our sex life became increasingly sado-masochistic. I would be drunk or high on speed most of the time and would provoke hostility from him. He would try to argue with me or hit me, and either I would get turned on and find the sex more exciting or he would force me to perform oral and anal sex. At other times I went for kinky sex—spanking, whips, belts, bondage, costumes. I sometimes masturbated after he went to sleep since I almost never had an orgasm with him. I didn't really know what an orgasm involving intercourse could be.

By now I could no longer deny the reality of how alcohol was ruining my life so I tried to stop my drinking. After thirty days on the wagon I took a drink at a job-related social and came home to find my best friend and drinking companion, a black prostitute, and my husband doing some drinking. After I did some cocaine and booze, my husband passed out and she undressed, started masturbating, then asked me to help her come. I felt I had to do what she asked. I had now progressed into marital swinging. There were several other bisexual and lesbian alcoholics with whom we had sex. It was never satisfactory.

I hit a bottom with alcohol and drunkenly and repeatedly told my husband to move out. To my surprise he did, and I humiliated myself by begging him to return. When he did not, I went to A.A., found a higher Power, and sobered up, but I swore revenge and tried to humiliate him by accepting as a sex partner every black man who called me from the bar my husband owned. I caught herpes and body lice, but I didn't tell my sex partners. I had sex with married men, had noisy sex in the daytime while my teenagers were home, gave money to sex partners, had group sex, and teamed up with another woman to do trios. One day I had sex with four different men. Eventually, I had sex with lesbians I met in A.A., and then I met Sheila, my addictive/abusive lover for five years.

Sex with her was guaranteed to make me come, and I came to need it like a drug. I felt only she could give it to me. I did everything she wanted in order to protect my supply. For someone who loved abuse, she was made to order. Once I was pushed out on her front porch naked with the door locked behind me until my screams brought her gay male roommate to the door. Another time I was thrown out at midnight without money or car keys. I had money stolen from me and my children, was threatened with exposure as a lesbian at my job, and participated in many other hysterical events. I always saw her as the problem and could not be honest about my own sickness, my need to be abused.

We finally broke up, and my anger kept me celibate for almost three years while I earned a Ph.D. During this time I held on to Sheila mentally since I had repeatedly said that in five years we'd both be ready for our great love to flourish. Well, in half that time I felt that I had earned some sex so I called her. She came immediately and, to my amazement, the insanity and the power of the disease had progressed in me. The symptoms were obvious. My job search lost momentum and I began to clean offices part time. I lost my car, ran up a lot of debt, and imposed on friends and family when running from her. I lied, cheated and stole in order to keep her for my sexual use. I manipulated her emotionally as had been done to me as a child. I hated myself and could not look at myself in the mirror.

On a geographical cure to Boston, I heard about S.L.A.A. at an A.A. meeting. I knew that I was addicted to sex and love so I went to a meeting. I had resistance to letting go of Sheila though, and for six months I kept calling her and playing games until she finally made the break final. When I realized it was really over, I wanted to die, but this time I let go absolutely. I did not tell myself that in five years we'd be together again. This time, I felt the feelings of withdrawal. I lost interest in living and let my appearance go. I binged on food and then starved myself, thereby continuing the abuse to which I am addicted. I had very little energy and needed lots of sleep. I imagined that strangers on the street wanted to attack me. My attitude was negative, I cried constantly, and I hated God for my situation in life.

However, a day at a time I adhered to my bottom-line of not calling Sheila. Today, my bottom line also includes celibacy with no masturbation for a period during which I surrender to the S.L.A.A. program and the Twelve Steps and learn to apply them to my life. The energy transformation that is occurring is incredible. All I have to do is turn to God for help, wait for the sexual feelings to pass, and not act out. I am being rewarded with the ability to make friends in the program, get involved in service at various levels within S.L.A.A., sponsor S.L.A.A. beginners, resume exercise and meditation, take up racquetball and running again, dance, learn typesetting, and accept a more challenging job.

My program comes first today. Anything I am tempted to place before my program and/or God, I am certain to lose. I do not know if there will be another lover in my life, but living one day at a time, I really don't care. I am learning to eliminate abuse of all sorts from my life. I have had to accept my character defects—my readiness to fight, the way I set myself up for abuse, my free-floating hate and anger. I have had to stop judging myself for having obsessive thoughts about another S.L.A.A. member. I have slowed down the punishing schedule I set for myself. I stick with the winners and learn from the losers. I give all I can, in whatever way I can, so that when the time comes that I get the insane urge to throw myself away on an abusive sex or love partner, I will be saved. S.L.A.A. and God can save me if I put them first before my sex drive and my need for love.

I believe that all my needs will be met if I practice a spiritual approach to life. I believe there exists a parallel world of the spirit which contains all the experiences of my childhood and the active phase of my sex and love addiction. When I stay sober and fully experience the pain and the joy of the present, I claim those experiences and grow towards becoming a whole person again. As I call upon God and S.L.A.A. for help, the power of the disease lessens and the reconciliation of love and abuse can take place. It takes place within me as I learn to accept and love myself. I am very grateful to be a recovering sex and love addict today.

I Never Knew I Could Live
Without an Iron Lung

I was in my early fifties, nine years sober in Alcoholics Anonymous, when I began to suspect that what I thought to be my strongest personal asset—that I was a loving, caring man—had always had a component in it that was turning this asset into my greatest liability. At the time, I was two years divorced from my wife of nearly 28 years—M.—whom I loved dearly, or thought I did—the mother of our several children. I had just moved out of the house of a woman— A.—whom I loved dearly, or thought I did, with whom I had been living for fifteen months.

My life was really a shambles. I was unemployed. My only possessions were a beat-up car, some decent clothes, a few books, and a little money as a result of some consulting work that had just ended. Nine years before, when I had come into A.A., I owned a nice home and a couple of cars, belonged to the local country club, was sending our kids to private schools and had all the outer trappings of "success." In A.A. I kept hearing, "Don't drink, go to meetings, and your life will get better." In the next nine years, I didn't drink, went to well over two thousand A.A. and Al-Anon meetings, worked to the best of my ability on the Twelve Steps, and my life just kept on unraveling. I thought I had hit my bottom in my seventh year of sobriety when, just for openers, I went through a divorce and bankruptcy and nearly died from an infection of an abcessed tooth.

I had moved to the opposite end of the country, gotten a job, met A., moved in with her, and for a while my life seemed to be working again. And now here I was, all but broke, out of work and once more alone. I could see that those fifteen months with A. had been a condensed replay of my twenty-eight year marriage. I began to admit that there might be something terribly wrong—not with M.—nor with A.—but with *me*.

Looking back on my life, I could see that for as long as I could remember I'd had girls about whom I had had romantic or sexual fantasies. From puberty on I'd always had girl friends, and if I didn't have one, the most important item on my agenda was to find one in a hurry. I could see that my major identity had always been determined by the relationships in my life and my role in those relationships. I was my parents' son, my siblings' brother, M.'s husband, our children's father, A.'s lover—but who was I all by myself? I had never found out. As an adult I just didn't know who I was without a lot of emotional, mental and physical involvement with women. I was a loving, caring man alright, but that loving and caring *had* to have its focus on a woman who fed the loving and caring back to me in the framework of a sexual relationship. Without that I was, figuratively, a polio victim without an iron lung. A major reason for the breakup of our marriage was that M. finally got tired of being that iron lung.

But I soon found another iron lung in A. I was totally oblivious to the realities of the job I held while living with her. It was a mickey-mouse job with a mickey-mouse company, but it gave me a legitimate front, a place to spend the day and an adequate income, while my *real* career was playing house with my new love. A. finally wised up in much the same way that M. had, and our relationship ended.

I knew something had to change, and knew that something had to be *me*. But *how?* I just couldn't imagine my life without a primary relationship, just as nine years before I couldn't imagine a life without alcohol.

Something outside my conscious awareness—call it the grace of God, my guardian angel, my deep unconscious yearnings, a higher Power—led me into contact with the only S.L.A.A. group in the country at that time. I think I am the fifth or sixth member of our fellowship who came and stayed.

I stayed, but it was, and is, a struggle. I tried just about everything imaginable not to have to face what I had to face. Long-term dependent relationships seemed to be what was causing me the most pain. I had long since learned that for me one-night stands, pick-up bars, prostitutes and the like were all bummers, but I still hoped there was a happy middle ground in a liaison of a few months' duration with no real commitment. So I tried a couple of those and they just turned out to be elongated one-night stands. I tried living as a housemate with a woman who was an old friend and that was the end of the friendship: we each became the dumping ground for the other's unresolved anger. There was a positive fallout, however, from what was otherwise a disastrous few months. I could no longer deny that I *did* have a huge amount of unresolved anger, very subtly hidden, and unless I got it out I would eventually be destroyed by it.

I had finally just had *enough*; enough of anger, enough of dependent relationships, enough of inner turmoil, enough of one-night stands, long or short. What I wanted more than anything else was freedom from the internal fetters that had bound me all my life. I'd hit a "bottom" and something within me just let go and said "yes" to whatever it was going to take to be a free man. I knew the first thing it was going to take was to live alone with no sexual contact.

The next year was one of real growth for me. I entered therapy with real commitment. The therapist and the therapy turned out to be just right for me.

Ever since I had first studied the Twelve Steps of A.A. ten years before, I had known that there was more implied in the Fifth Step than a simple confession. I had taken the Fourth and Fifth Steps several times over the years to the best of my ability, but always knew I had not yet gotten to the "exact nature of my wrongs." Finally, after better than a year of therapy, I was able to fully understand and internalize what that exact nature was.

As a small child, long before conscious memory, I'd had to learn to cope as best I could with a headstrong, eccentric mother who had troubles of her own and a hard-drinking father who loved her dearly and put up with her eccentricities. While there was no economic deprivation, I received some severe emotional and physical battering. The result was that I emerged from early childhood with a lot of unmet emotional needs and buried feelings of fear, anger, resentment, helplessness, and confusion. To deal with these unmet needs and unresolved feelings, I had developed a coping strategy.

This early coping strategy was at the very core of my adult personality—it had carried me straight through my growing-up years and on into my adult life. To use an anology, if I was a computer then that early coping strategy was my basic hard-wired program. The adult manifestation of that hard-wired program was a pervasive pattern of compulsion, addiction, and dependency, covered over by various strategies to hide the pattern even from myself. The heavy drinking was just the tip of a very large iceberg. It was just one manifestation. When I stopped drinking, other manifestations took over, even when the consequences were the last thing I consciously wanted to see happen. Who in their fifties wants to be alone, broke and unemployed? I was truly powerless. The huge amount of guilt and self-recrimination that occurred hardly needs telling. Twice I had seriously examined suicide as an alternative, the last time being in that seventh year of A.A. sobriety.

Since becoming sober in Alcoholics Anonymous, I had read enough philosophy and psychology to understand most of this intellectually, but it was only through therapy that I was able to deal with the hard-wired program at a deep emotional level. I had to look at those early coping strategies and learn to watch myself act out their adult manifestations. Once I could do that, I came to realize that I indeed did have a choice over whether or not I would continue to act out, and thereby gained some conscious control over my behavior.

There is one experience relating to my therapy which shows how resistant I was to examining that hard-wired program. After about ten months of one or two sessions a week, my therapist detected enough chinks in my armor to tell me exactly how things really were with me, which she proceeded to do. As she talked, I knew she was right on target, but that was just while the words went by. Those words simply went in one ear and out the other, and when she stopped, I couldn't have told you a thing she'd said. I was, however, taping my therapy sessions, and in the next few days I listened to the tapes three or four times. The words still would not stick, so I sat down and transcribed the tape on a typewriter—four pages of it. By the time I had done this and then read it over ten or fifteen times, I was finally able to "hear" what she had said.

The reader may wonder, as I did, why I was so resistant to this first real look at the hard-wired program. I'm convinced it was because that program, that outgrowth of the early coping strategies, was so deep in my nature I thought it was *me*—I thought it was my basic identity. If it *was* my basic self, then there couldn't be anything behind it to look at that basic self *with* if I pulled out. Yet here I was, looking consciously at what I had thought to be my basic identity with yet another part of my "self." A conscious part of me was now able to watch what I had thought to be my basic self. So what I thought to be that self wasn't *me* after all—it was only my program. Of course, I had known a lot of this intellectually, but to actually *experience* it was for me the difference between life and death—literally.

I think the most significant words in the book *Alcoholics Anonymous* are in the fifth chapter—"the results were nil until we let go absolutely." "Absolutely" for me finally came to mean *everything*—the last to go being the hardwired program that I thought was me.

Thanks to an upbringing in one of the more rigorous religious traditions, I had bought what has aptly been called the "Judeo-Christian guilt trip"—judgment and condemnation, guilt and punishment, heaven and hell, purgatory and penance. I'd bought these things, but I didn't have to keep them. I could now wrap all this garbage up in a package and take it to the dump. The "exact nature of my wrongs" was not wrong at all. There was no judgment, no condemnation, no guilt, no punishment, no heaven, no hell, no purgatory, no penance: just the adult manifestations of the coping strategy of a small child trying to survive as best he could in the situation in which he found himself.

In my new-found sobriety I started doing some things I had never done before—just for me. I bought a good camera which I had wanted for years, and I really enjoyed using it. I bought a bicycle on which I commuted every day to a job I didn't believe two years before it was possible for me to hold. I went skiing for the first time in six or seven years. I took some painting classes at a local gallery. And most important, I found I could do all these things and more all by myself, or with friends, without the help of the "iron lung" I always thought I had to have. With this came a tremendous sense of freedom that I had never before experienced.

But one thing came very hard—emotional withdrawal from my ex-wife. M. and I had had, looking back on them, many happy years. Ours was a monogamous, committed relationship for more then twenty of those years. Our divorce, while painful, had been without acrimony. We now lived at opposite ends of the country, but we were seeing each other briefly a couple of times a year, and I was in the habit of calling her on the phone every couple of weeks. Our children were supportive of us both. The divorce didn't seem to destroy the sense of family we had all experienced over the years. It was just that Mom and Dad weren't married any more and lived 3,000 miles apart.

I had thought that through time, the S.L.A.A. program, and the psychotherapy, I had let go of M., but I realize now that I had always been holding onto the shred of the fantasy that somehow, sometime, we could reestablish an intimate relationship. My withdrawal, therefore, was not unconditional. In it was a hidden agenda that read, "If I really clean up my act and live an indepedent life, then maybe M. and I can get back together in a new way."

This was brought home to me near the end of my therapy when M. and I spent four days in the same city, visiting each other, some of our children, and friends. At the end of those four days I realized that getting back together with her in *any* form just wasn't going to happen. Within the next week, after eleven months of celibacy, I found myself in bed on two occasions with two different women. I honestly wasn't consciously looking for it, but a couple of women happened to come my way and I responded. I'd heard in S.L.A.A. that we are always tested when we are the most vulnerable. I was vulnerable; I was tested; and I flunked. No judgment or condemnation, no guilt or punishment, no heaven or hell, no penance or purgatory—just a little kid coping with feelings of anger and frustration by going out and getting laid.

Sexual and emotional sobriety are self-defined in our fellowship. Of course, jumping in bed with two different women because of anger and frustration over my ex-wife's attitude did not demonstrate emotional and sexual sobriety on my part. But what would? Did I need to step up the level of my activities: put in longer hours at my job, set up a darkroom and develop my own pictures, join a bicycle club, go skiing more often, sign up for another art class? These are all "worthwhile" activities that I enjoy. But if I was using involvement in such activities as a mask for my own negative inner feelings of fear, anger, resentment, dependency, or loneliness, then these activities are not really so different from the destructive strategies I had used in the past. The basic motive, though not necessarily the conscious one, was the same. What I really needed was to just take it easy and experience my feelings as they really were, face them square on, and deal with them on a day-to-day basis, avoiding behavior that I'd come to identify as troublesome.

This latter approach seems to me the path to the ultimate freedom of not being driven to do *anything*—of acting from choice rather than from compulsion. The real key here is "a day-to-day basis." One day at a time. The past is gone, the future isn't here yet. Be here now. This theme is at the core of any recipe for happy living. It involves, however fleetingly, the experience of a total trust, a total faith, that basically everything is just as it should be at this moment, including my desire for it to be different in the next moment.

I cannot overemphasize here the important role that hard, repetitive work on the Twelve Steps (both in Alcoholics Anonymous and as adopted in the S.L.A.A. fellowship and other Twelve Step fellowships) has played in my ongoing recovery from life-long patterns of multiple addiction. My therapy was really nothing more than necessary professional help with the Fourth and Fifth Steps. But for "hands-on" experience of feelings without taking any measures to avoid them, for disciplined practice of "be here now," there is nothing that takes the place of regular disciplined meditation as suggested in the Eleventh Step. I have engaged in this practice for several years and consider it as of equal importance in my recovery as attendance at meetings and therapy. It is a vital part of my life.

I said at the start of this that I thought I loved M. and thought I loved A. I cannot define love. All I do know is that in my relationships with these two women I experienced a different dimension than I'd experienced in any others. I think that the difference came from the level of my commitment, which in both cases was total and unconditional. Both relationships had rich rewards. Both ended with acute pain for me (and the women) because of my iron-lung syndrome. I have nonetheless experienced the unique joys of an unconditionally committed relationship, and I know those joys to be real joys.

The commitments I've made in my life, including those to M. and A., have all had that same quality of gut-level, emotional response as the commitment I described earlier to do whatever it took to be a free man. As such, they have had a compulsive element in them—I had no choice but to say "yes." I now find I have increasing strength to say "no" to situations that I know are inappropriate and will lead to behavior I know from experience to be ultimately self-defeating, and to say "yes" to various other invitations from the circumstances of my life that I feel will be self-sustaining and self-freeing.

I now spend a lot of time in solitude—which I enjoy, even relish. Mixed with the solitude are experiences of loneliness in varying degrees. But as I observe the lives, the marriages, the relationships of many if not most of my contemporaries, I find an excellent antidote for the occasional twinges of self-pity that come my way. There is no one I really envy.

With the solitude has come an increasing sense of my human dignity, of my self-worth. All my life I've had a sense that way down deep I was a fake. In many ways I was a very good fake. I could almost succeed in hiding the fact that I was a fake, even from myself. But underneath I always knew.

I now know I am for real. That feeling alone has made it all worthwhile. None of us are ever completely free in this life, but those internal fetters that had me bound tight are loosened, if not completely fallen away.

I now feel I would like to share this freedom in a fully committed relation-ship with a woman who is also real and free—to have a sharing, growing part-nership in freedom. It will happen when it happens, if it's supposed to happen; and I am willing, if not yet completely able, to accept the fact that it might not. I can look for a parallel in my personal life for what has happened in my busi-ness life. There was just no way to get from where I was when A. and I parted to where I am three years later . . . just no way. But here I am, and it is real. It isn't fake. Whatever happens in my personal life will be just as real and just as rewarding, providing *I* stay real.

And so my life unfolds—one day at a time.

The Language of the
Emotionally Damaged

At forty-one, I was entering into, and trying to get out of, my fifth major relationship. I had only been single for two days since adolescence. The last fifteen years had been spent with men addicted to alcohol and pot. These men were sensitive, creative, self-involved, and emotionally damaged. My pattern was to use each lover to get away from the last, changing my destination by leaping off one train onto another, never bothering to ask where the next one was going. Since all these relationships were emotionally frightening, draining, and destructive to me, I assumed that the sex was not only my forte, but also the binding force and my prime motive. I later realized that I was on a series of emotional rescue missions, but that sex is often the only language that the emotionally damaged speak. Fortuitously, my latest lover was in his first year of sobriety from alcohol, and I was unable to drink, numb out the emotinal despair, and pour myself into bed.

It felt as if the damage to my loving capacity and self-esteem would be terminal this time. But after three break-ups in a month, I was still unable to stay away.

When my therapist suggested I was an "addict," it was as if a curtain had been drawn, and I saw my whole adult life fall into place.

With trepidation, I hunted down this meeting of sex and love addicts, which surely would be filled with weirdos and rapists, appropriately hidden in the depths of the octopine Lindeman Center, a local community mental health center.

A woman was talking about being raped while hitchhiking on her way home from being raped. I was moved, but felt out of my depth. I was disappointed. The meeting that day seemed to be 95% men, most of them gay, most of them dealing with promiscuity issues. This had nothing to do with me. And I didn't like the term "sex and love addict"—it felt self-damning.

I resolved to start a new group of women "love-obsessives." But while I collected myself to do that, I went to meetings.

The large meetings threw me back on all the old feelings that had perhaps dropped me into addiction in the first place. It was like being the new kid in grade school eating alone at recess, terrified people would see my aloneness.

Moreover, snubs were enormously confusing in this group context. If someone seemed short with me, the possible interpretations seemed infinite. They didn't like me; or they did like me; or they were afraid I would think they liked me; or they were afraid I liked them; or afraid I didn't like them. Beyond that, I had never had a male "friend" in my life, making casual friendly connections apparently impossible.

Meanwhile, I was hearing people say things they had never said to anyone before—not to their lovers, their spouses, their therapists. I was watching people change weekly, acquiring trust and a sense of belonging to the human race. I was hearing people praying for their lives, giving up the only reality they'd ever known for some thing they only hoped was there. I realized that if any group was going to work for me, I was going to have to surrender, not take control. So I stayed at S.L.A.A.

Thanks to the intimacy of the smaller meetings, I was beginning to feel a deep sense of connection, to have people I looked forward to seeing, was concerned about, prayed for, and counted on. I told my story. I started socializing after meetings. I took phone numbers.

But I didn't actually make phone calls. And I didn't get a sponsor. And I stayed in phone contact with the lover I'd left. And after ten weeks, I had a "slip" with him.

I had counted on feeling no guilt. And this was the case. I had not counted on a reawakening of all the yearning for him, the crying need of every cell in my body to bond again. I had not counted on having to go through all the tearing feelings of withdrawal again. I didn't feel as if I'd had a "slip." I felt as if I'd "broken out," like a whole herd of wild horses.

Although I still didn't feel ready to get a sponsor in the program, I used someone outside of the program for that purpose, and spoke to my lover once more to tell him that we would not be in phone contact for a long time.

Withdrawal was much harder the second time. The image that came to me was of having spent my life on a desert filled with mirages of lush watering holes which dried up on contact. I had spent years at the site of each vanished mirage, hoping beyond hope. Bordering the desert was a mountain ridge, beyond which lay the real but unknown valley of "recovery." To get there I had to pass through a long dark tunnel through the hills. The tunnel was withdrawal. It was a place of limbo. There was no light at the end of it yet. It was going to be a long walk. But I knew I wasn't walking through it alone.

It was becoming abundantly clear to me that if the program was going to work for me, I couldn't just put my old behaviors on ice and expect them to look any different when I thawed them out in a year or so. I was going to have to acknowledge the healthy needs and instincts that motivated my old patterns—and find a way of meeting those needs—to extract what had been vital and successful in those romantic and sexual bondings, and then integrate those qualities with the reality I was discovering and creating.

Most recently, after a meeting, a couple of S.L.A.A. members helped me to realize that it's okay to ask for help and to make phone calls from a position of need. I have surrendered with gratitude to the idea that I need a sponsor.

In maintaining my sobriety, I find it more useful to keep in mind what I call my top line rather than my bottom line. My top line is what I *do* want for myself, my program goals.

I want to integrate myself physically, emotionally, mentally, and spiritually; to relate to others from a state of wholeness; to live making decisions from a place of freedom and clarity rather than compulsion and confusion; to feel sufficiently safe to stay open enough to find the little realities of life moving, rather than needing to get dropped off a cliff to get a thrill. I want to be present, see things the way they are, and be glad to be alive. These things are beginning to happen for me.

As Subtle as the Force Behind
a Martial Art

I am writing my story in my first year of sobriety in S.L.A.A. with the hope that you too will gain something much needed, as I have.

I was raised in an alcoholic home and entered into a love-through-pain pact with myself that became as subtle to me at times as the force behind a martial art. My parents were Catholic and I was raised accordingly, going to parochial school, becoming an altar boy, spending most of my young life daydreaming and playing at athletics (which I think helped save me). I also can still remember, in my early years, my sister wrapping her warm body around me at night when I couldn't sleep, or watching her get dressed and feeling awe-struck at her beautiful body—dying to get some for myself.

I was subtly abused, physically, by my father when I was young, and mentally abused by the rest of my family, who figured being cruel was a form of having fun. As the youngest of five children, I grew up trying to be tough, but at the same time I was very sensitive to all the jesting at my expense that went on in the family. I didn't know that alcohol was already the main factor in my life (because of my father's drinking problem), and surely I didn't know that I was ever going to be affected, and later develop my own alcohol and drug problem.

I was pretty confused and spent a lot of time fantasizing about being the best boxer, fighter, football player, basketball player, baseball player, pole vaulter, etc. I was good enough at sports to keep these fantasies alive for years and years, until alcohol (which I initially hated but came to rely on) took over and filled in the gaps of love and happiness for me. But I am ahead of myself.

Around puberty I made the mental connection between my penis and girls' anatomy; I found a new ballpark to play in, and I was off and running. I can still remember masturbating in a field across from two older women's home (hoping both that they would and wouldn't see me), eking out a tiny bit of sperm, and hitting the sky with pleasure. Then I remember feeling pain from religion-derived guilt afterwards. However, I continued to seek the pleasure and relief at full force, and would do anything to get it.

The older I got the more confused I got—caught between the relief and the guilt, between being sexually driven and love-needy. By the time I was seventeen, I was using drugs enough to end up with hepatitis. I also was playing baseball, and my alcoholic father was the coach of the team. Around this time I got friendly with some guys in a rock band, and they asked me to audition as a singer for this band. I did, got the job, and moved in with them.

Then came the horrors at night—I was on my own, away from my abusive parents, and I was lost. What to do? Have a homosexual affair—*anything* that would help me endure my secret sickness. This affair worked for a while because it continued to make me feel a lot of the old stuff (pleasure, guilt, shame, etc.) that I had become accustomed to in the past.

So on I went until one night I got thoroughly raped by some people who were staying at my partner's place. I was devastated by this experience. Therapy, which I had started a while earlier, wasn't working. (I was drinking and smoking pot, taking sleeping pills and valium.) I continued therapy and continued to be confused as to where and what my problem was. I also continued to masturbate more and more, seeking oblivion from my discomfort.

This whole sludge-ball pattern ambled on for some seven years until I reached the point of being more and more panicky and couldn't escape my panic. I had joined another band during this period and got myself into all sorts of jackpots involving wives of the other band members.

Leaving the band in disgrace, I came back to Boston disgruntled and got a straight job. Then I met a girl whom I started dating while, on the side, I chased sexual oblivion for the next several years, intriguing with prostitutes and feeling guilty. I even started making obscene phone calls and got caught when my step-mother had her phone line tapped and the calls traced. I was busted with my pants down and laundry showing. I got away with a slap on the wrist, a one year "guilty without a plea" probation.

Amazingly, I found work as an alcoholism counselor, and I did well at work in the beginning. I seemed to be able to handle, through private masturbation, the sexual tensions which can arise in the counseling situation. Also, about this time I met my future wife. I was all screwed up, however, because although I enjoyed her, I didn't know what to do with another woman I thought I was in love with. Nevertheless, I broke off the other relationship and picked up with the new one. I also joined A.A. at this time.

I stayed in anger, fear, and guilt for some two years, wanting to act out sexually but staving it off because I didn't want to destroy this relationship. Then the lid blew off and I acted out with a couple of former counseling patients. I ended up owning up to this at work, and I was fired from my job.

I called my A.A. sponsor. He suggested going to an A.A. meeting in order to meet a friend of his who was in S.L.A.A. I had no idea what was in store for me but I was really desperate. Out of work, acting out, fighting with my girl-friend and everyone around me, I was out of control—and by now I knew it.

My girlfriend went to visit her mother (who lived outside the U.S.) and I was alone. She evidently always instinctively knew I was a sex and love addict although it had taken her a long time to trust what her intuition was telling her. She needed time away from me.

So off I went to S.L.A.A. I proceeded to get sober in this wonderful, open and honest program. I realize now how powerful the program is because I had been in therapy and trying very hard for over three years, with little progress. Then I came into this program and—wham!—I made progress starting from day one.

All I can say is if you've got a problem in any area dealing with relationships, or acting out sexually or romantically, you've come to the right place. I wish you lots of strength and fortitude. Remember—*you can do it, you can stay sober.* I'm sober nearly a year, making plans to marry, and rehabilitated as an alcoholism counselor.

The Only "Me" I'd Ever Known

I was born to very sick parents. I was hated and constantly told how no-good and sub-human I was. I was sexually molested by many adults in my life—this included parents, aunts, physicians, a deacon of the church, a psychiatrist, neighbors, and men my mother "sold" me to in the hopes of getting rid of me.

My mother would tie me up and torture me sexually. I would cry and hold myself at night, unable to sleep because of the pain in my vagina. I would try violent "masturbation," not for pleasure, but to try to alleviate the terrible pain.

My family was so freaky that people would cross the street to avoid walking past our house. My mother went to great lengths to make me look hideous. This was not her only manifestation of craziness, for she spent as much energy in making my sister look beautiful. For some reason, I represented to her all evil and hatred and my sister all good and love. I lived in the same house with my sister for six years and maybe caught glimpses of her that many times. My mother would scream violently if we accidentally entered the same room because I might defile my sister by laying eyes on her.

The way I looked really was absurd. Some very hardened people have had tears in their eyes upon seeing a picture of me as a child.

The neighborhood children would not play with me, would even run from me, call me names and try to beat me up. I was too freaked out to go to school and I never did—not even grammar school. I guess the school authorities thought my family was too crazy to bother with.

My father started going to nuthouses when I was three or so, so he was only around periodically. To the rest of the world he appeared the crazier of the two, but believe me, his abuse didn't come close to my mother's! He was also responsible for giving me the one message that saved my life for years, "Sex is great—go for it!" This, coupled with my mother's message, "Relationships are, at best, stupid, horrible, bad, etc., and to be avoided at *all* costs," set the stage for the way I've been relating to people ever since.

My first relationship started when I was six. The girl next door had endured the other neighborhood kids' rejection too, as well as name-calling, verbal abuse from my parents, and beatings from her father for playing with me. One particular day she had received a severe beating from her father for seeing me and had still sneaked back over. I was so afraid of losing her! I don't know how I knew, but I did, that I could keep her through sex. I said, barely audibly, "Wanta play nasty?" She jumped at the chance and thus started a three-year every day affair.

She was five years my senior and very experienced. Her older sister had just ended a five-year sexual relationship with her because she had discovered boys. F. and I did everything adults do—it wasn't just "playing doctor." It was mostly one-sided, with her making love to me. I was not yet orgasmic but it felt so good and took away the pain. I lived for my hours with F. and endured my life in total isolation and terror the rest of the time.

Right before I turned nine, we abruptly moved from L.A. to Kansas City. I was totally devastated—crushed—destroyed. I *loved* F.; how could I *live* without her?

In Kansas City I was put in a "special class" for "crazy" kids. There were ten kids in the "class" and no academic work whatsoever, only a "dollhouse," blocks and a sand pile. I spent my days in the "dollhouse" or coat room or bathroom doing to two other girls in the class what F. had done to me.

After three and a half months we moved back to L.A., but not near F. My mother had had me on drugs since I was seven. Now there were rounds of people she would "sell" me to or "share" me with. I *hated* this sexual activity with adults. The drugs increased in quantity. I also *hated* the drugs.

My mother finally got an institution to accept me three months before I was ten. I had known about the impending imprisonment and "throw-away" for seven months, and the anticipation was hell. The drugs increased until I was nodded out all the time. A neighbor had to come over and periodically carry me to the bathroom. I tried to persuade and beg my mother not to throw me away. I made promises to be good—whatever *that* meant. (Looking back, I *was* good!) I tried not to be seen or heard because bringing attention to myself only meant severe abuse.

Not quite ten, off I went to the asylum—a locked ward. That would be a terrifying place for an adult, let alone a ten year old. I can't begin to describe the terror and agony I went through. I was hysterical for three weeks—screaming and crying and writing letters, begging my mother to take me back. After three weeks I got strangely calm, walked over and asked the guard for a transfer to a minimum security ward, where I proceeded to go on my first sex-run. I compulsively engaged sexually every girl I could get my hands on, and kept at it with utter abandon. I kept getting caught and getting the ward "locked" and was beaten up by groups of girls for getting them punished, but I kept on with my sexcapades. I'd show my mother I didn't need her or anybody else in this whole damn world!

After a couple of months I escaped. I was a ten year old runaway, totally on my own, starting another pattern which would continue for many years. I would escape from an institution, be on the streets for a while until I got busted, go to some institution or another, stay a while, and escape again.

On the night of my first escape I met a pimp. It was the first time I drank and took drugs on my own, and with a vengeance, because I knew he was going to have sex with me and I didn't want to remember it. I didn't. The next day he put me on the streets to work. I left him after a week or two and never had a pimp again. Instead I later became one, at thirteen! I did this because I hated prostituting myself so much.

The next few years were just a normal story for a street addict. The only thing unusual about it was my age (but I looked much older). During this time I was careful to keep my sex with women "for free and for fun." I would never charge a woman, and I would certainly never turn one down!

One thing I liked about prostitution was that it gave me the privilege of saying *no* to men. I *despised* sex with men. I would also con, rob or otherwise abuse my men tricks. I had quite a following, because I always attracted masochists—both men and women.

When I would be in the institutions, I would spend most of my time in lockup, coming out only when I wanted to go on a sex-run or escape. My heaven would be when I was in a dormitory of twenty to fifty women. I'd go from bed to bed all night.

During these years I *did* have relationships, and up until recently I thought they all broke up because of my excessive drug and alcohol use. Not so at all! In an inventory I took, I found out that each and every one broke up because of my sexual addiction. No matter how much sex I had with a partner, I *had to* have everyone else too—in large quantities, in front of my lovers, everywhere, all the time. I was not into sneaking and looking over my shoulder. My lovers did tell me they didn't like it, but I honestly couldn't hear their complaints. Even if I had heard, I *couldn't* have stopped. I might have gotten more sneaky perhaps, but I couldn't have stopped doing it in front of them. It was not unusual for me to "bring the whole bar home" for an orgy, or for my lover to catch me several times a week, with different people, in strange places.

At fifteen I gave birth to a son. I can't tell you much about the next few years, because they were almost a complete blackout. Towards the end of my drinking, I was either attacking or raping people.

I went to A.A. at seventeen, then again, for real, at eighteen. I got sober, and immediately got into a relationship—wasn't that what you were "supposed" to do? She was *very* dependent on me, and I was dependent on her dependency. She knew how important sex was to me, and she serviced me sexually, which fed my ego very well.

I would stay "semi-monogamous" to her for three weeks or so, break up, go on a large sex-run, then go home when I was tired. Usually these "runs" consisted of thirty to forty women—more if orgies were involved.

Our relationship was also very sadomasochistic (S & M). When we were first together, I injured her several times in succession, requiring hospital visits, and swore off active S & M. However, I continued to beat her up regularly. This didn't fit too well with the "Wonderful Ms. A.A." image I had of myself.

From the first day I met her, I tried to break the relationship off for keeps, but I *couldn't*—I was addicted! I hated her, I didn't respect her. I didn't respect myself or what we were when we were together, yet I *couldn't leave.* Sex with her was fantastic, but everything else was shit. (I see now that it was much more than just good sex that kept me addicted.) This relationship lasted four and a half years, and I was nearly destroyed by the time I got out.

After that, she had another lover, but they couldn't make love unless my ex-lover would pick up a woman for me and call me over to make love to the other woman, so she and her lover could watch, and get off. I loved her supplying me with women, and I loved putting on shows, but I *hated* the hold that this woman, whom I despised, had on me.

After we were officially "not together" anymore, my life became a continuous sex-run. This was about twelve years ago, and even then I was beginning to see that "something was wrong" with me and sex. I found myself out in the rain "cruising," having to stop frequently at gas stations to masturbate. Before I even got a woman into bed, I would often feel panicked, saying to myself, "Oh my God, where am I going to get the next one?"

My son was, next to sex, the most important thing in my life, and the *only* person I ever loved. Yet I dragged him through hell, across the country, in pursuit of a piece of ass. I took him to orgies; I locked him in closets so I could cruise without having to be concerned with where he was.

In fact, my sexual addiction was, in a twisted way, partially responsible for my son's death. I was on my way to pick up a ring I thought I needed to help me cruise. I was very obsessed with the prospective partners who would be at the night's upcoming party as I yelled at my son, telling him to hurry up and cross the street. I don't know if it would have mattered, but chances are, if I hadn't been so orgasmically preoccupied and turned on, I might have seen the oncoming car.

About a week before his death, I stayed home one night. I was getting real tired and disillusioned by my sex life. He was so amazed. He kept saying over and over, with tears in his eyes, "You mean you would, *really,* rather stay home with me tonight, than go to a party?" I felt that way that night, I really did. But the next night there I was out again; *every* night I was out there.

After his death, for the first time in my life, I *didn't* want to have sex. I took his death as a punishment from God for all my sex. "Maybe 'those' people were right after all," I said to myself, thinking of all the "hellfire and brimstone" preachers who had ever cursed the likes of me. Yet, despite feeling sick of having sex, and sick at heart over my son's death, I again found myself sexually hooked, and with the very people I had managed to say no to before. And I was doing it for money now, with both women and men, trying to raise the money to bury my son. I felt used and taken advantage of. I started to use drugs again, then drank. I was even gang-raped, and got pregnant again. Miraculously, I managed to get sober again.

Newly sober once more, pregnant and terrified of having the baby alone, I was also really, really burnt-out on my sex life. So I picked up a woman who was also newly sober, moved in with her, and married her.

I didn't go out on her. Instead I obsessed about the pregnancy and the baby, moved us to a very small town so as to totally isolate us from other lesbians, and gained one hundred and twenty pounds.

I gave this woman sex, but she was really quite boring to me in bed, so I'd just wait till she was asleep and go in the bathroom and masturbate. Besides, with a hyperactive baby, a "mini-farm" to run, and my extreme obesity, I kind of had no time for sex.

I had used weight before as "insurance," to somewhat curb my sex-runs. I would shift back and forth between sex, weight and relationships. Weight never stopped me, only slowed me down somewhat, but I had never been that grossly fat before. I had previously been in O.A., and I went back and lost about eighty pounds.

We moved to San Diego and almost immediately broke up. I was in San Diego with no money, no friends, and a hyperactive two-year-old that no one would babysit. I couldn't even go to A.A. meetings because he was so disruptive. I was forced into what seemed to me to be celibacy, completely against my will. It was the worst year of my life!

Actually, it wasn't celibacy. I was just so much less sexually active that it seemed like celibacy to me. I would drive up to L.A. and leave my son with my mother—who I knew was crazy and abused him—so I could go on a sex-run. I *hated* myself for that.

After a year, I moved and found a permanent babysitter, and started up again. My kid was in nursery school all day, and I had thirty hours a week free babysitting at night. I was on welfare, so I could devote my entire time to cruising. But at times I still found it necessary to leave him, for hours, in the car parked outside the bar, so I could cruise. And I was still keeping my big sex-runs for when I would go to L.A., about two or three times a month.

Everyone had always known how "kinky" I was, but I then came to grips with, and admitted, my own S & M. After that, it seemed like every woman in the world was after me—I didn't even have to cruise. I had a reputation—which I spent a lot of time maintaining (to ensure that I had a never ending supply of partners)—of doing anybody's fantasy, no matter how bizarre. I had thousands of dollars of "toys" and "costumes." People used to come to my house in groups to have a tour of my "collection."

Things continued to go downhill more rapidly. I was living in the bars. I was burning out fast. I was prostituting myself again. And it was all so empty. I resented the women I was with for using me, and letting me use them. I resented myself for using them, and letting myself be used. I just resented the whole goddamned thing. But how could I blame anybody but myself?

I believe there was nothing wrong with any of the forms my sexual expression took—only with me—the *way* I used it. I have never had a single sexual experience that wasn't totally selfish, whether it was in my "bad" days when I would scare people into obliging, or my socially acceptable days when I took it upon myself to cure the entire female population's sexual problems.

My tricks were getting progressively sicker. I remember one night, while a woman and I were making love with a loaded gun, thinking, "Yeah, I guess that *would* be the ultimate orgasm," feeling sure that *that* was how I would die—and soon—in a scene.

I met D.; she moved in the same night. It got even worse! I decided to be the abusee this time, instead of the abuser. It was horrid. I was with her for two years and, true to form, was trying to find a way to leave the entire time.

It finally began to get through my thick, thick skull—I WAS ADDICTED. I was getting *nothing* I wanted or needed, and lots of trauma and drama I didn't need, and I still couldn't leave! I saw how it was *just like* being addicted to drugs. With very few exceptions, I didn't even go out on her, because I *knew* that sex was not the answer anymore.

I ended up, one more time, gaining ninety pounds, using drugs again, breaking my leg, and finally drinking again.

Then I was finally given the gift of being able to leave. And it most definitely *was* a gift—the Power *did not* come from me.

That was on December 16, 1983.

When I moved out, I *knew* I couldn't take another round of sex *or* relationships. I gave away my whole collection of "toys," moved to a small, red-neck infested homophobic town, and refused to lose my weight—all to protect myself from women and from myself. I went through loss and grieving, but I was, mainly, still anesthetized by my weight and isolation and the fact that I was so *grateful* to have been rescued from that relationship. It had been more demoralizing and humiliating than all my drugs, alcohol, and food combined. Only later did I realize that I had hit bottom and surrendered.

I got involved with the Adult Children of Alcoholics groups, and this finally started the ball rolling in my recovery—*at last*—after some seventeen years of being "around" various self-help programs but never really involved in a committed way.

I started to get honest—finally. I started talking at meetings about my sex and relationship addictions. I started taking inventories of my sexual and relationship history. I knew that I could no longer hide behind my weight, or the isolation in which I had been living. I also knew that as soon as I started to lose weight, the old sexual obsession would return—and to yield again would be my death.

I really had hit bottom; I knew that. Not only couldn't I engage in sex, I couldn't even flirt—or *talk* about sex—the way I had before. I knew that the pain of *not* indulging was less than the pain of indulging. The price of indulgence was too high—actually it always *had* been, but I hadn't known it.

I started spilling my guts at A.A. meetings (to which I had also returned). I shared with anyone who would listen. I didn't care what response I got—I was talking about saving my life!

The hardest time for me was when I burned my last "trick-book." I went through *physical* withdrawal with that! It was concrete evidence that I really *was* serious, and throwing away my past—not only my past, but *my total identity*—the only "ME" I'd ever known. Everything, to me, had been either sexual, or a prelude to sex, whether it was working on my car or going to the store. I was capable of turning every situation in my life towards sex, and had in fact done so.

I don't know if I can ever again have sex, or when, and at this point I don't particularly give a damn. I can't have sex now, and I am so eternally *grateful* to be relieved of *that* bondage that I don't care. Heaven knows, I certainly have had my share—and several other people's share, too!

After writing one of my sexual inventories, I called about thirty people and, coincidentally, no one was home. I finally ended up desperately calling a woman I *knew* wouldn't understand what I had written. When I finished reading it to her, she gave me the address of S.L.A.A.

I have been corresponding ever since, and devouring every bit of literature I can get, and (surprise!) people here have been coming out of the woodwork, wanting an S.L.A.A. meeting in San Diego, so we are starting one.

We are all baby-newcomers and really don't know what we are doing, but I know that—with the literature, correspondence, the friendship of other S.L.A.A.'s, and my higher Power—I will be O.K. I am so grateful.

I have had brief glimpses of "being," of just "living," that have felt so much better than any orgasm I ever had. I don't know what it is, but I do know that it is only a tiny, tiny glimpse of what is yet to come.

And you know what? I Am Doing It! Not gracefully, mind you, but *I am doing it.*

Notes

Notes

Notes

Notes